Creating Leaderful Organizations

Creating Leaderful Organizations

HOW TO BRING OUT
LEADERSHIP IN EVERYONE

Joseph A. Raelin

BERRETT-KOEHLER PUBLISHERS, INC.
San Francisco

Berrett-Koehler Publishers, Inc.
235 Montgomery Street, Suite 650
San Francisco, CA 94104-2916
Tel: (415) 288-0260 Fax: (415) 362-2512
www.bkconnection.com

Ordering Information
Quantity sales. Special discounts are available on quantity purchases by corporations, associations, and others. For details, contact the "Special Sales Department" at the Berrett-Koehler address above.
Individual sales. Berrett-Koehler publications are available through most bookstores. They can also be ordered direct from Berrett-Koehler: Tel: (800) 929-2929; Fax: (802) 864-7626; www.bkconnection.com
Orders for college textbook/course adoption use. Please contact Berrett-Koehler: Tel: (800) 929-2929; Fax: (802) 864-7626.
Orders by U.S. trade bookstores and wholesalers. Please contact Publishers Group West, 1700 Fourth Street, Berkeley, CA 94710. Tel: (510) 528-1444; Fax: (510) 528-3444.

Berrett-Koehler and the BK logo are registered trademarks of Berrett-Koehler Publishers, Inc.

Printed in the United States of America

Berrett-Koehler books are printed on long-lasting acid-free paper. When it is available, we choose paper that has been manufactured by environmentally responsible processes. These may include using trees grown in sustainable forests, incorporating recycled paper, minimizing chlorine in bleaching, or recycling the energy produced at the paper mill.

Library of Congress Cataloging-in-Publication Data
Raelin, Joseph A., 1948–
    Creating leaderful organizations : how to bring out leadership in everyone / prepared by Joseph A. Raelin
        p. cm.
    Includes bibliographical references and index.
    ISBN 1-57675-233-X
    1. Leadership. I. Title.
HD57.7 .R34 2002
658.4'092—dc21   2002028136

FIRST EDITION

08 07 06 05 04 03   10 9 8 7 6 5 4 3 2 1

Project management, design, and composition: BookMatters, Berkeley; Copyedit: Janet Reed Blake; Proofreading: Lisa Goldstein; Index: Ken DellaPenta

To my sons, Jonathan and Jeremy
My proudest feat from my own leaderful practice

Contents

Tables and Figures

Tables

FIGURES

Preface

This book is designed to develop "leaderful practice," a new paradigm of leadership for our organizations. Leaderful practice directly challenges the conventional view of leadership as "being out in front." In the twenty-first-century organization, we need to establish communities where everyone shares the experience of serving as a leader, not sequentially, but concurrently and collectively. In other words, leaders co-exist at the same time and all together. In addition, we expect each member of a community to make a unique contribution to the growth of that community, both independently and interdependently with others. In this sense, our leaders are inherently collaborative, which in turn they derive from their compassion toward other human beings. Their well-developed sense of self permits them to develop a deep consideration of others.

It may be somewhat ambitious to suggest that one book can produce an entirely new paradigm of leadership. However, I am convinced that when the audience of practicing managers fully reflects upon the significance of becoming "leaderful," they will join together in this quest to transform leadership practice as we know it. The turbulent world that characterizes our organizations today, staffed by increasingly diverse and skillful people, can no longer be pulled together by bureaucratic authority nor by charismatic personality. The only possible way to lead ourselves out of trouble in management is to become mutual and to share our leadership.

Why should we call our new paradigm "leader*ful*?" Can you re-call working with a team that hummed along, almost like a sin-gle unit? The experience was a joy. Team members each had a par-ticular functional role but seemed implicitly able to support each other when warranted. Any one of the team members could speak for the entire team. On occasion, you might have heard someone refer to this team as "leader*less*." Let's not call it leaderless. Let me rather introduce you to the revolutionary concept of leader*ful* practice.

As a prospective reader, you might wonder if this book applies to you. If you work with others in any capacity, you *are* capable of exerting leadership. You don't have to be the CEO or top gun. Managers and employees who work in teams and organizations might find this account especially useful. Why? We've entered an age of lean operations, of doing more with less. Managers may feel overwhelmed by technology or by contractors out to replace them. Meanwhile, employees don't find life any easier. They're given assignments that seem nearly impossible to accomplish in a specified time by supervisors who have far less understanding of the problem than they do.

It seems that leadership may be the most desperate problem we face in organizational life today. Yet, conceived in a different way, it may also represent the very solution to the ills of work in our turbulent times.

I invite you to read on about a form of leadership that can re-spond to our seemingly chaotic world in the only way that can bring out the best of the human condition. I'm not talking about leaders consulting with their followers. I'm not even advocating that leaders learn to step aside to let others take the reins. I'm talk-ing about a true mutual model that incorporates everyone in lead-ership, that transforms leadership from an individual property into a leaderful practice.

The book is divided into two parts. Part I introduces the new paradigm of leaderful practice. Part II uncovers the traditions and applications that underlie the four C's of leaderful practice. The four C's represent a transformation from the conventional to the leaderful approach; hence, leadership's former serial quality becomes *concurrent*, its individual focus becomes *collective*, its controlling orientation becomes *collaborative*, and its dispassionate nature changes to *compassionate*. The account in both parts will introduce you not only to new ideas that seek to reanimate your thinking about leadership but also to new tools that will help you try out explicit leaderful behaviors.

In chapter 1, I begin by illustrating how leaderful practice contrasts with conventional leadership and how it can accomplish the critical processes of leadership as, or more, effectively. Readers will first be introduced to the four C's in this chapter and will be apprised of the rationale for calling for a new paradigm of leadership in our era.

In chapter 2, I anticipate some of the maxims that may well be disturbed by the new paradigm; in particular, what is to become of such standard precepts as authority, bureaucracy, followership, and management itself? Chapter 3 takes up additional challenges that need to be addressed if leaderful practice is to succeed as a viable leadership approach. In particular, since people and groups are not necessarily standing around ready to adopt leaderful practice in their organizations immediately, it addresses how to prepare for it, how to distribute leadership roles, and how to respond to resistant employees. Learning how to develop individuals to assume leaderful practice becomes the objective of chapter 4, which acknowledges that it takes time, commitment, and skill to become leaderful. In chapter 5, I reveal the benefits of adopting the leaderful approach, both in terms of its contribution to the bottom line and its appeal to important democratic, human instincts. Leaderful practice ignites the natural talent of people to contribute to the growth of their communities while allowing them to remain genuine among themselves so that they can bring their whole selves to work.

Part II of the book provides full detail on the four C's of lead-erful practice. Concurrent leadership, covered in chapter 6, in-corporates the traditions of situational management and team fa-cilitation. You can't easily become leaderful unless you're willing to have others in your team step forward to provide leadership as the situation warrants. Collective leadership, elaborated in chap-ter 7, relies upon stewardship and meaning-making and also re-quires leaders to be learners. Leaders ultimately provide service to their organizations, which might also have them speak in a col-lective voice. This might entail probing below the surface to un-cover the assumptions underlying the team's values. Collaborative leaders, meanwhile—as chapter 8 reveals—seek affirmative changes for their communities, often facilitated through dialogue on well-considered points of view. They engage in mutual in-fluence processes, encouraging all parties to affect the flow of de-cision making. Leaderful leaders are also compassionate. As chapter 9 shows, they have a profound respect for the dignity of every human being. They're not interested in holding others in awe, as a charismatic would; rather, they seek to establish sus-tainable relationships with stakeholders that honor such values as humility, participation, and trust.

Finally, in chapter 10, I challenge readers to begin their own quest to transform their leadership. Since employees as well as managers can be leaderful, I offer suggestions to both parties on how to get started on this quest. It is one thing to talk about lead-erful practice; it is quite another to change your behavior. After reading this book, I hope everyone will realize his or her leader-ful capability.

Acknowledgments

As my readers might expect, having now become somewhat familiar with the leaderful perspective, I believe pulling off a project like this requires a number of leaders in addition to myself. Aspiring to be leaderful in my own life, I wish to acknowledge those who played an important part in the evolution of the leaderful concept.

Unfortunately, most of these leaders have to go unnamed because, having affected me in their everyday encounters, they are too numerous to name or to sometimes even recollect. Yet, whether through their example or through their argumentation, they have genuinely shaped the articulation of leaderful practice. There is a second unnamed group of leaders who have gone even further by agreeing to participate in this manuscript. These are my many graduate students who in taking my course on leadership have willingly shared their journals with me and have generously given me permission to quote them in exchange for their anonymity. If the account to follow succeeds in its practical nature enriched by real-life examples from practicing managers and employees and their leadership struggles, it is largely thanks to the personal generosity of these students.

There are some individuals who extended particular dedication to the craftsmanship of this book. First, the application of my leadership course to the content of this book was significantly impacted by the facilitators who staffed the course. For little or no monetary compensation, these facilitators moderated the learning teams organized to support the course and lent their wise counsel to the development of the traditions that eventually founded the leaderful concept. These facilitators are Tracey Madden, Louis Leyes, John McGillivray, Brenda Reed, Ken Chadwick, Dan Kerls, Laura Cannata, Dan Collins, and Fr. Michael Burns, of Edinburgh, Scotland, the last of whom served as a facilitator over two offerings of the course and who has continued to share his insights on leadership with me ever since.

I have also experimented with my leaderful ideas with participants in several so-called executive breakfast series. A number of individuals have helped me coordinate these series, namely, Sims Cooledge, Julie Whitmore, Phil DiChiara, and Mark Braun. I would also like to thank Bill Gjetson and Toby Casey for allowing me to challenge the executive staff at Caterpillar Paving Products with the novel implications of leaderful practice, and Colm O'Comartun and Brian Kane at Boston College's Irish Institute for giving me a platform to share my ideas on leadership through many workshops with their visitors from Ireland and Northern Ireland.

At Boston College, I benefited enormously from a research incentive grant awarded through the auspices of Dean Helen Peters and Assistant Dean Amy La Combe. I was also privileged to work with a superb research assistant, Carolina Charrie from Uruguay, over the full two years of the book's development. The many journal extracts used in these pages were largely hand selected by Carolina, as was the preparation of the graphics that spice up the text. In addition, the complete family of staff, participants, and alumni affiliated with the Leadership for Change graduate program have shaped my thinking about leadership over the program's nine-year history. It has been a pure privilege to have been associated with this dynamic program through these years.

My appreciation also goes out to the entire Berrett-Koehler

family whose members have demonstrated leaderful contact with me at every stage of the publication process. Jeevan Sivasubramaniam has been my supportive main contact person and Steve Piersanti my insightful editor. I am also grateful to the reviewers of my original manuscript, especially Jan Nickerson, who took the extraordinary step of visiting me at my house to supplement her insightful and bountiful written comments with a full verbal explanation and dialogue.

I am now privileged to have begun a new adventure at Northeastern University as the Asa S. Knowles Chair of Practice-Oriented Education. I look forward to promoting leaderful practice in my new environment headed by already leaderful President, Richard Freeland.

And finally, I am deeply grateful to my family for putting up with my perpetual experiments in leaderful practice, not to mention with my time away from them in preparing this book.

Joe Raelin
Boston, MA

PART ONE

Presenting a New Paradigm for Leadership: Leaderful Practice

JAMIE WATERS, CURRENTLY THE DIRECTOR OF RESEARCH AT A well-known technology company, almost left the company seventeen years ago. Though she held a Ph.D. from Stanford, her first job was with a supervisor who simply refused to listen to her ideas or act on any of her suggestions. Discouraged to the point of looking for a job elsewhere, Jamie was rescued by a research fellow who used a different form of leadership on his team. Rather than insist that the group follow his lead, this manager let people, in his words, "follow their heart." Team members worked on projects that energized them yet simultaneously contributed to the mission of the group. They decided together not only how to create but also how to serve their mission and how to contribute to the greater good of the company and its markets. They worked in sync yet their collaboration seemed effortless.

Jamie adopted this style of leadership and advanced to the directorship she holds today. Through her encouragement, many of her teams now operate just like that second experience of hers, which saved her for the company. Whenever new employees now ask her how she creates such leaderless groups, she's quick to point out that these teams "are not leader*less*. They're leader*ful*." They're not deprived of leadership; they're full of leadership. Everyone shares the experience of serving as a leader all together and at the same time!

Let's keep in mind, though, that this company nearly lost Jamie forever. That she stayed is in no small measure a reason for the company's continuing success. Jamie's case (based on a real-life example) represents a starting point for understanding why we need a new brand of leadership in our corporate, public, and civic environments today. One obvious reason is that without people like Jamie or her former research fellow, we'll lose countless talented employees.

Besides retaining good people, what pressures face those in

management positions? A close look across the organizational landscape reveals people in large measure overwhelmed, uncertain, and on the run. We've entered an age of lean operations, of doing more with less. Managers are pushed to use complicated technology to replace supervisory systems and labor. A lot of work is now assigned to teams that manage themselves. The expanding value chain leads in some cases to more work being outsourced on a product than completed in-house. Meanwhile, companies are entering markets and providing services that may not have existed at the start of the manager's career. At the same time, more sophisticated consumers and clients demand increased customization to meet their needs. It is no wonder that managers find themselves torn in many directions. How can they control an operation producing a dizzying array of special features, and using specialized technologies that they aren't even versed in?

Meanwhile, employees, like Jamie in our introductory example, don't find life any easier. Oftentimes, they're given assignments that are nearly impossible to accomplish in a specified time by managers who have far less understanding of the problem than they do. They feel undervalued, under-utilized, and often overwhelmed with "busy" work (work that requires them to be busy, not necessarily productive or challenged).

If these predicaments sound familiar to you, then you might agree that leadership is potentially the most desperate problem we face in organizational life today. Yet, conceived in a different way, it may also represent the very solution to the ills of work in our current era.

This is what this book is about. I intend to cast leadership in a new light, to potentially change your entire way of viewing it. As your thinking changes, I hope in turn that your practice of leadership—and, as you will see, you can practice leadership whether you're an employee or a manager—may also change for the better.

1 The Tenets of Leaderful Practice

What Is "Leaderful Practice"?

I would like to introduce you to an alternative paradigm of leadership: "leaderful practice." It directly challenges the conventional view of leadership as "being out in front." In the twenty-first-century organization, we need to establish communities where everyone shares the experience of serving as a leader, not serially, but concurrently and collectively.

Leaderful practice is unique compared to empowerment models that have become popular in recent years in that it does not merely present a consultative model wherein leaders in authority allow "followers" to participate in their leadership. Nor does it equate to stewardship approaches that see the leader step aside to allow others to take over when necessary. Instead, it offers a true mutual model that transforms leadership from an individual property into a new paradigm that redefines leadership as a collective practice.

It may seem somewhat ambitious to suggest that a book can produce an entirely new paradigm, but the recharacterization of leadership that I suggest is hardly a revolution. The subject in question is already in motion and, thus, has but to be brought into popular consciousness. In fact, although I had assumed that I had invented a new word—*leaderful*—I subsequently discovered that such authors as Robert Kenny, Jessica Lipnack, Charlotte Roberts, and Margaret Wheatley, as well as many other leadership

5

consultants, had already made many references to it. So, I am now convinced that when all of us in the working world fully reflect upon the metaphor of "being leaderful," we will collaborate in this endeavor of transforming leadership practice as we know it. The chaotic world of corporate affairs especially requires leadership that diverges from age-old conceptions of leading by control. The only possible way to lead our way out of trouble in management is to become mutual and to share our leadership.

What Is Leadership?

Before we get ahead of ourselves, I need to first provide a depiction of what *leadership* itself represents. Once we have a sense of what it is, we will have a base of operations to determine whether leaderful practice can accomplish leadership as effectively, or more effectively (as I contend), than conventional leadership practice. In other words, as we encounter the new ideas and behaviors of leaderful practice, however novel or inventive they may appear, we need to assess whether they nevertheless continue to accomplish the enterprise of leadership. A good place to start is to review four critical processes that are mobilized by leadership. The model depicted in figure 1-1[1] is iterative, so I could start my explanation anywhere, but for the sake of clarity, let's begin with setting the mission.

1. Leadership is concerned with setting the mission or direction of an enterprise. At some point, whether in the beginning of an activity or as it evolves, the community needs to know where it is going.

2. Accompanying the mission is the need to actualize the goals of the enterprise. A host of activities and tasks need to be accomplished to get the work done.

3. There is also a need to sustain the commitment and cohesiveness of the working unit. Community members want to feel that they are part of something.

FIGURE 1-1. Four Critical Processes of Leadership

4. While members need to feel cohesive, they also need to be adaptable to respond to changes that may require a shift in direction. As members entertain alternatives, the mission may become redefined; hence, the process begins anew.

The first critical process, setting the mission, defines the outcome to which the community becomes dedicated. A mission becomes a stabilizing factor in the face of pressure from forces, both inside and outside the system, to change it. Though subject to change from the adaptive process, the result of which may cause occasional shifts in the mission, the mission gives any system a consistent boundary for a period of time.

The interest among major firms to define strategic direction gives testimony to this essential process. Wal-Mart, for example, makes its mission very simple: "To give ordinary folk the chance to buy the same thing as rich people." Other companies are more specific. Federal Express states: "FedEx is committed to our People-Service-Profit Philosophy. We will produce outstanding financial returns by providing totally reliable, competitively superior, global, air-ground transportation of high-priority goods and documents that require rapid, time-certain delivery." In either instance, members of these corporate communities obtain a good sense of where their company wishes to go.

The second critical process, actualizing goals, is concerned with how a community organizes itself to extend social and political energy and shape its economic performance. Members of a community engage with one another to work on behalf of their mission. Failing to engage in the requisite tasks to accomplish a mission typically results in mission failure itself, no matter how noble the mission.

Let's look at one of the most important institutions in our society: primary and secondary education. The United States severely lags behind the industrialized world in standard indices of educational accomplishment, not to mention the pervasive criticism and consternation from American citizens that our schools have not done their job properly. In this case, the mission is not in question, though some may disagree about what the education of children should comprise (should it be, for example, the command of academic subjects or a comprehensive sense of the meaning and practice of citizenship?). By most accounts, the criticism against our educational system rests on how we structure our school institutions to deliver the best product that we can. We also seem stifled regarding what we should actually teach students and how we should assess their learning; when, where, and how long to teach them; how to prepare, supervise, and evaluate our teachers; how much to spend on educational resources and how to obtain these very resources; and how to manage the entire educational enterprise.

The third critical process, sustaining commitment and cohesiveness, addresses the need of system units and constituents to come together in a mutual adjustment process to support the system as a whole. The need to coordinate its parts faces any community as it grows. This can be partially accomplished by structuring processes. But leadership is also required to see that people remain engaged and supportive of one another, that they have complementary expectations, and that conflicts are brought out into the open and managed for the good of the whole.

Consider how a team within a Fortune 50 yarn-making plant responded leaderfully to a customer complaint.[2] Apparently, the customer had received a yarn shipment of incorrect size. The researchers first noticed the team literally "huddling" in response to this unexpected turn of events. Then, various team members launched into action. Through a series of phone calls, some members first acquired needed extra raw material from another part of the plant. Team members scheduled several periods of overtime to redo the order. Meanwhile, the customer was informed that the correct size yarn would ship in a matter of days.

The fourth process, responding to changes, is a boundary function that links a system with its environment. Any system not only has to organize itself internally but must also be prepared to change in response to new environmental conditions. Hence, communities cannot become overly cohesive or overly committed to any course of action that would preclude a shift in direction when necessary. Although not always active, a repertoire of available resources and actions should be available to facilitate a need to change course.

Digital Equipment Corporation (DEC), the preeminent start-up in the minicomputer era, was perhaps one of the most admired U.S. companies in the 1970s and early '80s. No less admired was its iconoclastic founder and CEO, Ken Olsen. However, DEC and its leadership missed the exploding demand for desktop computers that started in the mid-eighties, an oversight from which it never fully recovered. Though it found another niche, Internet-based computer systems installation and service, Compaq Computer Corp. eventually bought DEC in 1998.

In order for organizations to remain adaptable, leadership must occur in many areas, not just from the top. Indeed, many of our most adaptable responses arise from regular employees or from those in the organization who listen to their customers.

Microsoft's Internet applications are due as much to students and
to new hires, among whom were inveterate Web surfers, as to Bill
Gates. Starbucks's Frappaccino came from a store manager in
Los Angeles, and most franchise operators, like McDonalds, will
tell you that the best ideas come from the franchisees in the field
rather than from headquarters.

What Is Conventional Leadership?

Having identified what leadership represents, we next consider
the dominant approach to effecting leadership. As the reigning
paradigm, conventional leadership has qualities that are considered commensurate with leadership itself. As we shall see, there
is an emerging recognition that this dominant approach may be
listing as we prepare to manage twenty-first-century organizations. There are four tenets of conventional leadership.

1. Leadership is *serial*. Once one achieves the office of leadership, that position continues at least for the duration of the
   term of office. Only when one completes his or her term—
   or vacates or is forced to leave the office—does leadership
   transfer to the next leader, though it may return at times to
   the original person. Leaders are thus always in a position of
   leadership and do not cede the honor to anyone else. Upon
   acquiring power, most leaders attempt to sustain or increase
   it. Giving up or sharing power with others would be seen as
   abdicating one's responsibility.

2. Leadership is *individual*. That a leader is one person signifies
   leadership's solitary role. An enterprise has only one leader
   and normally such a person is designated as the authority or
   position leader. It would weaken or at least confuse leadership to talk about having more than a single leader or to
   share leadership because there would not be a concrete end-
   role for making decisions and directing actions.

3. Leadership is *controlling*. The conventional leader believes
   it is his or her ultimate duty to direct the enterprise and en-

gender the commitment of community members. To ensure smooth coordination of functions, the leader acts as the spokesperson for the enterprise. The subordinate role is to follow the guidance of the leader and to help him or her successfully accomplish the enterprise's mission. Leaders may choose to share their deepest beliefs but only with their closest associates.

4. Leadership is *dispassionate*. Although the leader may recognize that employees have feelings, the leader must make the tough decisions for the enterprise in a dispassionate manner. Tough decisions may result in not satisfying (or may even hurt) particular stakeholders, including employees, but accomplishing the mission of the enterprise must come first. Leaders are also the authoritative source when the operation faces problems, and they tend to exude a confidence that they are in charge and that subordinates can rely upon them to handle any challenge.

What Does It Mean to Be "Leaderful"?

In the opening vignette, Jamie Waters cautioned against calling groups leader*less*. In leaderless groups, there is no longer a need for a leader, or even a facilitator, because the group has learned to conduct its affairs on its own. It no longer has, or needs, leadership. The problem with this idea is that it suggests a group may at times be devoid of leadership. It can go on for a while, albeit tenuously, until there's a crisis. At that point, a leader may need to emerge to settle things down. Consider, though, that some groups don't lose their leadership when they work in sync like a well-oiled machine. Leadership at this point becomes distributed across all members of the community. It is not leader*less;* it is leader*ful!* As Jamie noted, it is full of leadership since everyone shares the experience of providing leadership.

Leading in Your Community   I would like to make a new reference to the unit that receives or conducts leadership. Let's refer to it as a *community*. A community is any setting where people congregate to accomplish work together. Hence, it can be a small group, an office, a plant, or a large organization. It can be in the private, public, or civil (nonprofit) sectors. I prefer to use the word *community*, rather than *group* or *organization*, because it is more hospitable to a notion of leadership that applies to the whole rather than to the parts or their sum. It also allows me to refer to leadership within any interpersonal context, rather than having to distinguish whether it refers to team or managerial or strategic settings. To say that leaderful practice occurs within a community comes with one qualifier: I am drawing attention to leadership's interpersonal character. The community is a unit in which members already have or may establish human contact with others. In this sense, it is a social structure that extends beyond the self, that links people together for some common purpose. Most of us can see ourselves as belonging to a number of communities. Some of them may not necessarily entail work; for example, people may assemble for recreational or spiritual purposes. In this book, I am most concerned with leadership that helps our communities work better together.

Some groups don't lose their leadership when they work in sync like a well-oiled machine. Leadership at this point becomes distributed across all members of the community. It is not lead-er*less;* it is leader*ful.*

The Four C's of Leaderful Practice   Leaderful leadership offers an alternative approach to conventional leadership that is ripe for the requirements of our communities in the current era. It is an integrative model that has been in the making for some time but for its coherence. In other words, it contains historical traditions that, without integration, have not been able to supplant the dominant heroic paradigm. Leaderful leadership can also accomplish the four processes of leadership in more settings and with more pervasive effectiveness than the conventional approach. Let's consider how the four tenets of conventional leadership can be replaced with what I have labeled the four C's. Leaderful managers are concurrent, collective, collaborative, and compassionate.

Figure 1-2 displays the two leadership approaches as a set of continua. I have chosen continua because most of us are not completely settled in one approach or the other. As much as I would wish for my readers to create fully leaderful organizations, it takes some practice to get there, as chapter 3 will point out. As such, some of you will find yourselves more leaderful compared to others but will also find that you vary in your leaderful tendencies across the tenets. For example, you may be a compassionate leader but believe firmly that leadership of the enterprise should gravitate to you as the ultimate single decision maker. Further, you may find that you embrace leaderful practice only under particular circumstances, such as when your colleagues are ready to share leadership with you. Otherwise, perhaps you tend to take control of the community.

As I expect that few readers will consider themselves entirely leaderful at this point, in this book I will attempt to both make the case on behalf of leaderful practice and illustrate some practical methods to help you become more so. It is not that I believe conventional leadership is invalid; it has served us well. I simply see the leaderful leadership approach as more practical and useful in managing communities in our new century.

The first tenet of leaderful practice, that leadership is *concurrent*, is perhaps the most revolutionary. It suggests that in any community, more than one leader can operate at the same time, so leaders willingly and naturally share power with others. Indeed, power can be increased by everyone working together. Since leaders perform a variety of responsibilities in a community, it is pointless to insist that only one leader operates at any one time. For example, an administrative assistant who "knows the

CONVENTIONAL   LEADERFUL

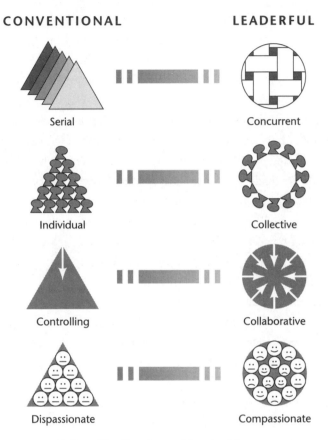

FIGURE 1-2.   The Continua of Leadership

ropes" and can help others figure out who is knowledgeable about a particular function may be just as important to the group as the position leader. However, this same position leader need not "stand down" nor give up his or her leadership as members of the community turn their attention to the administrative assistant. These two, as well as many others, can offer their leadership to the community at the same time.

Leaderful leadership is not only concurrent, but is also *collective*. Since we have dispelled the assumption that a group can have only one leader, we can entertain the view that many people within the community might operate as leaders. The community does not solely depend on one individual to mobilize action or make decisions on behalf of others. I include in this assertion the role of the position leader. This "authority" may have formal power conferred on him or her by the organization, but formal authority is not necessarily the most valuable to the operation. Decisions are made by whoever has the relevant responsibility. Leadership may thus emerge from multiple members of the community, especially when important needs arise, whether preparing for a strategic mission, creating meaning for the group, or proposing a change in direction. Although someone may initiate an activity, others may become involved and share leadership with the initiator. Have you ever experienced being in a team that was temporarily stymied in its attempt to solve a problem? Feeling disconsolate, members wonder if they will ever find a solution. Then, all of sudden, someone offers an idea, perhaps not a mainstream idea but one that has an immediate appeal, one that engages the community's imagination. Soon, everyone begins throwing out additional thoughts and tactics to build on the original idea. For a time, an almost breathless quality descends on the team's functioning as it becomes absorbed in this all-encompassing solution process. The team is experiencing collective leadership; it is not dependent on any one member, not the position leader, not the idea initiator—everyone is participating in leadership.

Leaderful leadership is also *collaborative*. All members of the community, not just the position leader, are in control of and may speak for the entire community. They may advocate a point of view that they believe can contribute to the common good of the community. Although they might assert themselves at times, they remain equally sensitive to the views and feelings of others and consider their viewpoints as equally valid. They thus seek to engage in a public dialogue in which they willingly open their beliefs and values to the scrutiny of others. Their listening to others becomes rapt. They also understand the difference between collaborating as a pretense and becoming fully involved. In pretentious involvement, you quickly discover that all the critical decisions seem to get made without you. Collaborative leaders realize that everyone counts; every opinion and contribution sincerely matter.

Finally, leaderful managers are *compassionate*. By demonstrating compassion, one extends unadulterated commitment to preserving the dignity of others. Shareholders' views are considered before making a decision for the entire enterprise. Each member of the community is valued regardless of his or her background or social standing, and all viewpoints are considered regardless of whether they conform to current thought processes. In practicing compassion, leaders take the stance of a learner who sees the adaptability of the community as dependent upon the contribution of others. Members of the community, not necessarily the position leader, handle problems as they arise. Compassionate leaders recognize that values are intrinsically interconnected with leadership and that there is no higher value than democratic participation. When people who have a stake in a community venture are given every chance to participate in that venture—including its implementation—their commitment to the venture will be assured. The endowment of participation extends to the wider community affected by the actions of an organization. For example, if building a new corporate complex will affect the existing ecology or serenity of a neighboring property, the compassionate leader will include the neighbors in deliberations concerning the construction.

Why Do We Need to Be Leaderful?

Leaderful practice has become an exigency for both managers and employees. Managers already are having to cope with new forms of organization. Information, reorganized now for decision making in the form of distributed knowledge, is gradually breaking down our bureaucracies. More people have access to information that was once the exclusive domain of top management. As every organizational member receives the necessary tools to run his or her immediate work function, he or she also sees how that function connects to the rest of the organization. When workers become more connected to one another, the entire enterprise becomes much more interdependent than in the past. Salespeople communicate customer preferences to systems designers. Nurses and dietitians become part of the same team. Expertise has become as much a function of the cross-functional unit operating together as intelligence professed by one single individual.

Each worker also likely possesses knowledge that may exceed that of his or her superiors. Take as an example the emergence of our military forces, which are becoming digitally networked, supported by unmanned spy planes and robotic sensors. In order to achieve its objectives of speed and agility this new technology pushes information down the line to the lowest ranking troops. The strategy, though, will only succeed if officers in the field can act on the available information without waiting for orders from command headquarters.[3]

In addition to becoming more interconnected, in order to unlock the knowledge of our workforce, organizations are becoming far more fluid, experimenting with virtual and network structures that have begun to even challenge our conventional notion of "internal" and "external." In such organizations, clear boundaries that distinguish the employees inside from customers, suppliers, and even competitors outside no longer exist. At Home Depot, for example, you might find a clerk who looks like a Home Depot clerk but who actually works for Georgia-Pacific. Why? By collecting detailed point-of-sale information, Georgia-Pacific expects to help Home Depot lower prices and reduce out-of-stock shelves while lowering inventory.[4]

Customers, meanwhile, whether businesses or individual consumers, now have greater leverage in our consumer markets owing to the access they can have to corporate units through information technology. As a result, they expect to work with corporate representatives who can streamline decisions and actions. They don't wish to be kept waiting for clearance from some corporate executive with whom they've had no contact. To operate in this way, boundary persons in such roles as service technicians, customer representatives, or purchasing agents need to operate with immediate authority to act in the company's interest.

Leadership, then, becomes operative as a collective property, not the sole sanctuary of any one (most important) member. Our corporate, public, and civic communities and teams still require leadership, however. Recalling the four critical processes, they still need to establish a mission for themselves, work collectively toward that mission, sustain their commitment, and face future challenges as they arise. It's just that the leadership of the unit needs to come from within the community, not from an ultimate authority imposed from the outside.

Meanwhile, how might employees participate in leadership? There is a good chance that if you're reading this book, you are part of the formally educated, knowledge workforce. You are, consequently, more capable, more independent, and more intrinsically motivated than workers of an earlier era. By this, I mean that you tend to respond well to open communication, fair treatment, and challenging work. But, most of all, you know your stuff. Consider the telecommunications industry as a compelling example. Executives of some of the major companies in the industry can remember a time when hardware meant telephones, lines, and switches. Hardware today means fiber optics, wireless devices, and internet infrastructure. Have these executives stayed so current that they can still solely determine strategy without the collective participation—not just input—of their technical staffs?

In the new century, we can no longer afford to have a mechanistic view of the world. We live in an age that is specialized but subjective, complex but relational. In such a world, we cannot rely on a coterie of subordinates to await their marching orders from detached bosses at the top who have sole possession on problem fixes, even across the remote corners of the organization. We need organizations that empower anyone with the capability and the willingness to assume leadership in the moment in his or her relationships with peers, team members, customers, suppliers, and other organizational partners. Alas, we are in it together. The essence of leadership is collaboration and mutuality.[5]

Abraham Lincoln liked to tell the following story (uncovered by Donald Phillips) to discourage managers from assuming almighty command.

> It seems that there was this colonel, who when raising his regiment in Missouri, proposed to his men that he should do all the swearing for the regiment. They assented; and for months no instance was known of any violation of the promise, that is, until a teamster named John Todd happened to be driving a mule team through a series of mudholes a little worse than usual. He thereupon burst forth into a volley of profanity.
>
> The colonel took notice of the offense and brought John to account. "John," said he, "didn't you promise to let me do all the swearing for the regiment?" "Yes, I did, Colonel," he replied, "but the fact was, the swearing had to be done then or not at all, and you weren't there to do it."[6]

If your boss insists on telling you who will do the swearing, as an employee, you'll probably leave. I say "leave," however, not only in the physical sense but also figuratively. If you continue to work under a controlling boss, you may bring only your subservient self to work. In this sense you may take little responsibility for anything outside of your own immediate job sphere. You may become inclined to focus on narrow tasks and duties and loath to extend any efforts to solve problems that are broader in scope. Especially during the early season of your employment, you might find yourself frustrated that the company is not using your full self. Over the course of time, you may become content to extend just that part of yourself that accomplishes the assigned task. The organizational culture becomes one of compliance, not commitment.[7] Later, if given the chance to participate in decisions or to bring your whole self to work, you will likely respond with mistrust, even resentment.[8] You may protest, "Now, what do they want from me?"

We need organizations that empower anyone with the capability and the willingness to assume leadership in the moment. . . . Alas, we are in it together. The essence of leadership is collaboration and mutuality.

I recall a story that has been attributed to Peter Drucker in which he presumably asked a group of senior executives to identify the "dead wood" in their company. Many of these executives were quick to nominate many of their direct reports as falling into this categorization, to which Drucker responded: "Were these people dead when you hired them or did they become dead wood?"

Placing exclusive power in an authority figure to determine the course of events in an organization without sharing leadership with others requires a dependence that relegates all employees to a subsidiary "yes boss" role. The net effect on adaptability and learning can be disastrous, as everyone but the boss has a cop-out in the event something goes wrong. Listen to how Trot Nixon, a baseball player from the Boston Red Sox, once feigned his displeasure at not being consulted. At one point during the 2001 pre-season, most Red Sox observers thought he would play left field once the right field position was granted to his teammate, one Manny Ramirez. A *Boston Globe* reporter asked Nixon why he hadn't been given the chance to play left field during spring training by then-manager, Jimy Williams. Nixon replied: "I have no clue. I'm not paid to think. Jimy always finds a way to get players some at-bats. I haven't thought that much about it. Earlier in the spring, I thought maybe I'd have the opportunity to play all over the place, but it's Jimy's team, he makes out the lineup" [March 23, 2001].

What Makes the Leaderful Experience New?

There is a view in our culture that we need heroes to guide us out of trouble. This is the main reason why leaderful practice may seem novel to many; it rarely calls for heroic intervention. There are also those who think they are leaderful, but, in fact, they are merely benevolent or they only get as far as espousing leaderful beliefs but inconsistently practice them.

Let's start with our hero fascination. In fairness, the heroic model does have historic roots. The Anglo-Saxon *lédan* means "going forth" or "standing out in front." The nineteenth-century historian Thomas Carlyle insisted that the one certainty that defines history is what "Great Men" have accomplished. Perhaps this is why the pull toward the heroic model of leadership in our culture persists even as we talk about the need to include other members of our communities under the leadership umbrella. Though we may advocate the value of participative leadership and other forms of organizational democratic practice, the drive to raise up a spiritual leader whom we can love and who can save us sneaks back into our consciousness just as we prepare to assert our own worth and independence. Part of the reason for this is that our culture still seems to value, even revere, individualism while preaching teamwork. Whatever the walk of life, be it a corporate setting, a professional sports team, or an opera, we tend to focus on the star performer even when he or she depends entirely upon the team to achieve prominence. Just listen to any advertisement about a sports contest and you will likely hear references to the competing teams' stars over the teams themselves.

We also like to point to exemplars of leadership during times of crisis. Whenever I ask people to name the greatest leaders, they tend to point to such heroes as Gandhi, Churchill, or Martin Luther King Jr. who seemed to have arisen during periods of great upheaval in their respective cultures. But what about the other moments when we, in our every day communities, operate in a time of stability and social order? Can we not witness the emergence of leadership during these moments as well?

Consider here the first of the many journal entries that I will quote to demonstrate the essence of leaderful practice. In this rather lengthy entry, a middle manager reflects on the derivation of the individualistic practice of leadership.

> As a small child in grade school, being the leader usually meant that one possessed a quality that distinguished themselves [*sic*] from the other students. The best read "led" the reading group; the best athlete was chosen to be the captain of the sports team; the best musician was rewarded with the solo. This pattern continues throughout our education and then follows us as we mature into adulthood. Or does it?
>
> During one of my past performance reviews, it was communicated that "I was good at the hard stuff, but terrible at the easy stuff." The "hard stuff" was the technical and professional requirements of my profession. Like a child, I had worked hard on distinguishing myself as a student of my own career and had done great work for the executive team. The executive team had no doubts about my capability or knowledge base, and in fact, I was regarded as one of the natural talents in my field. However, they were unwilling to promote me because I was not a leader. I was not a leader because of my inattention to the "easy stuff."
>
> The "easy stuff" was the regard and acceptance of those who worked beneath me. In order to be promoted, the junior and secretarial staff needed to recognize my abilities as well. Up until that point, most of my interaction with the support staff had been abrupt and directive. In response to my actions, none of the junior staff wanted to team with me on projects or felt that I could be a mentor to their own development. If I was to be promoted, I was going to need the acceptance of those below.

A provocative reason for our hero worship is what Jean Lipman-Blumen refers to as "existential uncertainty," an immutable reality that the future is unpredictable and largely outside of our control.[9] Even though we increasingly understand much of human existence thanks to advances in science and technology, many of us remain at times in a state of fear regarding what the future will bring. The tragic events of September 11, 2001, only serve to heighten our fear. Under this cloud of uncertainty, many people look to heroes, or surrogate parent figures, who can bring us comfort and assurance, who can inspire us and explain the future. Accordingly, we endow our leader-heroes with enormous power to make decisions on our behalf, only to take the power back when times feel more secure or as we realize that some of our leaders are getting out of control. Look at what we have done in our posthumous biographical extracts to expose such modern heroes as Franklin Roosevelt, John F. Kennedy, or Martin Luther King Jr. in order to bring them back down to earth.

The point is that hero worship is unfortunately outdated in our age; indeed, it might have become outdated ever since the common man was thought to be able to go out into the world and make decisions on his or her own. Relying on a single leader to "separate the seas" for us works as long as the leader can successfully diagnose the environment and make correct decisions. But what happens when this leader errs? What happens when his or her followers realize that they have the maturity to make decisions on their own? What happens when the environment becomes so complex that no single individual could possibly discern all its elements? What happens when the leader dies and no one is available to take his or her place?

We simply must graduate from our reliance on single heroes because sooner or later, they will need *us* as collaborators in leadership. Note that leaderful efforts to incorporate followers in leadership goes beyond benevolence. According to this view, leaders should be concerned about "their people" and assure them that their interests will always be considered. Although we welcome this human perspective, it still represents a sympathetic view that encourages dependence rather than interdependence. Subordinates are placed in a psychological hospital in which they can feel secure, knowing that the leader will take care of them. In the direct aftermath of the September 11 tragedy, many chief executives said that they felt at a loss because they didn't know how to "take care of" their people. Why could they not just use the precious moments after the tragedy to just "be" with their people?

I submit that we don't want dependent subordinates who are waiting to act based upon an impending signal from the leader. We want our colleagues to act under their own initiative, not as loose cannons but as members of a well-oiled community that trusts their independence and needs their interdependence. Naturally, these initiators will check back with their community as appropriate. But if we insist that they wait for the proverbial "go-ahead," they may have lost their chance to act by the time they receive permission.

Nor do we want subordinates only willing to act on the basis of the concrete rewards that they can negotiate from their superiors. The point is: people are not necessarily standing around waiting for someone to motivate them. They're *already* motivated. If you have to motivate "your people" to get them to do something useful in your community, you have already lost them. Consider the definition of leadership used by Frederick Smith, CEO of Federal Express. In a recent interview he said that what distinguishes leaders is that "they're able to get people to coalesce around organizational rather than individual goals. And if they're good leaders, they motivate people to do their jobs to the best of their abilities and not just the bare minimum to avoid getting fired." [10]

His view, in my opinion ensconced in old logic about leadership, is that people, without the motivation of their superiors, will pursue only their individual goals or will only work at a minimum level. In this same interview, Smith went on to laud the efforts of a courier who was delivering visas to a couple about to travel to

Russia to adopt a little boy. Apparently, the couple needed the visas right away because of the fickleness of the Russian authorities. Unfortunately, their expected package had been misaddressed and time was running short. According to Smith, this courier, on his own initiative, tracked down the package, corrected the address, and then went miles out of his way to hand-deliver the visas. Two questions: was this courier not a leader for FedEx? Did he wait for motivation from the top to perform this service?

This more expansive view extends leadership beyond the confines of the chief executive suite. Organizations need to act responsively in a diversified environment. They can't afford to wait for the command from the top, even if the commandment is the expectant, "Thou shalt change." Whatever form the change commandment takes, "total quality management," "process re-engineering," even "organizational learning," nothing will stick if it's seen as a commandment. Everyone has to be involved in leadership; everyone has to take part in the change.

As we shall examine in developing leaderful practice, it is not useful to consider leadership as a unidirectional phenomenon. It is not a straight-line communication from the leader to the follower and then, in benign circumstances, from the follower back to the leader. The latter condition is potentially an improvement since it suggests that the manager will entertain feedback from the subordinate. But oftentimes the feedback is merely an attempt to help the manager learn to communicate more effectively with the subordinate or to provide him or her with a second opinion about a planned or made decision. It does not necessarily suggest to the manager how to involve others in the process of leadership. The manager remains firmly entrenched as the mastermind, except that, with feedback, perhaps he or she delivers orders in a more sensitive manner.

Some may protest that our employees as followers do not want to participate in leadership. For example, there does not appear to be a groundswell clamoring for employee ownership or self-management. Historically, few employees take advantage of company suggestion systems. This argument, however, has its base in a common reasoning flaw that stipulates that an idea is not valid until it is shown to be practiced. We would hardly wish to give up our democratic form of government, even though fewer than 50 percent vote in national elections. The point is that people need to have an opportunity to practice leadership. The opportunity has to be real and persistent. If it is, people will commit themselves to their community.

In some instances, followers may not wait for permission to participate in leadership. Whether as a result of a pent-up need to declare their rights or of an abuse of power by those in authority, they may seize their own opportunity to express themselves. In the wake of the sexual abuse scandal that rocked the Catholic Church in early 2002, lay groups sprang up to practically force the church hierarchy to be more leaderful. For example, a group called Voice of the Faithful, representing middle-of-the-road mainstream lay Catholics, formed for the purpose of sharing in the governance of the church. One of its original members, in her plea for expanding leadership, explained: "We're trying to save the hierarchy from itself, from its own insularity, secrecy, and medievalism. They need us."[11]

For many practitioners and writers, the leaderful form of leadership would seem an attractive idea that they have already embraced. Yet, it is so much easier to espouse than to practice. Consider the views of two of our most notable writers on leadership, Warren Bennis and James O'Toole. On one hand, they degrade the outdated notion of charisma, equating it with an inflated ego. They understand that leadership consists of working with and through other people. Yet, on the other hand, they prescribe leadership as a destabilizing force because "real leaders are threatening to those intent on preserving the status quo. A leader [is someone] who can motivate people to change." They go on to say that "a successful leader generates such high levels of respect and loyalty among followers, the performance of his or her successor will seem pale by comparison."[12]

Wouldn't we rather have leaderful individuals who can affect the status quo, not by becoming a champion in from the cold, but by working with us to manage our own conflicts, by encouraging us to talk openly with one another to identify our needs and our wishes for our community?

Can you see that even for these great writers, there is a need to keep that great leader out in front? I maintain that the "smooth talker" who can win friends and influence people has outlived its usefulness. Nor do we need the inspirational leader, the Vince Lombardi, who can shake things up, who can motivate, who can be admired. Do we really want leaders who are so inspirational that no one can take their place when they "hang it up"? Wouldn't we rather have leaderful individuals who can affect the status quo, not by becoming a champion in from the cold, but by working with us to manage our own conflicts, encouraging us to talk openly with one another to identify our needs and our wishes for our community? Wouldn't we rather have someone who can just as easily step aside and let others participate in leadership as subtly force us into dependence? When we reach adulthood, it's a distasteful bromide to hear the dictum, "grow up!" But at some point, we must—otherwise we give ourselves up to the direction of others. The view that we all have an unconscious need to subsume ourselves to a dominant authority figure may work well under Freudian psychoanalysis, but it doesn't play well as a basis for creating leadership within our twenty-first-century organizations.

Consider as a second example of great writers who subconsciously subscribe to heroic views of leadership while espousing participative action, the words of David Bradford and Allen Cohen. They offer a view of leadership that they even label "post-heroic." Consistent with shared leadership, they believe that anyone in a team can become a leader, able to seize opportunities, correct problems, and be accountable for performance. Subordinates, in their view, should be working partners, sharing responsibility for the overall success of the unit. Furthermore, they exhort subordinates to take initiative and not defer to any boss. They should have a purview of the entire organization, not just their immediate work area. Finally, a leader managing post-heroically, according to Bradford and Cohen, shares control with a team because decisions made by a "competent group of individuals . . . will generally be superior to decisions made by a single person." Yet, in the same text that produced these thoughts, the authors, in considering the question of whether team members ought to be partners in the vision-setting process of an organization, offer the following:

> Solo vision formulation saves time and avoids the problems created by dissenting individuals. . . . In most cases, the leader should initiate and the team should be involved. The leader has to make it clear that the work of determining the vision is important and that it will be brought to resolution and implementation. Insisting on movement is not the same as dictating the vision.[13]

Although I may be presumptuous, it appears to me that Bradford and Cohen are unaware that they espouse in one place in their text what they decry in another. They may be unaware of the contradictions that defy the post-heroic leadership they endorse. In their statements, for example, they appear concerned that members of the team may be "dissenting." Although they wish to involve team members in visioning, they advise at the same time that these team members defer to the directionality of their leader, without whom the so-called visioning process appears doomed. What is it about our culture that makes truly sharing leadership appear so uninspiring? Are we ready for an alternative tradition of leadership?

2 The Distinctiveness of Leaderful Practice

The Concern about Authority

Although leaderful practice applies at all levels of the organization, it might well face its most direct assault not from those on the front lines but from those in the executive suite. Executives and their exponents might say, "Sharing and collaboration might work well among regular employees, but we must set the course and tone of the organization from the top." For example, Carol Hymowitz, who writes an "In the Lead" column for the *Wall Street Journal*, reports the experience of general manager, Cynthia Danaher, in an article titled "How Cynthia Danaher Learned to Stop Sharing and Start Leading." According to Hymowitz, the very talents that bring success to leaders at the entry and middle levels of the organization become counterproductive when one climbs farther up the corporate ladder. Presumably, one can no longer be an "involved-with-people" boss, nor can one promote teamwork at the upper levels. Danaher's rationale is that "[p]eople say they want a leader to be vulnerable just like them, but deep down, they want to believe you have the skill to move and fix things they can't. . . . Moreover, once a manager is in charge of thousands of employees, the ability to set direction and delegate is more vital than team-building and coaching."[1]

These assertions by both Hymowitz and Danaher are not only nonleaderful but they can also lead to both poor morale among employees and resulting poor performance, especially under turbulent market conditions. As I have and will continue to establish throughout this book, we cannot afford to have workers await their orders from detached bosses who have sole possession on problem fixes even across the remote corners of the organization. As I will also discuss in chapter 6 on concurrent leadership, Danaher misuses the notion of delegation, assuming that it means *tasking* others lower in the organizational hierarchy. In fact, delegation occurs when others are prepared to *assume responsibility* for work that typically resides above their level.

Whether the manager is a man or a woman (as in this case), being tough is not necessary for leadership at the top levels of an organization. There is room for compassion and collaborative activity no matter where one sits. Danaher appears relieved to have learned that when "there's a rat in the room, she can be the one to kill it." She believes as an executive her approach is superior to two other leadership approaches: (1) There's a rat in the room; let's devise a plan to kill it; and (2) Did anyone notice that there's a rat in the room? Danaher's approach may be the most futile under the condition when no rat exists. I fear that managers like Danaher might spend all their resources killing "rats," overlooking community members who, if given the chance, could point out that there are none to kill.

Although leaderful practice is not antagonistic to hierarchy, we need to recognize that the latter is not always the most practical structure in which to operate an organization. As we shall examine in more detail in the next section, organizations are becoming more knowledge based. Some organizations are also "professional bureaucracies," which are inherently pluralistic especially due to the need to satisfy external professional norms and values.[2] In these organizations, such as universities and hospitals, no one person may have formal authority, and legitimate strategic objectives may vary across a range of stakeholders. Such settings require collective leadership. Among hospitals, for example, a CEO may have to share authority with the board, the board chairperson, a medical director, and several clinical department heads. No one person assumes dominant power (in spite of possible attempts of some of these position leaders to do so), since each is responsible to a prominent set of constituents. The only way to function is to accept that one is part of a leadership constellation and to learn how to lead collectively, concurrently, and collaboratively.[3]

Hierarchy is nevertheless a popular organizational structure, and executives—at the top of the pyramid—are typically responsible for managing the organization as a whole and overseeing how it interacts with the external environment. In large multidivisional organizations, a series of other levels of management exist, successive to the top, with such names as group manager, business manager, or functional manager.[4] Many writers have demonstrated through the years that senior leaders more often engage in complex tasks, such as planning, coordinating, and boundary-spanning, than junior leaders.[5] They are also thought to have longer time horizons.[6] Yet these activities, though functionally important, do not address *how* leaders should interact with those within their immediate and wider communities.

For example, in determining whether to engage in a merger, a CEO can't perform the requisite analysis and initiate contacts all alone. Such problems are often too complex for any single individual to handle. Most likely, the CEO will assemble or call on a top management team (TMT) to undertake this activity. Such a TMT will typically include individuals who have diverse functional expertise and who can approach the problem in unique ways but who can also develop collective capacities to coordinate their functions toward a consensual decision.[7]

Other activities, perhaps of a less global nature, are similarly going on in other parts of the organization. A product manager may have to figure out how to lower costs in her supply chain in order to compete on price with a competitor. A supervisor in marketing may have to determine whether to use a known ad agency for a new release. That supervisor may also need to assemble a team to evaluate current and prospective contracts. Although many assume that decisions tend to require more complex conceptual ability at higher levels, as decision making in organizations flattens—as managers in their respective domains gain authority to make decisions in that domain—lower-level decision making most likely will require comparable conceptual ability to higher-level decision making.[8]

Managers at all levels in an organizational structure, therefore, will need to exhibit flexibility and adaptability in the face of dynamic environments. It is no longer useful to think of supervisors at lower levels carrying out the orders of those above; in many instances, lower-level managers face ambiguity as much as those at higher levels. They just need the "authority" to carry out their own operations as they see fit. This idea is hardly a new presupposition. For decades we've known the value of decentralization. Here's how Rene McPherson, former CEO of the Dana Corporation, described it.

> Let people manage their assignments. Whatever risk we may find inherent in this idea is due primarily to the insecurity of management. . . . Frankly, it is much easier for managers to rule with the force of total authority than to share with their people the challenge of accomplishing a task.
>
> There is no single style of management for involving people within an organization. Such a climate is much more difficult to develop, however, where authority is centralized. Having worked in both types of organization, I much prefer that which is highly decentralized, placing the operating and decision-making authority where it best belongs—as far away as possible from headquarters.[9]

Many organizations are also experimenting with relatively flat organizational structures, such as horizontal or circular configurations. These tend to produce cross-functional teams that have a relatively high degree of autonomy to determine how to carry out their mission, whether in customer service, patient flow, or plan integration. In addition, these teams are often self-directed, operating without a designated leader.

At Harley-Davidson, for example, their circle structure doesn't call for managers; rather each circle has a "coach," someone selected by the circle not for his or her authority but for "acute communication, listening, and influencing skills." Responsibility for carrying out the work of the team and communicating with other teams does not lie only with the coach; any team member may perform such a role when needed. In the words of former CEO Rich Teerlink and executive consultant Lee Ozley, "We did not expect a single individual to emerge as the leader of the circle. Instead, we anticipated that leadership would be a shared responsibility."[10]

Structural Foundations

Given the incredible degree of complexity in our organizational environments—complexity that borders on chaos since it defies the comprehension of any one mind—there is a growing suspicion that leadership itself does *not* matter. This "leader irrelevance" argument contends that forces outside the actions of any one leader—the structure of the organization, market conditions, chance events—have a far greater impact on business outcomes.[11] The problem with this argument is that it is still ensconced in the dated view that leadership resides in a single person. If we can see leadership as a collective property, admittedly one stimulated and developed by the actions of one or a few individuals, then clearly it can have major impact on the business. After all, any business needs to achieve the key processes of leadership, whether in establishing and accomplishing a mission, sustaining commitment, or successfully responding to the environment.

Leadership and structure should co-exist, though leadership is thought to preferably establish structure rather than vice versa. It has also become widely recognized that bureaucracy no longer provides an automatically useful structure to cope with the nimble requirements of life in the information age. We need to entertain forms of organization that rely on collective rather than individualistic properties. One such form, referred to as the "radix" organization, emphasizes lateral relationships across functions, business units, and geographic regions. Radix organizations have evolved through our increasing use of teams, contingent workers, strategic alliances, and outsourcing.[12] These characteristics, in turn, have required an organizational form that maintains fluid and permeable boundaries and is highly adaptive to its environment. As for leadership, managers find themselves increasingly without authority to direct the tasks of others; rather, they can do no more than guide cooperation toward task accomplishment. In Russ Ackoff's words, there has to be a change from "power-over," suggesting authority or command, to "power-to," suggesting the ability to implement.[13]

Another new form of organization is known as a high-reliability or smart system. A smart system does the right thing, regardless of its structure. In a study of the modern nuclear-powered aircraft supercarrier, a megaorganization that could be characterized as "a million accidents waiting to happen," Weick and Roberts contend that its historically reliable performance has hardly been based on the actions of heroic, autonomous individuals.[14] Rather, the success of such an organization depends upon dense and sustained interrelations among the operating crews. The culture is represented not by macho heroics but rather by a collective mind involving cooperation and heed. Indeed, it is expected that organizations in the future will increasingly require reliability as much as efficiency and thus will require leadership that encourages collective practices over independent action.

Here's how Roberto Testore, President and CEO of Fiat Auto, puts it:

> For too long we have had a model of leadership founded on the power of the person. We are trying to change this by saying: "it's not important that the individual is brilliant, but that the team is

brilliant and successful." This is one reason for the current short-age of leaders. To get the leadership we want requires a cultural change—away from the individualistic model toward a team approach.[15]

In order to reduce the suffocating effects of bureaucracy, some very large organizations try to make themselves small. Consider Virgin, a company of more than 25,000 people that prides itself on becoming a global brand name. Some have referred to it as an amoeba, continuously dividing and reproducing. To keep itself lean, it organizes itself as a subtle network of interrelated companies held together by its values, speed of service, and customer orientation.[16] Similarly, Cisco Systems tends to split up units in the company as they become increasingly successful. According to its CEO, John Chambers, this allows for a more focused approach to the customer; however, it can only work if you allow the managers who are close to the customer decide how to grow the business.[17]

Alain Godard, former CEO of Rhône-Poulenc, adds that managers need to learn to accept uncertainty and a certain amount of imperfection in order to cope with the chaos of twenty-first-century organizations. In fact, he would encourage his managers to make decisions, 20 percent of which could be considered calculated risks. Otherwise, they would only continue to do the things that they are comfortable with, which, in turn, would likely lock them into a routine.[18]

An organizational metaphor that represents the structural difference between leaderful practice and leadership might be soccer compared to football. Tom Kelley, general manager of the product design firm, IDEO, claims that in soccer you have "a group of people flying in formation as opposed to a quarterback and the people supporting that person."[19] On the other hand, football is changing. Consider the actions of the New England Patriots during Superbowl 36. During the pre-game introductions, the St. Louis Rams sprinted through the tunnel first as the PA system announced their starters. When it came time to introduce the Pats, defying a league custom, they ran onto the field together, refusing to have the announcer single out their most notable perfomers. The subsequent MVP (most valuable player), quarterback Tom Brady, professed that they had no key individuals on the squad; they had only "team"!

Leadership and Followership

Leaderful practice takes a fresh look at followership and suggests that followership and leadership are in essence part of the same process. If we have reached a point in our organizational evolution that we no longer need leaders "out in front," then in the same vein, we no longer need our followers "back in line." Followers and leaders are interchangeable parts in the conduct of leadership. It is counterproductive in most of our knowledge enterprises to even use the concept of *follower* since it connotes "doing what you are told" because you are less valuable than the leader. Ridding our culture of this distinction between followers and leaders can go a long way toward directing attention away from ancient personalistic accounts of leadership and toward its rightful place as a mutual, social phenomenon. It characterizes the group as a whole, not the heroic attributes of single individuals. Leaderful individuals can create leaderful communities.

If we have reached a point in our organizational evolution that we no longer need leaders "out in front," then in the same vein, we no longer need our followers "back in line."

Consider the qualities that Robert Kelley describes for making an effective follower. He claims that such people

> have the vision to see both the forest and the trees, the social capacity to work well with others, the strength of character to flourish without heroic status, the moral and psychological balance to pursue personal and corporate goals at no cost to either,

and above all, the desire to participate in a team effort for the accomplishment of some greater common purpose. [20]

How many of you would like to see these same characteristics in your leaders? I hope you all would. These characteristics make for promising commitment to any community and are certainly as much a part of leadership as they are of followership.

A cluster of studies highlight the false dichotomy between followers and leaders, without this explicit intention. They start by suggesting that some followers have more value to the leader than others. Indeed, a theory known as "vertical dyadic linkage" (VDL) purports that leaders establish "in-groups" and "out-groups."[21] The former represents those granted greater access to the throne, which, in turn, accords them special privileges and responsibility. In-group members receive greater attention from the leader but in return must pledge their loyalty, work hard, and help the leader perform some of his or her administrative chores. In-group members also need to attend to their relationship with the leader in order to sustain it into the future.

Given that theories of this nature are antagonistic to leaderful practice, it is comforting to report that studies have revealed the obvious: choosing favorites creates feelings of resentment among members of the out-group and, moreover, undermines cooperation and teamwork within the work unit as a whole.[22] Needless to say, it is unproductive to intentionally create divisions within your community on the basis of favoritism. We need to uplift everyone in the community to contribute toward a collective mission. The last thing leaders need to do is polarize our communities, pitting team member against team member.

I think the time has come to radically adjust the notion of followership in our organizational lexicon. By this, I am suggesting that followership is plainly outdated if we wish to create meaningful communities with members empowered to act on their own behalf and on behalf of the community. Communities of this nature also tend to be committed to developing their own capabilities and learning from stakeholder feedback how they can continuously improve their performance. The endeavors of such communities don't seem to matter, whether making yarn, manufacturing silicon wafers, or processing insurance claims.[23] What is critical is not what such teams do but how empowered their members are in sharing the leadership of the enterprise. So, let's reserve the term *followership* for those instances when people truly need to follow, as in boy scouts learning new outdoor skills from their troop leader or new recruits obeying commands from their drill sergeant. But when it comes to working *together* to create something of value, let's see if we can replace the concepts of leadership and followership with leaderful practice.

Surprise: Managers Can Be Leaders

Another thing to clear up is to rid ourselves of the romantic distinction between a manager and a leader. I can never get over how willingly MBA students will demean their present and future selves by subscribing to views that depict managers as boring. Let's put it simply: leaders can emerge anywhere, at any time, and *be anyone*. Abraham Zaleznik submitted perhaps the most chauvinistic of accounts in his *Harvard Business Review* classic, "Managers and Leaders: Are They Different?" in which he depicts the manager as rational, bureaucratic, dutiful, practical, and unimaginative but the leader as visionary, restless, experimental, even "twice-born."[24] By twice-born, he suggests that leaders emerge because, having had an insecure childhood, it gives them a second shot to shine. I, for one, don't particularly care to have a brooding, social misfit in my group who fancies him- or herself as my savior.

John Kotter followed Zaleznik with his enumeration of distinctions between managers and leaders, though his classification is more benign.[25] Kotter feels that organizations needed both managers and leaders, but each has a different role to perform. The manager copes with complexity, while the leader handles change. Hence, managers focus on planning and budgeting, follow with organizing and staffing, and finish with controlling and problem solving. It is interesting to note that these functions fall into traditional control tasks long associated with bureaucratization. Leaders, meanwhile, have a different set of functions, namely, setting a direction, aligning people to the direction, and motivating and inspiring them to fulfill the direction. Although Kotter didn't demean the manager's functions compared to the leader's, the latter's certainly sound more exciting.

Let's move on from the archaic notion that managers do one thing and leaders another. It is true that managers are usually bureaucratically appointed and thus have position power throughout the middle of the organization. But they don't have to be "hired hands" (the root word for management is *manus* from the Latin for "hand"), condemned to a life of unimaginatively carrying out corporate goals or endorsing the status quo. Managers are hardly limited from leadership. They need to work with their peers, bosses, subordinates, and others and in this constant interaction, they have opportunities to emerge as leaders. A manager in a large financial services company journalized as follows on the proper setting for emerging leadership:

> I have tended to think of leaders as being part of something larger than the rather mundane corporate world. I realize now that leadership can come in many forms and on many platforms. Seemingly simple activities such as pushing a new report through the development process and into production in fact require a degree of leadership. I have come to appreciate that those in my organization and myself, for that matter, may exhibit some of the skills needed to lead effectively on a day-to-day basis. The larger backdrop of the political or religious arena is not necessarily the only stomping grounds of leaders.

I would add that the leaderful manager doesn't need to exert leadership as his or her sole responsibility. Leadership can emerge from any of the individuals with whom the manager comes into contact. What might be most leaderful about the manager is not that he or she takes the reins, but supports others to take them as the situation warrants. In 1998, the Conference Board prepared a report called *Bridging the Leadership Gap*, based on four hundred responses to a survey sent to Fortune 1000 companies.[26] The report concluded that leadership has become paramount to success in the global environment, but that sadly nearly half of the survey respondents rated leadership in their company either fair or poor. But where did the survey look for leadership? It looked for those in "leadership positions," namely, the senior, mid-level, and frontline managers. Is it possible that the Conference Board looked in all the wrong places?

Ironically, it has become increasingly difficult to find people to take managerial jobs or "leadership" positions. Middle managers especially are torn between competing demands from the top and from the bottom. Middle management positions, furthermore, tend to lack security, being often the first to go during times of retrenchment. Companies try to respond to the cynicism surrounding management positions by offering management development programs designed to "develop your leadership." What are the implications of this message? Such development programs imply that in order to become a leader, one has to take the program or the course. Between these programs and consecutive experiences in a variety of managerial positions, one may eventually make it as a "leader." Yet, we all know that leadership can exist anywhere, without a course to make it happen.

I'm not suggesting that we cannot teach leadership. It's just that leadership development has more to do with surfacing one's emerging leadership tendencies than with introducing particular skills that constitute someone's list of leadership qualities. We need managers to be nominally responsible for certain contractual and operational responsibilities in an organization, but it is short-sighted to train them to be leaders if leadership exclusively means taking charge. The leaderful community takes charge. Everyone in the group can occupy the representative role, when necessary. In the leaderful organization, training managers for leadership can be severely counterproductive. Rather than training one person in the community to be the "leader," it is advisable to train everyone to be leaderful.

Narrative Example

To cap off this chapter, I invite you to follow an exchange I had with my good friend, Robert Kittrell, former principal of Leadership Solutions. Robert represents very well the perspective of the sensitive leader, the one whom subordinates can go to when they experience either professional or personal problems. Our exchange evolved from a story that Robert asked me and others in an electronic forum to comment on. In it, the protagonist J. T. Malone from Carson McCuller's *Clock without Hands,* dying of leukemia, could not find a sympathetic friend to listen in his time of greatest need. Robert asked: "What do the people whom you lead want most from you?" My answer follows.

> Robert, my first reaction is that the way you ask the question may predispose an answer. You ask what do the people whom *you lead* expect from you? This may set up the leader, in some of your commentators' minds, as someone out in front, someone who has the vision and the answers, someone who will take care of us, someone who is sympathetic.
>
> However, the leaders of today can no longer be these heroes with the answers, these benevolents who will take care of us. Rather, they need to be team members who can work with each of us to face our own conflicts without illusion. They are people who can truly listen and learn from us. They help us face our own vulnerabilities as they are willing to face theirs. They are empathic, not sympathetic. They recognize the leadership in each one of us; they don't have to be our saviors.

Robert then replied.

> Joe, in my view, the leader is out front. It is he or she who is in, perhaps, the most vulnerable spot of all. The rest of the group de-

cides whether what he is offering is in their individual and collective best interests.

In the final analysis, no matter how collaborative they are, they have a constituency who is looking to him in some way to provide focus and direction for the group. If they decide that he is more interested in power than in dialogue, they will ultimately reject him. But, in the meantime, it is my view that followers do have expectations of their leaders. I do not believe this "out front" role precludes collaboration. Nor does it have to mean only benevolence. Groups go somewhere because someone risks taking on the role of focusing the group, and of providing an articulate vision.

For example, when you stand in front of your classroom, you are the leader of that group. I'll bet you that everyone in that room wants something from you. What, you say? You may decide the What arbitrarily, or you and they may discover the What together. If you are not the focal point, through which the group finds direction and vision, then someone else will fill that role. Is there any such thing as a leaderless group? Is there any such thing as pure consensus? When human beings come together, one person or many will not get all of their way. If the group moved only when everyone was completely satisfied, it would not work.

In response, I tried to clarify my position.

Robert, my response arises from some views of leadership that are not always popular (just listen to any talk show, for instance, and you'll hear people clamor for a new coach who can come on in and get all these players motivated!), but perhaps they will cause some necessary rethinking as we look at the new organizations and gatherings moving into the new century. Admittedly, the leadership to which I refer is not appropriate for a new group or for a group of dependent followers, but it may well be appropriate for a community of mutual learners and creators.

There do exist communities where leadership can be a shared phenomenon; where vision is co-created and not concocted only in the private mind of the leader. In such a community, leadership is something that the entire group has; it need not reside in one individual. No one has to motivate others; people are already in motion. When needs arise, any one of the members may emerge to fulfill a given responsibility. And one such need may be to articulate, from time to time, what the meaning is of this entity as it does its work together.

Yes, in a classroom, I am the designated leader, but there are such things as inquiry groups where everyone can share expertise; indeed, the greatest generative learning may arise from such a setting of collaborative learners. In such a setting, anyone can speak for the group. There need not be automatic consensus. Objections to anyone's position are accepted without fear of retribution or without worry about embarrassing the other party. Dissensus is thus built right into the process of ongoing inquiry. No leader is required to give the green light on critical inquiry since all the members are leaders; each feels empowered to advocate and deeply listen.

Robert topped off our dialogue with a query.

Joe, I cannot disagree with your last response back to me. It seems to me that you have articulated an ideal group composed of equally self-actualized, self-motivated, and self-confident people, all of whom know what they want, or all of whom have no fear of disclosing to the rest of the group what they don't know, or what they are unsure of. It seems to me to be a true portrait of all-for-one and one-for-all, with no hidden agendas. It is a picture of human beings in balance.

My presupposition, on the other hand, in asking my readers to reflect on the story of J. T. Malone, and in my response to your earlier inquiry, is that very few human beings belong to groups, or a group, which is so balanced, as to be in a state of "homeostasis."

In my view, as long as groups are populated by individuals, each of whom brings his or her private issues to the table, someone(s) will rise to be the chief among equals, and others will fall to be the lesser among equals. Such conditions do not preclude genuine give-and-take, nor true consensus building. These conditions, nevertheless, call for someone to be the official focus and visionary person in the group, even if s/he is informally or consensually designated as such. It is my belief that this kind of balancing happens in even the most sophisticated of groups.

Joe, is it that you are articulating and arguing the ideal, and I am being far more practical? Are we disagreeing because our beginning frames-of-reference are so different? What do you think?

I believe that leaderful practice is a very practical idea whose time has come. Our organizations are no longer populated by combat battalions that need their marching orders, even from sympathetic bosses. Robert, though, offers a challenge that will become one of the purposes of this book: to demonstrate the relevance of leaderful practice in day-to-day management. Perhaps after finishing this book, my readers, including Robert, will decide whether I have achieved this mission. In the meantime, I would like to finish this section with an additional comment on Robert's vision of a sympathetic leader whose primary interest is knowing what followers expect from him or her.

I would admit that leaderful managers may face their greatest challenge in giving up control, but not just coercive control. That may indeed be the easy kind to give up. More difficult is giving up on one's sympathy. Who knows, it might even mean giving up a human instinct. Yet, I am surely not arguing for callousness. To be empathic is not to be callous; on the contrary, empathy demonstrates the highest form of respect and compassion. It says to the other: "I know that you can solve your own problems, and if you're willing, perhaps we can solve them together. I trust you to decide what you wish to share with us in our community that will advance not just your cause but our mutual benefit as well."

3 The Challenge of Leaderful Practice

Preparing for Leaderful Practice

Leaderful practice may not always be specified as the first leadership behavior exhibited within the community. Take, for example, the case of a hospital unit team who, having put up with a heavy-handed supervisor for fifteen years, got a chance to try out a self-directed team approach when the supervisor left the hospital.[1] The unit chose as its team leader someone who had strong interpersonal skills and who it considered a much kinder and gentler person. Originally, the team was excited about performing some of the administrative functions that the former manager had previously handled. The new team leader worked right along with the other staff in the unit, sharing administrative responsibilities. Over time, however, the team members began to push a lot of the shared responsibilities back onto the team leader. They reverted to their old ways and began to insist that the new team leader take on many of the former manager's tasks. What happened to the self-directed team concept?

This case brings up the challenge of introducing leaderful practice when people and institutions aren't ready for it. Individuals and communities are not generally standing by, primed to assume leaderful behavior. They need to evolve both an appreciation for and an ability to adopt leaderful practice. Although I am advocating that teams adopt a leaderful approach, I recognize that communities cannot become leaderful overnight.

One way to begin is to have the official leader promote shared leadership, teamwork, and collaboration within the community. Shared leadership becomes possible when everyone agrees to pitch in to "cover" the leadership of the team. The existing leader would have to convince the members that he or she does not plan to abdicate leadership. Given their relative degree of experience with democratic teams, the members may or may not agree with the leaderful offer of sharing leadership in the first instance. There also may be members who agree to share leadership but are not yet ready to tackle this role, whether in part or on the whole.

Ultimately, in self-directed communities, members agree together how to approach the whole job. In the early stages, however, the official leader may need to take on more of a traditional leadership role: to assume some of the functions associated with standard supervision, such as calling meetings, setting agendas, coordinating tasks and schedules, and the like. This same leader may also initially need to work with the community to solve the easier technical problems—how much inventory to carry, what educational qualifications might be necessary to post a vacancy—before turning to the thornier behavioral or strategic issues. By the time the team becomes involved in critical policy matters, they will be on the right track to assuming authority for their own actions. In this instance, they may become involved with such issues as determining the life expectancy of a major product line, whether to build or buy a new component, whether to expand into a new country or region, or even whether or how to retain employees in the event of a downturn. Once members become more comfortable with making such decisions, they develop a sense of community responsibility. From this point, they also typically begin to see the value of distributing a variety of leadership roles and functions among themselves.

In some cases the official leader may not have to intervene excessively to stimulate leaderful adoption. Robert Lussier and

Christopher Achua reported on a critical event at a company called Valena Scientific in which it took a facilitator merely two days to bring together a small group of scientists and technicians who had been at odds about a particular manufacturing process.[2] The facilitator helped the scientists talk across their traditional disciplines, share their vision for the key project they were all working on, and develop a consensus on the proper approach to the critical manufacturing process in question. This leaderful function, referred to as the relational approach, is also known as developing social capital within a community. Social capital is created between individuals who essentially generate resources for themselves by establishing networks of mutual acquaintance and recognition.[3]

One CEO who was committed to but initially thwarted in his attempt to introduce relational leaderful practice was Rich Teerlink of Harley-Davidson. During Teerlink's tenure at Harley, the company came back from the brink of disaster to become a very successful American manufacturer. Although Teerlink admitted to having had to use a top-down approach during Harley's turnaround, he believes he is hardwired to share power rather than exert it. Yet, in his own words, he often found himself as CEO to have expected more participation from his employees than they actually wanted or were capable of. He recounts a story about bringing the company's sixty senior executives to an off-site meeting for purposes of mutual learning and collaboration.[4] During one activity, the executives, now formed into cross-functional groups, were asked to reflect on what strategic change they would like to see occur. As he visited each of the groups and observed their work on flipcharts, Teerlink was dismayed to find that most of them had prominently written down, "What does Rich want?" He was taken aback that the teams weren't quite ready to assume responsibility for corporate strategy. Perhaps they had the ability, but their cultural consciousness still expected a command-and-control mode from their "leader."

The challenge of preparing a community for leaderful practice may initially require, then, a facilitation role—one that raises awareness of the natural dynamics of groups and organizations so that members realize not only the challenge but also the benefit of mutually developing their team. This approach suggests that teams will vary in how quickly they can transition into leaderful practice based on such variables as the foreknowledge members have of each other, their degree of sophistication regarding working in groups, or their collective orientation and interest. Some individuals, for example, simply do not like working with others, preferring to do things on their own. Other members may actively seek or compete for social status within the group that might give them particular privileges, such as the right to initiate and direct conversations, the command of "air-time," or the prerogative to confirm or dispute others' views.[5]

Similarly, managers need to consider a host of contingencies in deciding when to release members of the community to assume greater leadership responsibility. The service industry, for example, has found that empowering service staff depends on their time and experience together, on the complexity of customer needs (e.g., how many choices the customer has in choosing a product or service), and on the complexity of the task in servicing these needs (e.g., whether the service is highly standardized—as in a McDonald's restaurant chain—or variable—as in a fine dining establishment).[6]

Another critical contingency in developing teams is the cultural values of the workers to begin with.[7] North American workers, for example, when compared to South Americans, tend to be more individualistic rather than collectivist. This means that they tend to respond more favorably to individual rewards rather than team rewards, feel as comfortable working alone as in teams, and are content to make decisions on their own. Collectivists, on the other hand, more often value harmony in a group, do not like being singled out in front of their peers, and feel content to work with a group of others. At the same time, North Americans are thought to have less power distance compared to South Americans, meaning that they are less inclined to accept status and power inequalities as a normal aspect of life in society. These cultural values suggest that unless North American workers are exposed to the individual benefits and opportunities of working in teams, they will likely resist being "thrown" into them and will not readily appease their management by merely going along with team-based strategies.

Consider two short cases presented by a consultant friend of mine. She believed that she practiced democratic team leadership with her consulting teams; yet, she was surprised when they seemed reluctant to take ownership of their teams in her absence. Here is how she described the situation.

> I had an interesting experience that I'm still trying to understand. Some years ago I had a consulting firm in my country, and we were a group of six or seven. I was the "owner" and leader, and they did the delivery work. I developed clients, looked for opportunities and wrote, and they took over once there was a possibility and provided services and maintained contact.
>
> Then I began the transition into moving into this country and thought: what better than letting them continue the business they have learned? Just keep up the good work, the contacts, the good delivery, and begin also looking for new opportunities. I didn't think I had a dominant leadership style in terms of not empowering the people, however I soon realized my style was stronger than I suspected.
>
> Well, to make a long story short, I invited them to become joint "owners," with the more senior person of the team (and well respected professionally) as the leader. Result: Total flop. Panic, questioning, crisis, drama. The rationale: "We cannot assume the owner's risk." We had no debts at that time and I was not selling the business to them—just giving it away!
>
> I couldn't explain enough that there was no risk other than not getting income, as it had been in the past. To me it was not such

a big step because we were a good team, they were in my opinion very empowered and although they frequently approached me with questions on what to do, I tried to avoid direction and always asked, What do you think you should do?

That seemed to work so well! So, this was five years ago. These days I think that I had more leadership influence than I thought, and that although our decisions at that time were jointly made, and they were autonomous, there must have been something more "symbolic" about my being around. They didn't believe it was possible without me.

Some two years after, a similar thing happened with another team. I was 80 percent owner of a business and had a 20 percent partner plus a team of seven people. I wanted to get out and invited each to acquire 13 percent of the shares and become community owners of the business. Another panic and crisis. Similar rationale: We don't want to pay (in this case they had to buy shares) for a business that we don't know will work (yet, it depended on them!). The team almost collapsed and some ended up leaving. The 20 percent partner took on the leadership with me from a distance and it took her over one year to get the team back to work.

So when I hear about shared and collective leadership, I evoke this nightmare. This is what I was persuaded could work, but it didn't. I still need time to understand what happened.

These cases point out quite dramatically that one can't just "show up" and expect everyone in the community to take over the leadership. It also suggests that consulting or sharing with others is not necessarily the same thing as empowerment and full participation. The situationalists perhaps have it right (we will examine the situational model in depth in chapter 6). One needs to develop a team to such a point of delegated responsibility that the nominal leader can virtually leave to work with other teams and tasks, checking in with the team every now and then to help it with its resource needs. In this instance, the leader's initial job is to help members over the course of time prepare to assume community leadership roles. One questions whether my friend was willing to let go of the ultimate control over her teams. If she were sincerely interested in letting go, then it would have been just a question of preparing them for a day when they ultimately might "own" their own company.

Working with Resistant Employees

Although I sincerely believe that most people will embrace leaderful practice if given the opportunity and preparation, some individuals will remain forever skeptical and resistant. I'm not necessarily referring to "problematic" employees, that is, bullies, substance abusers, harassers, racists, or generally disgruntled workers who are difficult to manage no matter what the leadership approach. These individuals are often subject to discipline and other legal procedures governed by human resource policies that are well documented elsewhere.

Some who may resist include temporary workers, who may have little interest in leadership since they typically have only a casual relationship with the unit to which they are assigned. Certain occupations might disincline employees or managers to leadership as well. Knowledge workers in our e-economy, for example, may be resistant because, socialized in their professional occupation or craft, they tend to align themselves more with their profession than with their organization.[8] They are thought to seek employability over employment. In search of venues in which to practice their fine-honed skills, they often become dissatisfied when forced to work in routine environments that don't stretch their skill set and imagination. They resist, then, only to the extent of their being confined to procedures and standards not defined by them.

My main interest lies in those employees who have every positive intention to contribute to their community but who do not believe it is their role to participate in its leadership. One of the first tasks in working with such resistant employees is to determine whether the individual's beliefs or the situation has caused this resistance. The latter is often easier to overcome. You might have a willing employee, ready to tackle new responsibilities, but who is working for an overcontrolling supervisor who squelches any attempt by any employees to exhibit independent action. In some cases, you may have a willing employee who lacks the necessary resources to assume a leaderful posture. A receiving clerk may be interested, for example, in ordering supplies for his unit. Not only does he know the requirements, but he also has first-name familiarity with the vendor. However, he's never had the authority nor been given the necessary forms to make procurements.

It is also possible that someone has never had the chance to assume leadership and thus, though inclined, simply doesn't know how to proceed. It may turn out that an employee, though fully capable of taking more responsibility for community decisions, may just lack confidence. Conversely, someone may have the willingness to go forward but may lack some baseline skills, whether technical, as in how to manipulate code in the unit's software, or behavioral, as in how to assemble staff and run a productive meeting.

It is more difficult to overcome attitudinal resistance—especially when based on internal beliefs rather than on external forces—to leadership practice. In this instance, it is first important to determine if the attitudinal resistance is solitary or public. Although it is disheartening to experience someone who chooses not to live up to his or her leadership potential, it is less problematic than interacting with someone who promotes blatant animosity against leaderful adoption. If the latter occurs, you may need to take action before the resistance spreads and sours the attitude of the entire work unit.

Although resistant individuals are not always open to personal intervention, as a leaderful promoter you may need to have an honest conversation with the individual. You might find that the person has personal or family problems outside of the work environment. In this case, you might determine if the individual needs professional assistance or just provide an open ear. Whether you're a peer or supervisor, it becomes your business when an individual's behavior affects the unit as a whole.

If you determine that an employee's resistance is not personal and is not disrespectful to you or to others, you may now have a legitimate issue about which to dialogue. Perhaps the individual simply does not believe that leadership should be collective or collaborative. It is unfortunately common for those of us who are enamored of a new approach to label resisters, referring to them as complainers or as negative influences. However, they may have a legitimate gripe against the new approach.

Initially, there is no substitute for truly listening to a resister's concerns. He or she may reveal an instance when a leaderful attempt failed, despite good intentions. Perhaps at one point an employee was reprimanded for assuming too much authority by a manager higher up in the hierarchy. Perhaps the resister truly believes that most people do *not* want to assume leadership.

It could be that resistance of this nature represents a test, albeit often an unconscious one, to determine whether the leaderful offer is legitimate. It may also represent a fear that extra responsibility will simply result in a lot of extra unrewarded work. Although leaderful adoption should be monetarily rewarded if, as expected, it ultimately leads to improved unit performance (see chapter 5), it should not distress employees. People should not see it as a way for overworked managers to off-load their administrative burdens. Rather, this approach tackles the relationship between people, uplifts the power in everyone, and seeks to honor the dignity of each contributor within the community.

If you find that the resister is an honest opponent of leaderful practice, then as a leaderful manager, you can do no more than engage him or her in productive discourse. Let the resister express his or her reservations and acknowledge them. You may discover useful data in these reservations regarding other sources of resistance within the unit or organization. Although you can affirmatively express your point of view, you need not convince your opponents nor should you pull rank to force them into a leaderful disposition. That would represent the height of hypocrisy. Agree to disagree and keep the lines of communication open. There is also no need to spend an inordinate amount of time in trying to persuade another party of your noble cause.

On the other hand, if someone in a managerial position persistently blocks a willing community from transitioning into leaderful practice and if you have authority over this person, you may need to confront him or her with your perception of the mismatch. In this instance, the manager in question represents not so much a worthy philosophical opponent as a real live blocker of a potentially critical cultural shift. You may prefer to reassign such a manager to a unit that is not as inclined to embark on a leaderful journey. Perhaps retrospectively seeing the psychic and economic benefit to his or her former unit will in its own right teach more about the values of leaderful practice than any lecture from an ardent boss.

Sharing the Roles of Leadership

I have proposed that leaderful managers may have to introduce community members, especially the most resistant ones, gradually to some of the requisite leadership roles of managing a community. Initially, the community may simply need to assess itself on its accomplishment (or lack thereof) of these key roles. The position leader might thereupon note that it is critical for the group as a whole to determine how to get these roles done, rather than to rely on him or her to do them all. As members take turns in contributing to the accomplishment, they may begin to appreciate the value and freedom of acting collectively.

According to one model, members may need to learn to self-manage four critical leadership roles (note that these roles are consistent with our earlier cited four critical processes of leadership).[9]

1. **Envisioning.** This first leadership role entails seeking to identify and articulate the meaning for the community, which, in turn, offers the group a set of goals to strive for. In most settings, teams know why they are assembled, but envisioning may give members a sense of higher meaning regarding their work or may provide them with a sense of stability as their mission shifts from time to time. For instance, an arborist hired by a parks and recreation office was able to demonstrate proper design and tree planting in a densely populated urban area, which gave a work crew a new sense of purpose in caring for the colorful saplings they'd planted all across the city. Envisioners often also facilitate the generation of new ideas or help recraft goals that have become stale over time.

2. **Organizing.** Beyond the envisioning goal, groups also need leaders who have a practical orientation, who can mobilize teams to set up a useful structure, and who can focus on the details of their operation. Although this role may sound somewhat mundane, it can give the membership a sense of order, especially if the group's assignments are complex and interrelated. Organizers sometimes use a creative approach. For example, in a commercial banking team, one of the members suggested that they all consider becoming specialists by client type rather than accepting assignments on a first-come, first-served basis. She also suggested that this might necessitate dividing up the bonus plan by team rather than by individual, since certain client types were known to generate higher yields. The team tried out the new system on a temporary basis and discovered that, with some adaptations, such as a rotating plan, it made everyone feel more engaged in the work and more committed to learning.

3. **Spanning.** Spanners bridge and link the goals of their community with interested parties or external stakeholders. They represent the community in the outside world, whether with groups or individuals internal or external to

the organization. Those often acting in some official capacity can secure critical resources for the community. Sometimes, the request for resources comes without official sanction. A chemist in a pharmaceutical R&D team by his informative and systematic briefings to the director of research was able to secure incremental funds for genomic research that members of the team believed could lead to an entirely new line of revolutionary products.

4. **Maintaining.** The maintaining role looks inward to ensure that group members' needs and concerns are addressed and that they are developing into a healthy working unit. The maintainer tends to have good process skills and understands the natural dynamics of group functioning. Often such an individual will model effective communication skills among members, such as giving nonjudgmental feedback or demonstrating active listening. He or she might also show particular sensitivity regarding the participation of all members, assuring that quiet individuals, for example, get their views aired. Maintainers also recognize that voicing emotions in groups is natural and healthy and can assist others in working through them.

Belbin presented an expanded list of eight team leadership roles (see Table 3-1).[10] These roles can also be applied to the four critical processes of leadership. As team members begin to assume more and more responsibility and rely less on the position leader, leaderful practice can come within reach. In the table, the Belbin roles—arranged in chart form to correspond to the critical processes—are defined. Team members should be able to determine their strengths and weaknesses in each of these roles.

It is important not only that members share leadership roles but also that they recognize that they need to be differentially emphasized during the various phases of the community's life. For example, those members with maintaining or team-building skills tend to be quite valuable during the early stages of team

TABLE 3-1. Belbin's Eight Team Roles

Critical leadership process	Belbin's roles	Definition
Setting the mission	Shaper	Sets objectives and priorities for the team; establishes a pattern for group processes and outcomes
Actualizing goals	Implementor	Turns concepts and goals into practical working procedures; carries out plans systematically
	Coordinator	Sees that the best use is made of the team's resources; recognizes the strengths and weaknesses of team members
	Completer-finisher	Protects the team from mistakes of commission and omission; searches for aspects that need greater attention; sees that work gets done
Sustaining commitment	Monitor-evaluator	Analyzes problems and evaluates ideas and suggestions so that the team is positioned to make balanced decisions
	Team builder	Supports team members; improves communication between members and fosters team spirit generally
Responding to changes	Creator	Advances new ideas and strategies; looks for new ways to approach problems
	Resource investigator	Explores and reports on ideas, developments, and resources outside the group

Adapted from the work of E. Meredith Belbin, *Management Teams: Why They Succeed or Fail* (London: John Wiley, 1981).

TABLE 3-2.   The Dimensions of Leaderful Development

Task	Low discretion	← →	High discretion
Decisions	Seeks permission	← →	Autonomous
Sphere of activity	Over own tasks only	← →	Beyond the job
Commitment	Calculative	← →	Intrinsic
Culture	Control-oriented	← →	Trust-oriented

development to help members learn to work through their differences and openly share their expectations with one another.

As a final approach to learning how to share community leadership, let's consider a multidimensional view of leaderful development.[11] In Table 3-2 above, five dimensions are represented as continua displaying relative development toward leaderful behavior. The development role of any supervising manager who has committed to developing his or her team can be construed as facilitating the movement of each community member to the far right on each continuum. This might mean giving members greater discretion in how they interpret and transact the tasks inherent in their jobs. Individuals would gradually assume more autonomy about the key decisions in their work, requiring less need to seek permission. They would feel empowered to affect decisions and actions beyond their own sphere of work. Their motivation would become not just calculative, based on monetary incentives, but also intrinsic, meaning that they would show genuine caring about their job, team, and organization. Finally, they would gradually prefer a work culture characterized by a trust orientation rather than a control orientation.

4 The Development of Leaderful Practice

Self-Awareness First

Since leaderful practice will likely require a change in outlook, especially regarding questions of control and participation in your community, it requires initiators who have become comfortable in their own inner world. Change may need to start with the "reflective stance," which merely asks you to pause sufficiently to gain some awareness of your own actions. Ask yourself such questions as: Who am I, and what am I trying to achieve? What impact do I hope to have on the people around me, on my community, or on my society? Am I willing to share control with others? Do I believe in the capabilities of my associates? Am I willing to accept honest feedback on any experiments I wish to undertake in my leadership? Am I prepared to learn from my mistakes and examine my assumptions? Can I show my own vulnerability and even admit to others that I may not have all the answers?

Questions such as these require courage to ask of yourself privately, let alone in the company of others. Becoming leaderful, then, starts with doing work on yourself, especially learning how to "let go." Dr. Iva Wilson, former president of Philips Display Components Company and coauthor of *The Power of Collaborative Leadership*, displays this inner struggle.

> [Y]ou can't do this work without devolving power. So while you're trying to make that transition, there are going to be difficult moments for both yourself and the organization until you reframe

and are truly seen as a leader that is not using power in the old ways. This is where the need for collaboration comes in, because you will need other people to make this transition successfully.

As a leader, you have to be humble and accept that you do not have all the answers. But knowing when not to act so that things will come out better than if you did act is difficult. I wish I had more practice in letting go, having faith in the flow of things, and realizing that we're not the center of the universe. . . . We become so self-centered—not in self-interest, necessarily—but in believing that we alone can do it.[1]

"I wish I had more practice in letting go, having faith in the flow of things, and realizing that we're not the center of the universe."

Leaderful practice begins, then, with a personal awareness of your capabilities. Many of us placed into line positions eventually learn to operate on what Prasad Kaipa refers to as "autopilot," a set of mental models that represent a rather stable view of reality.[2] We tend to rely on patterns that "got us there" in the first place. Unfortunately, if these behavioral patterns lead to ineffective performance, we may have lost our ability to bring them to a level of awareness. In our efforts to achieve success, many of us have forgotten who we are. We live in a world of images, of self-interest, and control. We need to be awakened. Our world can become more fulfilling if we allow compassion, authenticity, trust, and openness to guide us. We need to awake from the autopilot of success and achievement in order to rediscover our selves.

In undertaking the process of self-discovery, we need to appreciate the mixture of life experiences that have led to our present way of being. Many of us may discover that we need to find an inner purpose to guide our everyday activities. Others need to become more aware of the gaps between our intentions and our behavior. This requires both an ability and a willingness to retrace our reasoning and the behavioral steps that have led to the actions that play out in our lives. It requires the courage not only to examine ourselves independently, but also to open our experiences to trusted others.

Barbara Mackoff and Gary Wenet believe that leadership capacity can arise from key life experiences, available to us if we but reflect on how we can integrate these experiences into our leadership lives.[3] They refer to this process as "inner work." Among the sources of these experiences are our parents, exemplars who championed our ability or served as models, and life-changing events that shifted our perspective.

Robert Lee and Sara King add a number of other dimensions to further the search for self-awareness.[4] They would have you determine what truly motivates you to engage in leadership. Do you become involved for the rewards, for impact, for service, or for deeper meaning? What competencies do you bring to the table? Are you effective, for example, in building trust, in forging teams, in creating networks, in getting things done, or in working through ambiguity and uncertainty? What leadership qualities most distinguish you, and what personal characteristics align most with these qualities? For example, a calm and easygoing demeanor tends to align well with resilience under fire. A cheerful and affectionate disposition tends to align well with the quality of fostering teamwork.

Kevin Cashman talks about the need to access not only our conscious beliefs—which are known to us—but our *shadow beliefs* as well.[5] Shadow beliefs are manifestations of hidden, unexplored, or unresolved psychological dynamics. We often unconsciously construct them from secrets that we don't wish to examine. Unfortunately, shadow beliefs, if left unexamined, can produce such ill effects as addictive behaviors, relationship difficulties, imbalanced lifestyles, and health problems. Further, they often go undetected because they are associated with leadership behaviors that others may see as strengths. Consider, for example, the trait of charm. Although normally seen as a strength, some may use it as a means to succeed, no matter what, even if they have to manipulate others. Similarly, conscientiousness, though typically well regarded, can degenerate into compulsiveness and perfectionism. Unless we bring the shadow beliefs underlying so-called strengths to the surface, they may lead to consequences that can derail an otherwise productive and contented individual.

Fortunately, you do not need to undertake the process of self-discovery toward a more open, leaderful perspective on your own. You can and should reach out to other colleagues to work through experiments in leaderful practice. This means turning to others not just for unconditional support but also for honest feedback about your personal transformation. No one is immune from self-deception. We all believe that we practice what we preach, but without feedback from trusted others, our reflective processes will inevitably break down. We need to persistently test ourselves and question whether we are behaving as we wish when it comes to our impact on others.

Feedback of this nature goes beyond the popular "360-degree" feedback process. According to Cashman, we should focus on what he calls "720-degree" feedback.[6] In 360-degree feedback, you obtain impressions about your performance from immediate stakeholders, typically your boss, peers, subordinates, and even customers. However, Cashman is concerned that such feedback may only help individuals learn how to create themselves in the image of others. This *outer* feedback may help you learn how to adjust your outward manifestations toward others. However, without adding inner 360-degree feedback, you may not come to appreciate how your inner, authentic self may produce the behavior in question. Hence, it is not enough to know that others see you as perfectionist; it is just as critical to learn that you have become obsessed with an overdriven will to succeed at all costs, perhaps to achieve beyond a level attained by your brother, who may have been the "favored" son in the family.

Self-discovery through feedback requires reflective space to evaluate and interpret the information that you obtain. Given the fast pace of organizational life today, finding such a reflective space may be easier said than done. Many companies rely on coaching or mentorships to facilitate the process of incorporating feedback. If nothing else, a coaching session provides time to slow down and reassess yourself. Coaches and mentors can also help you distinguish behavior from personality since the former is easier to change and to develop. They can provide a frame of reference to help you understand the contextual factors that the organization values. For example, a competitive culture might stress the need to hoard information, whereas a leaderful culture should emphasize sharing. Coaches and mentors can also help you convert feedback into developmental goals that can contribute to further professional and personal growth. They may also suggest methods to help you manage conflicts with others and to overcome unwarranted resistance to change.[']

Finding a reflective space doesn't have to be a private affair. Some people might benefit from the collective reflection that can occur in the company of impartial peers with whom you share common hopes as well as frustrations. Such a gathering can also give those in managerial positions a chance to receive feedback, unfortunately an often scarce commodity in the corporate environment.

Discovering our inner selves means peeling back the external images we have learned to rely on that in many cases block our self-discovery. These images may correspond to our everyday achievements or to occasional stimulations—such as bungee jumping—that may falsely give us a sense of identity.

We need to look inside ourselves to find our real selves. Thomas Merton notes:

> We are warmed by fire, not by the smoke of the fire. We are carried over the sea by a ship, not by the wake of a ship. So, too, what we are is sought in the depths of our own Being, not in our out-

ward reflection of our own acts. We must find our real selves not in the froth stirred up by the impact of our Being upon the beings or things around us, but in our own Being which is the principle of all our acts.[8]

In learning to engage in leaderful behavior, it is not sufficient just to know ourselves. We must also know how we impact others. Only through this interpersonal awareness can we engage in the necessary preparation and imagination that will allow us to change ineffectual patterns. It is not that we are never allowed to be grouchy; that would deprive us of our humanness. Rather we need to recognize when we get grouchy and how it affects others in our immediate community. In some instances, we may need to retain that grouchiness. In other cases, we may be able to temper our mood so as not to infect those around us with toxic behavior.[9]

As a general rule, most communities flourish when the overall mood tends to lean toward humor and kindness. Leaderful managers attempt to learn how to reinforce this cultural predisposition. A good first step is to remember the requirements, according to Carl Rogers, for creating a climate of personal growth within a team.[10] He called for people to be genuine with one another, to express positive regard toward one another, and to practice empathy, namely to try to experience reality as another.

Such self-awareness becomes requisite especially to persist against organizational circumstances that may not necessarily favor leaderful practice. In this instance, individuals may have to display unusual determination to stay the course. Phil Carroll, formerly with Shell Oil and Fluor Corporation, puts it this way:

> If you're going to go into this as a leader, you have to have an intensity of belief in what you're doing that is very high. You have to honestly say to yourself that if I cannot do this—if the organization rejects my efforts to make change—then I have failed. If leadership above me will not support it, if my boss or whatever key support I need won't let me do this, then I'm better off out of here.[11]

From Self-Awareness
to Self- and Team Leadership

Once you have a sense of personal mastery, you can work on mastering self-leadership. What is self-leadership and how do you introduce yourself, let alone a resistant boss or an apathetic community membership, to it? Manz and Sims, in their conception of "superleadership," explain that self-leadership arises from personal "behavior-focused" and "cognitive-focused" strategies.[12] The former entail such strategies as self-observation, self-set goals, self-reward, and self-criticism. As an individual, it is important to understand and observe yourself before you can advise others. You also need to reward yourself for accomplishments in self-leadership, but be willing to solicit feedback, even criticism, from others regarding your experiments in self-direction. Among the cognitive strategies, Manz and Sims essentially advise people to talk to themselves and, in so doing, build natural rewards into tasks or become increasingly aware of personal beliefs and assumptions. Natural rewards are intrinsic in character; consequently, they result from activities that can instill a sense of competence or self-control over life and work.

Having mastered a degree of self-leadership in themselves, position leaders can begin to model this behavior for others.[13] They can encourage their associates to experiment with similar behavioral and cognitive strategies, such as setting self-goals and using natural rewards. In some instances, position leaders may choose to assume a coaching role with some of their subordinates. Although this represents more of a formal approach to mastering self-leadership, it gives a clear message to members of the community that self-development and learning are valued.

It is important to note that self-leadership does not prescribe achieving individual goals at the expense of the community. People do learn to take care of themselves, but they are also encouraged to take care of each other. One of my students, who had been a Peace Corps volunteer, suggested that the link between self-leadership and community leadership is formed through stewardship (which I shall cover in depth in chapter 7). People need to share their learning with one another as a gesture of commitment to the greater good of the community to which they belong. A relevant passage from this student's journal follows.

> It would have been easy for my farmers to simply learn and enact the projects that we were working on and not to share their knowledge with others. However, every one of my farmers actively sought out others with whom to share their new knowledge. They did this, not for me, but rather because they understood why I was there working with them, and they believed in the value of the project. They knew that the more far-reaching the project, the more far-reaching the benefits for all.

Having mastered a degree of self-leadership in themselves, position leaders can begin to model this behavior for others.

The link between self- and team leadership is enhanced as members see their teammates become willing to take responsibility for their actions, including soliciting feedback regarding contributions they make to the overall team effort. They also see the power of collaborative action, acknowledging that there is generative potential in teamwork. People can do together what they may not see themselves capable of doing as individuals. Consider these words from a journal of one of my students: "Through reflection I came to the conclusion that my personal lens of viewing a piece of data is more helpful if combined with the lenses of other [teammates]. I realized that my lens is a *limitation* if used in isolation, but a *strength* if used with others."

Personal self-leadership skills may well be necessary before teams are prepared for the official leader to hand over responsibility to the community itself. Many people have heard of the unusual experiment in leadership that has characterized the W. L. Gore company, the maker of Gore-Tex. Gore calls itself an "unmanaged" company because it has no hierarchy, no structure, and no titles except for what is required for incorporation purposes. Its founder, Bill Gore, once proudly declared that "leadership is defined by what you do, not who you are." As a result, it comes as no surprise that at Gore in annual surveys conducted by the human resource department, more than 50 percent of associates, as they are called, answer yes to the question, "Are you a leader?"[14]

At any point, company associates can start up a project by recruiting members until a team, and even an entire plant, has formed. A company like Gore can only work, however, if everyone chooses to take responsibility for his or her behavior as a self-leader, someone who can both manage him- or herself and, at the same time, contribute to the success of the company as a whole. Gore associate, Bert Chase, was quoted as having said: "This place is for people with hound wings who want to fly."[15]

The behavioral and cognitive skills of superleadership are relevant in the case of transforming a culture to a team environment. Individuals need to establish goals for the team, engage the team, and then continuously solicit feedback regarding the contribution they are making to the overall team effort. Thinking team thoughts can also be useful. Fisher and Sharp suggest that people interested in adopting collaborative strategies consider repeating to themselves such slogans as "ACBD—Always Consult Before Deciding."[16] This particular slogan wouldn't have to be adopted for every decision, but at least it highlights consultation as a consideration.

In a study of some 100 teams in four different organizations, Kirkman and Rosen found four levers or steps that management, interested in a self-directed team environment, can take to ensure the likelihood of success of any team empowerment venture.[17] The first step, boundary management, essentially asks that the official supervisors of the team learn to stay out of the way once team members show themselves capable of solving their own work-related problems. The second step, procedures and systems, calls on the teams to establish their own production and service goals and standards, including the handling of customer relations.

The third lever, human resource management—perhaps the most difficult—calls on the team to determine its own compensation system as well as such human resource functions as hiring, appraisal, development, discipline, and discharge. The last element, social structure, permits teams to access whatever strategic information they need, including even the resources of other teams, to perform their job.

The Kirkman and Rosen study found that implementation of self-directed work teams would be doomed to failure if it didn't take into consideration some of these steps, which all together attempt to untangle the effect of centralized bureaucratic control systems. Control needs to be decentralized for team leadership to occur.

The chairman of AES Corporation, a Virginia utility that participated in the study, said: "We want people to take ownership of the whole—the way you care about your house. You run it; you keep it up; you fix it. When something goes wrong, you own the problem from start to finish. And nobody has to tell you to do it because the responsibility is all yours."

Preparing an organization to embrace leaderful practice requires efforts at the organizational or system level as well as at the individual and team levels. The top management of the organization has to look deep inside itself to determine if it is prepared to turn over the reins of power to individuals and teams, especially when it comes to according them access to information and the freedom they need to run their own affairs. If the organization is tightly hierarchical, for example, any pronouncement on behalf of collective decision making will be viewed with suspicion. Similarly, employees have a sense of the defining values of their corporate culture. Democratic values are most compatible with leaderful practice. In a company that values production at all costs over employee development, or that values the use of political currencies ("who you know") to get ahead over advancement on the basis of performance and commitment, calls for greater participation in leadership will likewise fall on deaf ears.

One of my students, an investment banker, wrote about his firm's attempt to push self-directed work teams. He wryly framed his firm's efforts.

> We have started out with very small groups, and the groups are tackling some of the firm's simpler quality issues. The idea of self-directed teams was rolled out a year ago and there was and still is skepticism among senior management. My Managing Director asked, for example, why we needed to ask the teams what needed to be done; he would be more than happy to tell them exactly what needed to be done and how to do it!

At the supervisory level, facilitators of self-directed teams can exhibit a number of behaviors that can help the teams become more self-reliant. Perhaps the most important of these behaviors entails monitoring the social and political environment affecting a team so as to run the necessary interference to ensure that the team can do its work. In some cases, this might mean acquiring the necessary resources (materiel or information), obtaining support or clearance for the team, or even providing technical assistance. As an example, consider this case of a facilitator working through some problems with his team having to do with the development of a new piece of equipment. It takes place at a durable goods manufacturing plant in the Midwest U.S.

> After he [a team member] showed me different things, I said that I'll make some sketches of what I think you want, then I'll talk to the first-shift person, the second-shift person, and then the third-shift person and see what their ideas are. I also came in on the off shift. The following week I brought three sketches in. I also wanted the other facilitators to be part of it, so I gave them

a copy, too. And I asked them all to choose which one. The choice was unanimous.

I should point out that this same facilitator, who was highly rated by his team, subsequently took this information to the appropriate sources in the broader organization and obtained support for building the new piece of equipment.[18]

Besides working on the boundary of the team, facilitators also initially work inside the team to prepare its members to develop their team leadership. For example, facilitators need to help team members build trust toward one another, to display interest and flexibility regarding the decisions they make on their own, and to coach them in managerial skills if needed. The latter might include skills in communication—such as listening and providing feedback, managing conflict, and conducting meetings—as well as skills in human resource management—such as recruitment and selection, performance evaluation, and discipline.

Employees need to have sufficient ability and willingness to accept a self-directed approach. Are they prepared to have a team control its own strategic goals and operational decisions? Are they receptive to cross-training so that they can interchange their functions on occasion with each other? As noted earlier, a team orientation is collectivistic in character, emphasizing team goals and performance over individual accomplishment. A certain level of altruism is required for people to become willing to give up some of their individual benefits on behalf of the team. Organ refers to this form of altruism as organizational citizenship in which workers are as likely to recognize and respond to the needs of their co-workers as to themselves.[19] Examples of such citizenship behavior include volunteering for additional team duties, assisting colleagues, being punctual to meetings, or, more generally, actively participating in organizational matters that do not directly benefit yourself.[20]

Besides preparing people for team self-direction at the individual level, the teams themselves as well as the wider organization need to be ready to support an evolution toward collective functioning. At the team level, for example, are members prepared to coordinate their heretofore independent duties with one another? Are they prepared to learn together as a unit? At the organizational level, are top managers willing to share formerly undisclosed strategic information that may be critical to the team? Are human resource policies in place to turn over traditional hiring and evaluation functions to the team?

As a summary of the aforementioned preparedness dimensions, I have distilled the readiness characteristics for leaderful practice down to four principles that apply across the individual, team, and organization levels.[21]

1. Be sure that leaderful individuals and communities have the necessary resources—whether information or monetary—that will allow them to assume accountability for their empowered decision making.

2. Add a learning component, both in skills and in attitude, to prepare all involved to assume shared responsibility.

3. Ensure that there is a commitment, especially on the part of management, to allow leaderful behavior to proceed without taking back control at the first misstep. Leaderful practice requires trust in the first instance. It also requires time to take. Managers and supervisors must be truly interested in sharing power and decision making and thus willing to abide by the decisions of the group or community that has assumed responsibility.

4. Be selective—leaderful practice should be accorded to those most ready to assume the challenge. There is no "one size fits all" category; for each individual or community, the extension of shared power and authority must proceed on a case by case basis.

5 The Benefits of Leaderful Practice

WHY SHOULD ANYONE ATTEMPT TO BUILD A LEADERFUL COMMU-
nity? What are the consequences of leaderful practice? Why do
we expect leaderful practice to produce beneficial outcomes?

Leaderful behavior is inherently collaborative. It is control by
the many rather than from the few. For most problems in our era,
two heads *are* better than one. So, it should come as no surprise
that leaderful practice is in the eyes of this writer a more effective
approach to community leadership than the classic alternative of
"being out in front." It builds capacity to take mutual action. It ignites the natural talent in people to contribute to the productive-
ness and growth of the community.

Bottom Line Impact

Those people in a community who are encouraged to fulfill their
potential are often inclined to dedicate some of that potential to
their organization, if given a chance. In turn, such a contribution
can have "bottom line" business effects, whether in established or
in start-up organizations. A study at Cap Gemini Ernst &
Young's Center for Business Innovation, for example, found that
a principal reason for new companies failing to exceed their IPO
prices was their inability to engage employees in corporate goals
and provide a satisfying work environment. A Gallup survey
found that the most "engaged" workplaces (those that involved
people in doing quality work, in fulfilling their talent, in demon-

strating compassion and commitment to employees' growth), compared to the least engaged, were 50 percent more likely to have lower turnover, 56 percent more likely to have higher-than-average customer loyalty, 38 percent more likely to have above-average productivity, and 27 percent more likely to report higher profitability.[1]

A study by Kravetz and Associates found that Forbes 500 companies that engaged in what they called "progressive" human resource practices (such as participative management, decentralized structures, employee development) exceeded their nonprogressive counterparts' growth in sales by $190 billion and their profits by $56 billion. The study also asserted that 80 percent of the progessiveness factors involved no cost at all; rather, they just entailed a corporate focus on people-oriented leadership.[2] It just stands to reason that when the chips are down—were the company to be blindsided by a competitor, by a new technology, by a sudden shift in market preferences, or even by a crisis or tragedy—it is imperative to manage with an engaged community, one in which members practically volunteer their services.

To Gary Hamel nothing short of revolutionary practices to deliberately upset the status quo will suffice to build the future in which modern companies will compete.[3] Moreover, the revolution cannot be led by a few at the top; it has to be a democratic practice in which anyone, the administrative assistant and the CEO, can challenge standard orthodoxies that prevent the firm from generating new ideas and strategies. Organizations need to pay as much attention, then, to human processes—how people openly dialogue with one another, whether they can challenge their superiors without adverse repercussions—as to bottom-line results. Leaderful practice recognizes that the means to accomplishment should be stressed as much as the ends themselves. Otherwise, we risk the enduring health of the enterprise for a short-term gain.

Since leaderful practice is a new characterization, there are not yet studies that link it to bottom-line results. However, an abundance of research on related social experiments in teams and organizations exists. For example, studies of participative management in all its forms—job enrichment, total quality management (TQM), empowerment, organizational learning, and the list goes on—have revealed impressive economic results, when implemented properly. The last caveat, *when implemented properly,* simply means that any leaderful approach must take into consideration the ability and willingness of the workforce, the nature of the product or service, the orientation of the organization, and existing cultural values.[4]

Let's take a closer look at these conditions. As I discussed in chapter 4, leaderful practice requires people to be engaged— to have the ability, motivation, and confidence to participate in leadership. Although most products and services today require an increasing level of knowledge and skill, many jobs can still be structured in simplified ways that may not require much discretion or judgment. My own preference is for management to minimally consult with the workers affected to see if restructuring jobs for increased responsibility would be feasible or desirable. If so, mobilizing workers for leaderful practice would likely require support, as we have mentioned, in the form of access to information, resource provision, and learning opportunities. It is also imperative that the organization and its managers endorse leaderful practice, in both their actions and words. Further, the degree to which leaderful practice is adopted throughout the organization will shape its acceptance. Finally, leaderful practice as an enduring philosophy needs to be sanctioned by the values of the existing culture.

If these conditions are met, bottom-line results are likely to accrue to the organization through a number of intervening processes.[5] This means that leaderful practice may not directly affect the bottom line, but may be a key precipitating factor. For example, we know that if workers feel empowered and fairly treated, they feel better about their jobs, which, in turn, reduces the rate of turnover and absenteeism. The link to performance and productivity from reduced costs associated with turnover and absenteeism becomes obvious. As further substantiation, if leaderful conditions result in having the people who implement decisions gain access to all the knowledge available guiding these decisions, then decision making as a whole should improve.[6]

Some of the important intervening factors that I propose to be directly affected by leaderful practice include:

- **Quality.** Leaderful conditions are expected to lead to pride in one's craftsmanship.

- **Innovation.** Full involvement leads to the contribution of one's heart and mind to new problem-solving processes.

- **Change.** Trust and support increase the adaptability of the community and reduce resistance.

- **Flexibility.** People feel challenged trying out new ideas and methods.

- **Learning.** Members of the community look to continuously improve their performance.

- **Supervision.** Greater use of self-management leads to reduced need for direct supervision.

- **Resiliency.** Leaderful individuals persist even when faced with adversity.

- **Proactivity.** Operating proactively, people tend to anticipate problems and are inclined to act independently and interdependently.

- **Output.** As people commit to their mission, the rate of output should increase after an initial learning period.

- **Commitment.** Increased satisfaction and commitment generally lead to greater attraction and retention of employees.

Data also show both a perceived and real direct link between participative programs and bottom-line results. For example, two studies by Lawler and his associates of Fortune 1000 firms found that employee involvement not only produced better operating results for the sponsoring organizations but also increased their industry reputations.[7] These studies broadly defined employee involvement as involving all levels of employees in the organization in four key factors: power, information, knowledge, and rewards. The first factor, power, is most consistent with leaderful practice since it entails consciously bringing employees into the process of managerial decision making. The contrast would be choosing to make decisions on your own within the confines of the executive suite. President Richard Nixon said of this decision-making style: "I would not think of making a decision by going around the table and then deciding on the basis of how everyone felt. Of course, I like to hear from everyone, but then I go off alone and decide. The decisions that are important must be made alone."[8]

Leaderful practice calls for participation in leadership and decision making at all levels and in multiple decision processes. Although it has to be developed, as was cautioned in the last chapter, its effectiveness will be enhanced as its reach is extended. So, to achieve positive bottom-line results, it may not be enough to merely consult employees on possible solutions to a problem. It may not be enough to involve them in the planning, design, and evaluation of an intervention but not in its implementation. The benefits of leaderful practice will accumulate as individuals, who are willing and able, concurrently and collectively participate in *all* phases of leadership.[9]

Bringing Your Whole Person to Work

Even though the potential of having leaderful practice affect the bottom line is robust, one could argue the case from an ethical point of view. To put it simply, allowing people to share in the leadership of their communities is simply the right thing to do. It is inherently human to wish to affect the endeavors to which we dedicate our time and commitment. Leaderful practice inspires genuineness among community members, enabling them to bring their whole person to work. Employees don't need to fragment their work and their personal selves. Many if not most of our important social relationships are formed at work, and we want these relationships to be genuine. Genuineness can contribute to worker satisfaction and retention. A 1999 study of more than 6,000 workers by Randstad North America, for example, found that the top reason employees gave for staying with their current company was affection for their co-workers (71 percent).[10] People don't want to "play a role" *within* their own community. Unfortunately, some of the current guidance on leadership argues for this very role-taking behavior. Focusing on developing the self for leadership, the book, *Discovering the Leader in You*, warns prospective leaders that they are no longer "one of the gang."[11] The authors caution leaders to prepare to lose their long-lasting, genuinely comfortable relationships, to instead expect a feeling of "aloneness." They further advise that the higher you climb in an organization, the more you need to tightly control your feelings and your words. "You may want to relax and joke around. . . . But relaxation becomes a scarce commodity. You must be more conscious of your image. A show of anxiety might easily spread anxiety among your direct reports."

The book, *Executive Leadership*, focuses on subordinate behavior. Its author advises subordinates, due to their inferior posture in the organization, to be guarded. They need to make themselves heard, particularly when plans are in the idea phase, but they also have to "suffer silence when the executive's decisions go counter to [their] idea of what is operationally correct or personally desirable." The author goes on to counsel subordinates, if they need to be critical, to be "critical in a deferential way, even though the actual feeling may be deep resentment."[12] This type of counsel strikes me as contrary to the sense of integrity and genuineness that leaderful behavior calls for. Although it is reasonable to ask subordinates to be fair and understanding, perhaps even polite, it is unreasonable to ask them to be deferential in the face of decision making that they oppose. Surely we don't need communities constituted of subordinates who spend a fair amount of their time suppressing their deeply held opinions and carrying around their deeply felt resentments.

Not only do we want the members of our community to express themselves, we want them to *be* themselves. Further, the experience of work need not be a deviation from your personal development or from your rightful personal enjoyment of life. Work can be fun and personally enlightening. Herb Kelleher, former head of Southwest Airlines, has said that he hopes that when employees think back about their experience, when, for example, they're talking to their grandchildren, "they say that Southwest Airlines was one of the finest experiences they ever had; that it helped them grow beyond anything they thought possible."[13]

There is already ample gamesmanship that seems expected in our talks with external constituencies, though we may wish these relationships also to develop to a point of greater authenticity. Most of us, consequently, prefer a relatively high level of authenticity among members of our immediate communities. As people feel more authentic, they feel more liberated to be all that they can be. They become, as Gilbert Fairholm likes to put it, "thinking contributors, not just physical extensions of the managers' capacities, ideas and creativity."[14]

We can all benefit from spending more time to get to know our colleagues compassionately—to consider them well beyond the organizational role that they may happen to perform. Think about this story that Max De Pree, former CEO of Herman Miller, likes to tell about his father, founder of the company.[15] D. J. De Pree would visit the family of any key employee who passed away. He would go to their house and spend time in the living room, typically in awkward conversation. One day the millwright died, and D. J. went to the home of his widow. She asked D. J. if she could read some poetry aloud. He agreed, so she read some selected pieces of beautiful poetry. When she finished, the young De Pree commented on how poignant the poetry was and asked who wrote it. She replied that her husband, the millwright, had written the poems. To this day, Max and many others at Herman Miller are still wondering whether this man was a poet who did millwright's work or was a millwright who happened to write poetry.

The ethic of authenticity and compassion inspired by leaderful practice is unlikely to evolve naturally due to unfortunate expectations on the part of both managers and employees. We commonly expect that anyone assuming leadership authority has to behave differently because of the trappings of the managerial position. Yet, this almost implacable assumption attending to the rite of passage into leadership is no longer useful or necessary in our knowledge era. Perhaps it will come down to merely informing managers who have an instinct of building community with their teams and organizations to recognize that they *can* be genuine and good leaders at the same time. Tony Watson and Pauline Harris have written a fascinating account of this dilemma through in-depth interviews of people new to the managerial role.[16] Their respondents, almost to the person, report the ambivalence of losing contact with their peers and feeling like they could no longer be themselves. For example, Carol, a new executive officer for a civil service agency, lamented:

> I still felt like one of the girls, if you like. And I knew exactly how they thought because I used to be one of them . . . and I used to say to them, "Look, I know how you're feeling," as if I wanted to say, "Look I am one of you." And I wanted to be sort of with them, but I think they felt distant. Whereas one time, they'd be able to tell me how they felt and how they thought, [they now] think, "Well, we can't say that to her now, because she's one of them."[17]

Carrie, an educational director said: "You can't be social any more. I can't be me any more. I hate that. That's the biggest drag

about it. . . . They don't open up because they don't trust me."[18]
And Marion, a new school administrator, pointed out:

> Yes, they do want you to be approachable and considerate and
> different [from] the person that they had before, but you are not,
> at the end of the day, one of the staff. And that's true, you're not.
> You have a different role. And the buck stops with me and so does
> the ultimate power really. And that does make you different.
> Whether that is acceptable to you or not is another matter. I
> think it perhaps wasn't to me initially, but it is now.[19]

From these accounts, you get the sense that the leadership role
requires distance or separation between yourself and your own
community. Yet, you also get the sense that people wish it could
be different. Leaderful practice asks the obvious, blunt question:
Why can you *not* be yourself?

As was explored in the last chapter, moving to a point of complete mutuality comes after a developmental process; it may not
occur over night. But this developmental process does not require
manipulation by management of community members. Nor does
it require engaging in reciprocal processes, such as tit-for-tat. In
another interview, Watson and Harris reported how Andrew
Shepherd, heading up a new banking branch, found himself
questioning whether his genuineness was in reality a subtle form
of managerial control, whether he was using his interpersonal
skills to get something more out of his people.

> One, I wanted to go and support her, but two—and I hate to say
> this—I knew what the impact would be when I went to support
> her. . . . I knew she'd volunteer for something else next time and
> I'd get it back. So I almost saw that as an investment, not only in
> her but for me as well. That's the slight dilemma. She thought
> how wonderful to see me and I was thinking yes how nice to see
> you, but there's more to come. Somewhere in my mind, I was
> thinking "Well, she'll go to the wall for me now," and that's nice
> to have.[20]

It is no wonder with tensions like the one Shepherd experienced that it has become difficult to find people to take managerial positions. Ultimately, I don't believe that people wish to behave inauthentically, no matter how much the acculturation. It does a number on your psyche, if not your soul, to behave instrumentally . . . to believe that the only way you can generate good will is via tit-for-tat. Leaderful behavior releases people in managerial roles from becoming a self-recognized charlatan. You can be a leader and you can be yourself.

Indeed, behaving authentically can have a dramatic effect on an organization. Tex Gunning, former chairman of Van den Bergh Netherlands, a foods division of Unilever, was credited with transforming the company from near bankruptcy by his "performance" at a retreat with two hundred senior managers.[21] He did nothing more than speak from the heart about the death of his father, his abusive family, the highs and lows of his schooling, and his career. After his story, one of the attendees shouted out, "Thank you for sharing that, Tex. It's good to know you better." The managers then shared their own life stories with one another. Another attendee summed up the experience of authentic dialogue this way:

> For me, the experience represented a major turnaround . . . the way leaders and then all the people of Van den Bergh showed something personal about themselves. The example showed that I am more than just a "working" person in the company. The "whole" person would be welcomed.

People learn to count on others because they have learned that each member, even the weakest, will be kept in mind as decisions are made and actions are taken.

A collective and compassionate approach expresses a humility that seeks to serve others, that does not seek power for its own sake. People learn to count on others because they have learned that each member, even the weakest, will be kept in mind as decisions are made and actions are taken. Most people resonate to those they deem trustful, who display their humanness. Those who try to sway others with glib speeches eventually get exposed. One doesn't need speech writers when speaking from the heart. Ken Melrose, who in 1981 took over as president of the near-bankrupt Toro Company, serves as a fine example of someone who engendered trust in people.[22] The company had slashed its headcount from 4,200 employees to 1,800. It had terminated the entire management except for Melrose. Morale sank to an all-time low. He decided to address the remaining employees all together. Here's how he put it:

> We're in a very severe crisis, and you're wondering what went wrong. Well, management has let you down, and the entire management team is gone except for me. If you have to blame someone, then blame me. If you want to be part of the solution, then join me, and we'll bring this company back from the ashes.

Melrose's personal appeal to his community (to call it a speech would devalue it) led to a cultural transformation at Toro. In four years the company returned to solid health, in large measure thanks to what we might call Ken Melrose's leaderful practice.

PART TWO   Uncovering the Traditions of Leaderful Practice

THE LEADERFUL CONCEPT IS NOT ENTIRELY NEW; IT HAS EMERGED from the work of many practitioners who have realized that we no longer need to inspire from the front. In part II of the book, I am going to present some of the noble traditions that found this new concept and should reinvent how we think about leadership. More important, these traditions will reveal some incredibly useful ideas about how to develop your leaderful practice.

So, how should you begin? As I suggested when I introduced the four C's of leaderful practice in chapter 1, some of you will already be more or less leaderful on these four dimensions. Although I encourage you to read the full account from here, you may wish to concentrate on the particular C that you find most controversial, most interesting, or perhaps most in need of development. To do the latter, you will need some means to assess your relative predisposition on each element of leaderful practice.

Accordingly, I have developed the Leaderful Questionnaire, depicted in figure II-1. At the time of this writing, it has not been scientifically validated, but completing the questionnaire may give you an informal sense of where you stand on leaderful practice.

You will find the questionnaire easy to fill out. The twelve scales each have two descriptions that characterize some views about leadership. These descriptions represent the outermost values on a scale of 1 to 5. Mark on the scale where you stand on the leadership view presented. You might find it useful to think of a specific job or work situation as you answer all the questions. You may wish to fill out the questionnaire now.

After you've completed the questionnaire, use the scoring instructions that follow to assess your leaderful potential on each of the four C's. You can graphically represent your responses for each of the C's by going back to figure 1-2 and plotting your scores. The endpoints are represented by the outermost values of 3 on the conventional side and 15 on the leaderful side. Your score will

FIGURE II-1. The Leaderful Questionnaire

Instructions. Mark where you stand on the twelve contrasting leadership views presented, using a scale of 1 to 5. Mark 1 if you completely agree with the left viewpoint, 5 if you completely agree with the right viewpoint. Values 2 and 4 suggest that you somewhat agree with the given viewpoint, and 3 would mean that you fall in between or feel neutral. There is no correct answer; the questions merely attempt to characterize your leadership predispositions.

a. Once you're a leader, you don't relinquish it to anybody else   1—2—3—4—5   Once you're a leader, you share it with others who may also be leading at the same time

b. Leadership resides in one member of a group   1—2—3—4—5   Many people within a group may operate as leaders

c. A leader's duty is to direct the operation   1—2—3—4—5   The direction of an operation should arise from the entire group

d. A leader has to make the tough decisions for the enterprise first even if it hurts some stakeholders   1—2—3—4—5   A leader will consider the dignity of the stakeholders first before making a decision for the enterprise

e. Once acquiring power, you attempt to sustain or increase it, not lose it   1—2—3—4—5   Power is acquired and increased by everyone working together

f. Authority is the principal basis of power in leadership   1—2—3—4—5   Power in leadership can come from many sources beyond authority

g. A leader should speak for the entire group   1—2—3—4—5   Subordinates should feel comfortable to speak for the entire group

h. The leader is the authoritative source when problems arise in the operation   1—2—3—4—5   There is no one authoritative source in the group; all viewpoints must be considered when problems arise

i.	Sharing power as a leader would be abdicating responsibility	1—2—3—4—5	Sharing power as a leader is a natural and desirable activity
j.	One person should ultimately make the decisions on behalf of others	1—2—3—4—5	Decisions should be made by whomever has the relevant responsibility
k.	Leaders should share their deepest beliefs with only their closest associates	1—2—3—4—5	Leaders should engage in a public dialogue that opens their deepest beliefs to the scrutiny of other group members
l.	A leader's job is to assure subordinates that they can rely upon him/her to handle any problem	1—2—3—4—5	A leader encourages subordinates, not him or her, to handle problems as they arise

---

SCORING INSTRUCTIONS

To compute a score for concurrent leadership, add your responses for a, e, and i   ____

To compute a score for collective leadership, add your responses for b, f , and j   ____

To compute a score for collaborative leadership, add your responses for c, g, and k   ____

To compute a score for compassionate leadership, add your responses for d, h, and l   ____

To derive a total leaderful score, add your scores together for the four components above:

TOTAL SCORE

KEY

For the individual components, you are inclined toward conventional leadership if your scores are less than 9; you are inclined toward leaderful leadership if your scores are greater than 9.

For the total leaderful score, you are inclined toward conventional leadership if your scores are less than 36; you are inclined toward leaderful leadership if your scores are greater than 36.

Concurrent
- *Situational Manager*
- *Team Facilitator*

Collective
- *Steward*
- *Learner*
- *Meaning-maker*

Collaborative
- *Change Agent*
- *Mutual Influencer*
- *Dialoguer*

Compassionate
- *Noncharismatic*
- *Conscience*
- *Social Caretaker*

FIGURE II-2. The Traditions Comprising the Four C's

likely fall somewhere in between. You may also wish to retake the Leaderful Questionnaire after you've tried out some of the techniques and practices suggested by the book. For now, you can use the results of the questionnaire to focus your reading, perhaps concentrating on those tenets of leaderful practice that you would most like to develop.

Before resuming your reading, take a look at figure II-2. Here you'll find the specific traditions that underlie the four C's, to which I'll refer as we shape the contours of leaderful practice. The ensuing chapters each correspond to a C and contain full explanations and numerous examples that illustrate how each of the traditions contribute to creating leaderful organizations.

6 Concurrent Leadership

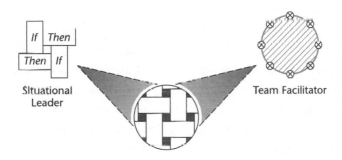

Situational Leader

Team Facilitator

IF THE POSITION LEADER OF A COMMUNITY HAS EITHER INHERITED or developed a group whose members can work effectively both independently and interdependently, then leadership can extend beyond the mantle of authority. People within the group can participate in leadership at the same time as the position leader.

As a revolutionary concept, concurrent leadership may threaten position leaders with loss of status or function, or even their very jobs. However, in a leaderful organization, they continue to occupy critical roles, though roles often discrepant from traditional bureaucratic authority. Among their responsibilities is to release everyone in the community to assume concurrent leadership. This does not mean they should "off-load" administrative responsibilities. Position leaders may well retain such duties initially and even after community members exhibit other leadership roles. The key difference is that these responsibilities—whether coordinating tasks within the unit or between the unit and external stake-holders, acquiring resources, or recruiting new members—need not reside entirely within the office of management. People share responsibilities as the situation warrants.

Since most management cultures worldwide do not typically sanction concurrent leadership, the position leader needs to fa-cilitate its emergence. A number of concrete activities can, over time, lead to a state of self-direction. Initially, it is important for facilitators to diagnose the readiness level of their team and re-sponsively intervene. For example, teams may be at relative states of readiness depending on their effort, task performance, knowl-edge and skills, or group process.[1] If they exhibit an insufficient level of effort or motivation, the facilitator (or facilitating mem-ber) might have the group reflect upon its behavioral norms. For example, if members have adopted a so-called preferred value norm of just doing what it takes to get the job done, but no more than that, then they may need to engage in a dialogue about what might be preventing them from trying to achieve at a higher level. If they have a problem with task performance, one might reconsider the design of the work team itself. Perhaps subteams might accomplish work that formerly had to wait until the full group was assembled.

If they have an inadequate knowledge or skills base, one might need to review the competencies within the membership. The team might discover hidden skills right under its nose. Or perhaps members might need to enroll in programs that offer training and skill development. Finally, if there is a problem with group processes, the facilitator might need to encourage members to take some time to work through their interpersonal difficulties, whether through a feedback session, a conflict management ac-tivity, or a genuine reflective dialogue.

Concurrent leadership also has an external role: to interact with stakeholders that provide key resources to the community. In some instances, the boundary role requires the position leader to "run interference" for the team, to protect it from outside influences that might disturb its internal functioning. For example, a team of R&D scientists on the verge of an important discovery might need their R&D manager to seal them off from competing demands for their time that could lead to breaking up the team.

Position leaders as boundary managers can also perform the critical role of knowledge brokering. There are many cases of learning lost because particular teams were incapable or unwilling to share some of their work processes or technologies with the wider organization. In such instances, a boundary manager can link members from various teams who have compatible interests and resource needs or can merely inform other groups in or outside the organization about accomplishments by particular teams that might bear on the work of others. For example, a dean at a community luncheon reception happened to be sitting next to a local hospital administrator who was complaining about some scheduling difficulties in his emergency care department. The dean referred him to an operations researcher on the faculty who, along with two colleagues, was working on a queuing model. Although not originally conceived for that purpose, it applied quite successfully in the hospital setting.

Reaching a point of concurrent leadership is not necessarily a natural process in cultures that elevate authority as the primary basis for control within communities. In such instances, situational management can help community members develop their leadership potential. As members develop themselves, the position leader may need to learn team facilitation skills so as to enhance the self-direction of the group as a whole.

As a fundamental tenet of leaderful practice, concurrent leadership represents perhaps the most critical idea to release us from the shackles of classic bureaucratic control, often outmoded in twenty-first-century organizations. The following two sections will detail how to prepare for concurrent leadership within your community.

The Leader as Situational Manager

Since the multifaceted, dynamic organizations of the modern era require nimble and behaviorally complex managers, leaderful managers are needed to perform a variety of leadership functions and vary them with the situations that they encounter. They also need to operate with equal dedication whether working with peers, subordinates, superiors, external stakeholders, task forces, or cross-functional teams or whether working to shape strategy, manage conflicts, structure the organization, or perform other functions. They also successfully resolve the fundamental values conflict between the management of task and the management of people by "doing" them both. This doesn't mean that they take full responsibility for each task and each process; rather, they work toward a point in time when this responsibility may rest with their community. As I suggested in chapter 4, the situational element becomes critical as a developmental basis for building a leaderful community.

Let's review the logic of development briefly. Leaderful groups rarely, if ever, just show up. They have to be built. Members arrive on a team with varying degrees of ability—experience, education, understanding of the job in question—and of motivation—confidence, willingness to do the job, sense of responsibility. The situational manager recognizes these differences in people and accepts two fundamental assumptions underlying the situational approach.

1. that he or she can diagnose varying conditions in the community, such as the nature of the membership, the amount of time available to accomplish a given assignment, the style or culture of the surrounding organization, the authority vested in the manager, the complexity of the task at hand.

2. that on the basis of the diagnosis, the manager can adjust his or her managerial style accordingly.

The life-cycle approach of Hersey and Blanchard specifies four styles that managers can adopt in developing their team members to accept leaderful conditions.[2] In the early phase of individual and team development, they specify a "tell" style, wherein the manager provides specific instructions and closely supervises performance. In the second phase of development, they prescribed a "coaching" style, wherein the manager explains his or her decisions or decision-making processes and provides an opportunity for members to ask clarifying questions. In the third, "joining" style, the manager shares ideas with his or her staff and facilitates their making decisions on their own. They refer to the final style as "delegating" behavior, at which point the manager can virtually turn decision making over to the staff.

The situational model of Hersey and Blanchard is essentially a followership model, since the four styles depend on the nature of the readiness of the manager's followers. What do Hersey and Blanchard mean by readiness? They propose two dimensions that characterize the nature of any leader's followers: their ability and their willingness. The ability of followers is defined by such elements as how much experience they have on the job, how much knowledge they possess about the job's requirements, and how capable they are in fulfilling these requirements. The willingness dimension represents how interested followers may be in taking responsibility, how much achievement motivation they may have, how committed they are to the job itself, and how much confidence they have in fulfilling the job requirements. Like a number of other leadership scholars, Hersey and Blanchard see leadership as a relationship between leaders and followers.[3] Hence, you need to find out as much as you can about your followers—their personality and preferences, for example, as well as their situation—so you can adjust your style of leadership accordingly.

Here's how one manager successfully adapted her management style using the situational model as a guide to understanding how to match her leadership with a follower's readiness:

> I have recently had the chance to experiment with some leadership skills. I have always preferred to be led by a "Theory Y" manager. That is because I like to take responsibility for my own job and dislike working in an environment that is tightly structured and closely supervised. I always assumed that this was the "best" way. I now realize this may be due to my readiness level.
>
> Recently, I delegated a couple of tasks to two different people in my group. As a result of my poor assumptions that everyone wanted to be led by a Theory Y manager like I do, I was ineffective in achieving satisfactory results from one of the employees. This individual's task was to construct a report that would regionalize our current month's support revenue. I forwarded along a copy of an old report as well as the raw data. The only other information I provided to this employee was a due date. I had expected this employee to take the raw data and use the old report I had forwarded along as a guide to create a new report and had expected few questions. I was immediately surprised by the amount of detailed questions I was receiving from this employee. I could not understand why he was having such a difficult time with this task. It wasn't until after understanding the situational model that I have come to understand what the problem was. Although this employee had the education necessary to complete the task, I now realize that his experience was inadequate for this type of leadership. This is mainly due to his being fairly new to our department. I now realize that I should have taken more time to explain exactly what would be expected of him.
>
> Fortunately, the other employee I delegated a similar task to completed it on time and accurately. I now realize that this was due to her high development level. She has been in our group for over a year and understands exactly what is expected. I have learned a valuable lesson from these events. It is extremely important to change your leadership behavior depending upon the

situation you encounter. You cannot be a successful manager if you are unaware of the needs of your followers.

The situational model's developmental approach comes into play when dealing with workers who have varying degrees of ability or were brought together from diverse arenas. They may require some initial structure and direction. People within the community, however, must have the chance to develop on their own and in concert with others. During the early phases, the manager should provide continuing support and encouragement. Once the members of the community reach a level of mutual support, they should be given the opportunity to work as a leaderful group.

Throughout the developmental phase, the situational manager may need to alternate between a coaching, joining, and even delegating style. Recall the familiar story about whether one should catch fish for someone or give him a rod to teach him how to fish on his own. In a similar vein, you may need to determine whether your colleagues need you to become more active, either by intervening directly in the problem that they are working on or by helping them through skill development to prepare themselves to find a solution on their own. Once someone has learned to fish on her own, the supervisor can leave this person alone for long stretches of time.

Situational leaders need to demonstrate a sense of personal and collective reflectiveness in order to remain effective. They need to check on their diagnoses to ensure accuracy. Yet, they need not hold their conclusions to themselves. In the spirit of dialogue, they can ask their followers, for example, whether direct supervision is as frequently required. In a journal, one manager put it this way: "As I continue to experiment with Terry, I am paying particularly close attention to any signs of frustration or anxiety on her part to ensure that I don't overdirect or annoy her with detail. This reflection has been critical to the constant adjustments that I need to make."

The leaderful style is more akin to the joining style than to the final delegating approach. This is because I don't see the manager leaving the group per se as is characterized in delegating. In organizations moving toward leaderful practice, the position leader remains part of the group. However, any member can serve in a leadership capacity when called for. One of the leadership roles may be to intersect with other units, perhaps in an official managerial capacity. But the members or member who occupies this role does not operate outside the group. This person remains a member of the team and may fulfill other roles that require full operating participation in the work of the community.

In a manufacturing plant that had adopted a self-managing team structure, one team had to prepare to move its assembly line to another location in order to have more space to expand and to add new features. Since the supervisor had already delegated authority to the team for most of its operation, she had to decide how much of a role she would play in the line setup. Here's how she described her role.

> They came in and set up their equipment. They very much had ownership. [They] knew what we needed to do and took it from there. This needed to be their baby. I was there to help them, came in, and got greasy setting things up, but they were going to be pleased with it if they did it themselves. It's an independence thing. Everybody came. There wasn't one person hanging back and letting the others do the work.[4]

Such situationalists as Victor Vroom have found that the modern era seems to be calling for greater application of participative leadership styles, as in the team described above.[5] For Vroom, participative choices are called for when decisions have critical and significant impact, when the leader needs the commitment of the group but the group may not be inclined to merely go along with the leader, when the leader lacks the sole expertise to make the decision, and when the group has a history of working together effectively.

We can think of the delegating style, ironically, as a last vestige of hierarchical authority in the face of a fully functioning, self-directed work team structure. The organization may still see the need to appoint supervisors to externally coordinate the teams, though these managers may no longer become directly involved in the teams' internal affairs. Delegating may also be called for in organizations requiring wide spans of control in which supervisors manage many different groups. If supervisors can succeed in adopting a delegating style with certain talented individuals or with one of their groups, they are released, so to speak, to spend more time with those requiring more attention. Some organizations may prefer to have representatives from teams meet, say as a cross-functional team or council, rather than appoint managers to fulfill this function.

Whether adopting a joining or a delegating style, traditional supervisors have an inherent antipathy, though oftentimes unconscious, to giving up control. Max De Pree reminds us that delegating means "sent and empowered," or "to entrust to another." Yet, he declares that delegation "requires that a leader clearly state the corporate vision, a vision to be fully shared and discussed and scrutinized. Understanding and acceptance must follow."[6]

Leaderful managers realize that once you have developed sufficient trust in others to engage them in delegation, you no longer need to oblige "followers" to accept a vision. In true delegation, people become empowered to develop their projects in any way that they see fit. Naturally, any significant variance will lead to further dialogue with involved stakeholders, including the nominal leader. In this sense, delegation and participation become aligned. Since the leader has not technically gone "away" to some distant office but remains part of the community, he or she is always available for participation in the project at hand. What makes leaderful practice so distinct is that others truly gain an opportunity to concurrently lead within their purview and interests without the need to observe explicit norms of conduct ahead of time.

The Leader as Team Facilitator

There's a well-known case of a bomber crew going out on a survival training exercise and encountering the harsh conditions of
the Colorado Rocky Mountains. During the training, an isolated enlisted man from West Virginia emerged to get the crew
through the exercise through his experience as a mountaineer.
The pilot of the crew had stepped aside to let the crew members follow the suggestions of the "mountain boy." Who was
the leader of the group? Was it the pilot or was it the West
Virginian?

Under the tenets of leaderful practice, this is a trick question.
The pilot does possess a component of leadership based on his
authority or legitimate power. He also happens to have what is
known as "referent" power, based on his pleasing personality. Yet,
the West Virginian also possesses leadership due to his expert
power. So, we now see that both were leaders of the group at the
same time.

Both were, at least if you are willing to adopt the leaderful
consideration that leadership may emerge from anyone in the
community at any time. More than one leader may operate
within a community. Given the diverse exigencies of organizations having to operate globally with increasingly customized
and complicated product lines, self-directed team leadership is
good news for this century. Although there is no definitive
count, I have heard reliable estimates say that close to 80 percent
of our largest public companies have self-directed groups in their
midst.

It is important to understand that since there can be more than
one leader on a team, the leader who operates with bureaucratic
authority does not necessarily *give up* his or her leadership when
exerted by someone else. In the survival training case, we might
even say that the pilot acted as a particularly effective leader since
he recognized the leadership offered by the mountaineer in the

situation. He didn't hold the crewman back for fear of losing his authority. In this setting, the pilot became more of a facilitator of team interaction than a supervisory authority.

It is important to understand that since there can be more than one leader on a team, the leader who operates with bureaucratic authority does not necessarily *give up* his or her leadership when exerted by someone else.

It seems that everyone these days has heard of Sir Ernest Shackleton, renowned Antarctic explorer, whose exploits left us with a legacy of portentous leadership practices, among them some critical lessons about facilitation. Consider how Shackleton recruited for his voyages. He wanted people who could complement their technical skills with such important attributes as team spirit, optimism, and a pleasing, even humorous, disposition. But when it came to the need for expertise, Shackleton was quick to hire on people who had all the technical skills that he lacked. Not only did their superior education and expertise not intimidate him, but he also encouraged them to pursue their own projects.[7]

Team leadership recognizes, then, that any member may lead at the right opportunity. The way Bruce Avolio puts it: "If [the team] identifies with what's important, who cares who is leading, as long as it's the best person or people for the task at that particular moment in time."[8] Manfred Kets de Vries refers to this person as the "authoritative" leader, the one who can contribute at a moment in time or who can "walk the talk."[9] Perhaps no one puts it better than Herb Kelleher, former head of Southwest Airlines.

A financial analyst once asked me if I was afraid of losing control of our organization. I told him I've never had control and I never wanted it. We're not looking for blind obedience. We're looking for people who on their own initiative want to be doing what they're doing because they consider it to be a worthy objective.

That I cannot possibly know everything that goes on in our operation—and don't pretend to—is a source of competitive advantage. The freedom, informality, and interplay that people
enjoy allows them to act in the best interests of the company.[10]

We are inclined to think that a firm leader is one who can
demonstrate real command, especially at the outset of his or her
term of office. Yet, team leadership based on the idea of concur-
rency may have a more responsive effect since it assures people
that the organization will not neglect their expertise and contributions; indeed, the organization will both accept and embrace
their leadership. Consider the approach that former food executive, Robert Eckert, used when he took over the then-troubled
toy manufacturer, Mattel.

As the new guy, I realized that every first encounter with a Mattel
employee had the potential to be fraught with tension, and I felt
it was my responsibility to do everything possible to reduce it.
Surprisingly, I found that in each situation, recognizing my own
lack of knowledge about the company's people and culture—in
effect, allowing employees to be the "boss" in certain situations—
actually helped me lead.[11]

Organizational teams are usually given a nominal leader as
their official manager. Often this manager initially designs the
team—for example, determining its size, its skill diversity, its core
strategy, its task objectives, its reward structure, and the avail-
ability of resources. If the team succeeds, this person gets the
credit; if the team fails, this person gets held accountable. But the
bureaucratic requirement of authority does not require supervisory control as the prevailing leadership behavior. Once the team
is in place, this individual can be just as effective coordinating activities within the team as controlling its members. This calls for
facilitation skills more than traditional supervisory ability. The
team facilitator provides resources when necessary, builds infrastructure—for example, by organizing role responsibilities—and

brokers interfaces with external stakeholders. The way Kimball Fisher puts it, the facilitator works *on* not *in* the system.[12]

At GE, Jack Welch used to refer to this boundary function of the leader as "managing less." Once the internal members of the team were ready, the job of the manager was plainly "to get out of the way." Not that the manager would miss bossing, according to Welch, since, in becoming a team facilitator, that manager would have more time to do the things the company really needed, namely to think big thoughts and transfer knowledge to other GE businesses.[13]

The boundary role of the leader adopted at GE is echoed at Intel's research and development labs in Hillsboro, Oregon.[14] Since 1998, Intel's technologists at Hillsboro have been working on the TeraHertz chip, one that they expect to run ten times faster than what's currently on the market — without consuming more power or generating more heat. Although Intel executives had to be satisfied that the labs were working on the right problem, they have left day-to-day decision making in the hands of the scientists and engineers and their immediate managers. In fact, so far, whenever they have heard about bottlenecks, executives have provided the necessary resources to head them off to the extent possible.

Team Development   The team facilitator also has an internal function, namely, to raise awareness of and to help the group manage its natural dynamics so that members realize not only the challenge but also the benefit of developing their team. Just as we discussed in chapter 4, we can use developmental theory in this case to consider particular styles of intervention to move groups through their natural stages of development. There is no unanimous concurrence that all groups go through the same stages; such variables as the purpose of the group, its constitution, duration, and organizational context will cause a fair degree of diversity. Yet, the classic study of Tuckman, with its rhyming stages, has gained a great deal of credibility among "team-building" aficionados.[15]

Tuckman's model outlines four stages that groups must contend with in their life cycle. A group will achieve greater effectiveness to the extent it can manage the unique challenges attending to each stage. In the "forming" stage, members begin to determine what is acceptable behavior within the group and how to approach their task at hand. As they orient to the task, they begin to establish some group rules, yet they tend to become dependent on the designated leader or authority figure (if one exists). They also begin to test their individual styles and personalities as they see whether others will accept them.

During the "storming" stage, as the group redefines its task and members try to agree on objectives and strategy, conflict inevitably results. Members may find that their styles do not coincide; in addition, they may differ in the amount of time they want to commit to a particular task, the priority they assign to it, or even the means to accomplish it. As a result, this tends to be a time of high emotion and tension. Members may compete to establish their personal preferences for the group and to achieve their desired position or status.

During the "norming" stage, members begin to come together as a coordinated unit. The jockeying behaviors of the storming stage now begin to give way to a precarious balancing of forces. Members begin to resolve their differences by exchanging their interpretations and opinions about group operations and, as a result, begin to act more cohesively. Team norms and roles also become accepted at this juncture as members display an increased willingness to listen and to contribute to the team. However, for some members, holding the group together may take precedence over responding to environmental influences. It is thus possible at this stage for the group to become an exclusive club that cannot accept inquiries and even criticism from external forces.

By the fourth stage of group development, the "performing" stage, the integration begun in the prior norming stage is completed. Members not only dedicate themselves to the tasks of the group but also simultaneously support one another. A sense of "common good" permeates the team that may occupy as much attention as individual need. There is energy for developing ways for the group to continuously improve and renew itself. The group structure becomes stable yet fluid, disagreements are handled in creative ways, and members become motivated by group goals. Further, members understand and accept their individual and collective responsibilities to other units in the wider organizational environment.

It is often this last practice that distinguishes the norming from the performing community. The former in its unity and self-sufficiency can become so autonomous that it can become isolated, often by choice, from the rest of the organization. If problems arise in its performance, it may even assume an "us-against-them" mentality, refusing to acknowledge these problems to outsiders or ask them for help. This phenomenon occurred at Nut Island, a treatment plant in Boston Harbor, to such an extent that a former director began to refer to it as the "Nut Island Effect." He describes in one example how an environmental consultant found that the plant's digesters were failing to convert an acceptable amount of sludge into fertilizer because of excess acidity. When he brought this to the plant's attention, the consultant reported:

> Their initial reaction was hostility—they didn't like me sticking my nose into their business. Besides, they insisted, there was nothing seriously wrong with the digesters. The wide fluctuations in acidity were just one of their little idiosyncrasies. Instead of addressing the root causes of the variances, the team would impose a quick fix, such as adding large amount of alkali to the tanks when sample readings (which may or may not have been reliable) indicated high acidity levels.[16]

It is often when one experiences the security of full membership in a team that one can relate most effectively to the wider community of the organization. At this point, not only might the individual support the team and the team support the individual, but both individual and team can support the organization and vice versa. This "holomorphic" characteristic can occur when there is support for a fully performing team structure as well as an appreciation for a common meaning that cuts across all teams.

Alain Godard characterizes the performing stage of group development in his depiction of some attributes of the most effective teams in a highly successful division of his former company, Rhône-Poulenc.

> I have been convinced that the strength of a team is not necessarily proportional to the sum of the individual qualities of its members. If these qualities are not put to the service of a shared objective, we witness some striking individual feats, but these may not necessarily serve the common interest. The team is lived through like a World Cup type of event, where the tension and the galvanization of [its members'] spirits enable the individuals and the teams that they make up to surpass themselves, fulfill themselves, and ultimately act in the service of an objective truly shared and understood by all.[17]

What Godard is saying is no more than the aphorism that many of us have grown up with but fail to practice, an aphorism repeated in the popular book, *High Five!*[18] In a performing team, no one person is as smart as the combined team. Team members reach a point at which they seek to improve themselves, not so much to satisfy their own egos, but to make a more effective contribution to the team and to the wider organization.

Facilitation Behavior   According to the situational model, applied here to group development, facilitators might deploy different degrees of two principal behaviors in working with groups.[19] Task behavior is relatively prescriptive about member roles and assignments and about what the group needs to do. Maintenance behavior is concerned with providing support and encouragement to group members, facilitating their interaction, and involving them in decision making.

We know from situational leadership that leaders can adapt their style to fit the situation. Hence, the proper combination of task and maintenance behaviors will depend on the stage of development of the team in question. Essentially, the facilitator can help move a group through the four stages previously described. The four stages may also be depicted in terms of the amount of work expected from each stage as well as the morale or socio-emotional tone of the group. The amount of work accomplished steadily increases through the stages. On the other hand, morale starts out high during the forming stage but takes a dip during the storming stage as the expectations of the members confront the stern reality of trying to reach a high level of task performance without having worked through the requisite maintenance functions. As members discuss and begin to define norms in this and the subsequent norming stage, morale begins to pick up until it reaches a high level in the performing stage.

Table 6-1 depicts the four stages, the relative degree of task and maintenance behavior advised for each stage, and the leadership style recommended for the facilitator. The "telling" style is most appropriate at the forming stage of group development as the team struggles to clarify its task and to set realistic and attainable goals. Telling provides for low maintenance behavior, just enough to establish a climate for members to accept one another and to initially introduce the process goals of open communication and shared leadership. The telling style may also require facilitators to inform the team about its own development so members can initially understand cognitively what may evolve as the team matures. Facilitators may need to help members gradually open up to one another in deciding on agendas for meetings, on plans for action, on developing a system for documentation, on distributing workloads and roles, and on determining critical success factors.

TABLE 6-1. Situational Team Leadership and Group Development

Stage	Forming	Storming	Norming	Performing
Task	High	High	Low	Low
Maintenance	Low	High	Moderate	Low
Style	Telling	Coaching	Joining	Delegating

By the storming stage, the facilitator has to increase the level of maintenance behavior to balance task provision. Essentially, a "coaching" style is called for as the facilitator trains team members in the skills and knowledge associated with task performance and group process. The goal at this stage is to work toward less dependency on the facilitator and more self-sufficiency within the group. This may entail such task behaviors as pointing out concealed problems, be they overexpenditures or portentous trends; broadening the group's repertoire of problem-solving skills or quality tools, such as force-field analysis or pareto diagrams; making suggestions about performance improvements; disseminating company-wide information potentially important to the group; or providing informal rewards or reinforcement when the group assumes responsibility for its own tasks. Coaching also delves into process behaviors such as modeling active listening, showing concern for team members' well-being, acknowledging difficulties and natural conflicts that arise among team members, and focusing on building supportive member relationships and group cohesion.[20]

During this stage in team development, certain members may see themselves as "natural leaders" and prematurely attempt to take over the group. Others in the team may perceive this type of behavior as presumptive or even coercive. Although the facilitator needs to allow some of these dynamics to play out on their own, he or she needs to ensure that they indeed get played out.

This may require the facilitator to encourage some of the quieter members to voice their concerns about unchecked controlling behavior on the part of the more vocal or assertive members. In coaching, the facilitator is attempting not to stifle the natural energy in the vocal members but to give them an opportunity to listen to others and help them reflect on their operating behavior.

The "joining" style aligns with the norming stage as the facilitator significantly diminishes emphasis on task and goal clarification. The facilitator at this stage may also be seen as encouraging group members to assume more and more of the maintenance functions that were once his or her province. As this stage evolves, then, the facilitator applies only moderate maintenance behavior since group members can assume more of the process work. However, the facilitator needs to be alert to some members' inclination to avoid conflict and disagreement for fear of losing their newfound cohesion. The facilitator needs to encourage continued free expression, balanced participation, and valuing of differences among members.

In the last performing stage, the facilitator uses a "delegating" style as the group itself begins to take responsibility for task and maintenance functions. Although the facilitator continues to monitor the goals and performance of the group, he or she can become more of a resource for individuals and for the group as a whole, for example in providing technical support for members' projects. The facilitator also has to be aware of the need to become more involved as conditions in the team change, for example when new members enter or a crisis, such as the loss of a key client, occurs. There may also come a time when the group will need assistance in preparing for its possible dissolution.

Rather than use a developmental approach built on situational behaviors or roles that respond to group maturity levels, another tack identifies the individual resistances to the adoption of team leadership. Once the resistances are identified, the facilitator can take the appropriate action to attempt to counter the resistance in question. Likely sources of resistance to team leadership include:

- **Managerial support.** Will the team get the appropriate infusion of resources, whether in terms of information, technology, or human resources, from management when necessary?

- **Trust.** Is there a sufficient level of trust to commit to the new structure, or do members fear that management will take advantage of them?

- **Role clarity.** Will team members be able to decide what they need to do to function as an effective unit and to carry out their responsibilities?

- **Cultural values.** Do team members buy into cooperative norms, or are they acculturated to work as individuals consistent with a surrounding culture that emphasizes individual freedom?

- **Tolerance for change.** Are members open to a new method of leadership, or do they prefer a more customary directive approach?

- **Workload distribution.** Will the workload be divided fairly?

- **Social support.** Are members willing to support one another for the good of the team?[21]

If facilitators identify one or more of these resistance factors, they can invent adaptable responses that may take varying periods of time to take effect. Consider the issue of trust, as an example. In one reported incident from a small midwestern company, the president thought he would start the process of giving employees more responsibility by invoking a flexible work hours plan.[22] As a result of rampant distrust in the organization, many employees immediately believed that the new plan would require them to work whenever their supervisors asked them to—including evenings and weekends. In such a predicament, the managers would first have to clarify the full details of the plan. Next, they would need to find out what has caused such a high level of suspicion of managerial initiatives to begin with. After that inquiry, an organization with this degree of distrust would most likely have to undergo a process of individual and collective healing. For people to move on, they often need to surface their feelings, take responsibility for their role in creating the climate that exists, and begin to reframe the experience to learn from it.[23]

In another example of resistance to self-directed teams, some employees expressed resentment that they would have to work with other team members when they felt content to work on their own. Their individual freedom was being usurped, in their view. It turns out that these individuals had worked before in teams that had a number of "freeloaders" who had taken advantage of their commitment. The managers in this instance had to assure these employees that the new team structure would not sanction freeloading and that they would install mechanisms to ensure that people would feel free to voice concerns about fairness. In this example, we see that the managers had to respond to two interacting resistances: the cultural value of individualism and complaints about workload distribution.

Whatever model a facilitator uses to prepare a team for self-leadership, there is usually a concern regarding when to cut the strings to allow the team to operate on its own. Delegating behavior, which effectively requires periodic noninvolvement in the team, can present a particular challenge to managers who have gotten used to having their teams rely on them for direction and support. On the other hand, when teams are prepared to take control of their tasks without a need for interference, managerial control can become especially ineffective. Consider a case from a project manager who had initiated a project to consider a new raw material (a type of copper) for use in a motor safety device.

A group of design engineers were assembled to test this new material. Here's how the project manager retrospectively described his leadership of this group.

> Early in the project I found myself very heavily involved in the testing aspect of the approval process. My deep involvement finally drove one of the senior engineers to approach me and express his concerns. He stated that he had been doing this type of work for thirty years and that he knew what needed to get done. He felt that I didn't need to get as involved as I was and that I should allow him and the team to run the testing aspect of the project. He would keep me informed on all progress and make me aware of any potential problems. I realized that he was right and then lessened my involvement. Reflecting on the situation, I realized that I had in fact mismatched my leadership style to the readiness level of the group, which had resulted in their frustration with me. They were a highly competent group of engineers with a high readiness level. I should have essentially delegated this responsibility to them; instead I found myself trying to micro-manage, which led to unnecessary tension.

Boundary Management   Boundary management, defined as coordinating the internal and external functions of a team, also encourages the concurrent sharing of leadership within the team. However, the team must have developed itself to a point where the position leader can adopt minimally a joining, if not a delegating, style.

Although I am interested in having teams develop to a point of concurrent leadership, the process cannot be rushed. For example, we know from an understanding of the norming phase of group development that teams can become overcohesive or "pseudocohesive" and thus fall victim to groupthink or similar tendencies to reinforce agreement and suppress dissent. Under this condition, although the team may appear self-managing, it can feel oppressive to those members who disagree with the reigning view or preordained method. In this situation, the facilitator or a leaderful member of the team may need to model the value of encouraging dissenting points of view to counteract the often dysfunctional behavior of forced agreement.

Sometimes a position leader may become guilty of overdelegating. This occurs when the leader assumes that the group has the necessary socio-emotional readiness and knowledge capacity to handle its own problems. As a result, the leader may leave the group alone too long. One of my students illustrated this very predicament.

> In my previous position with the company, I had a manager that particularly focused on boundary management. He was always working on ways to help us to help ourselves. He tried to improve the environment that we worked in and helped develop contacts throughout the organization for us to utilize in order to better perform our jobs. However, a problem arose out of his attempts at boundary management. Often, it seemed as though he were aloof and distanced from the problems that we faced on a day-to-day basis. Because his entire focus was working on the system and not in it, it seemed to those of us that were in the system that he was not focused enough on us and our daily tasks. At times a leader needs to work *with* the people in the system in order to remain "grounded" and focused on the group. I think that a good leader needs to find that right balance.

Perhaps the prototype of the boundary manager can be found in the life of Harold Ross, the famed and iconoclastic editor of the *New Yorker* magazine. Under Ross, the *New Yorker* became arguably the most influential magazine in America and the stan dard for contemporary literary journalism. It can be credited with changing the face of modern fiction, humor, and comic art. Although nonleaderful in some ways—his writers knew him to be so finicky that they likened his editing to a pasteurization process—he nurtured and championed them at every opportunity. Even if he didn't grasp their ideas or agree with their linguistic usage, he saw his ultimate role to be in their service. His commitment was both professional and personal, extending, for example, to covering emergency hospital bills or securing a larger apartment for a writer with a pregnant wife.

Ross seemed to have an intrinsic understanding that creative people—writers and artists—for all their insight and brilliance could also be quite vulnerable, so he would protect them from bruised advertisers, hostile theater producers, or exploitive book publishers. It was Ross, an editor, who pioneered the then-heretical idea of reassigning the rights to a story or artwork to its creator after it appeared in print. The ultimate facilitator, Ross operated the *New Yorker* as a learning laboratory in which his associates could pursue their craft individually as a great experiment, yet collectively in pursuit of a common cause.[24]

7 Collective Leadership

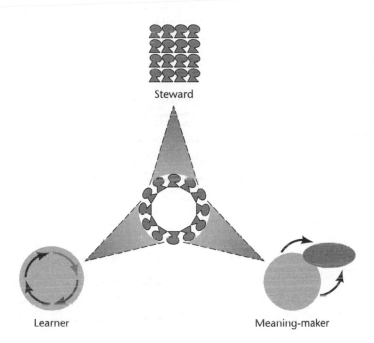

Steward

Learner

Meaning-maker

LEADERSHIP IS BEING SEEN MORE AS A PLURAL PHENOMENON, something that the entire community does together. It does not need to be associated with the actions of a single operator. People in the community assume leadership roles when necessary, and through this collective action, leaderful practice occurs.

Consistent with the adaptive process of leadership, collective leadership may make its most important contribution to leaderful practice in promoting learning for the entire organization. Learning occurs as we make ourselves available to alternative perspectives of understanding. Although we tend to be willing to alter our perspectives on an individual basis, we also tend to resist exposing our vulnerability to others. Doing so requires a humility that seeks as much to serve as to achieve and to defer as to supersede. Creating a learning culture in an organization is easier said than done. No one can dictate openness to another; no one can demand someone's vulnerability. Rather, it must pervade the culture of the organization.

Organizations that support collective leadership need to be designed for learning.[1] People brought into the community are supported for being learning inclined. No one needs to feel embarrassed for speaking up. Indeed, members willingly seek feedback, openly discuss errors, experiment optimistically with new behaviors, reflect mutually on their operating assumptions, and demonstrably support one another.

The collective learning process extends to the critical role that meaning has within a leaderful commuity. We see the meaning for a community represented not so much from its rules and procedures but more typically from the words and metaphors that characterize its collective purpose.[2] The meaning-maker possesses the ability and, most particularly, the courage to attempt a framing or a reframing of the situation at hand. The leader's first attempt may not work. People in the group may be contending with vague and conflicting feelings. However, in speaking on behalf of everyone and from the heart, the meaning-maker may provide a path that can guide the group through its contested terrain. What seemed indefinite can become clear. What felt conflictual can become harmonious. The collective leader, by the sheer act of framing reality, consolidates the prevailing wisdom of the entire community.

I imagine that many readers remember the Apollo 13 space mission, especially due to the popular 1995 movie directed by Ron Howard. Though scheduled as the third lunar landing, an explosion in one of Apollo 13's oxygen tanks and collateral damage to other systems resulted in an aborted mission. It was just after the explosion that Commander James Lovell transmitted the historic message, "Houston, we have a problem . . ."

The movie, based on the full account of this historic mission, contains many examples of collective leadership, but one particularly compelling scene involved the dangerous buildup of carbon dioxide in the spacecraft. To save the lives of the crew, the technical staff on the ground had to figure out a supplementary carbon dioxide removal system using only items available in the spacecraft. The brainstorming session that transpired revealed true collective leadership. As we witness the session, we see no sign of rank or privilege. Everyone becomes involved and leadership emerges out of the entire team, not from any one individual. Gradually, the staff built a mock-up of a removal device from parts of a lunar suit, plastic bags, cardboard, and a lot of tape.

In order to operate collectively, then, position leaders need to demonstrate how they and others can serve the community when necessary. Leaderful practice begins when people look to serve a common good as much as their own self-interests. This ethic of stewardship is supported when people see that actions within the community can be interpreted as learning opportunities. As people in the community adopt a learning orientation, they can begin to see that the visioning function of leadership should rightfully be co-created as a meaning-making process.

The following three sections demonstrate why and how to develop collective leadership within your community.

The Leader as Steward

Leaderful practice subscribes in part to the stewardship view of leadership, which begins with the stance that no one person has an automatic right to a position of power. Although stewardship theory, unlike leaderful practice, recognizes the role of follower, it views followers and leaders as intimately interconnected. Indeed, the roles may be reversed as the situation warrants. So leaders who "stand out in front" in the conventional sense do so at the pleasure of those "below." They hold their leadership in trust on a temporary basis while exerting their special skills or tasks on behalf of the group. When they complete their job—whether representing a team as their manager to those in the upper hierarchy or coordinating the tasks of a team or of several teams—they may resume their role as a regular member of the community.

The stewardship process in a highly developed group thus promotes collective leadership, though the process is quite implicit since the orchestration of responsibility flows to a natural rhythm. Those who need to exert classic authority do so as needed and then recede into the thicket of the community when their duty is over. No one possesses the credit to the exclusion of others; indeed, leaderful members tend to be uninterested in directing credit toward themselves, preferring to see credit shared among the community. When asked why he hadn't taken credit for not only the stability but also the reinvention of his company during the dot.com demise, former CEO Jim Kelly of UPS responded:

> I think CEOs are terribly overrated. The whole concept of the superstar CEO is nuts. When you look at successful companies, there are a whole lot of folks doing a whole lot of things to make them successful. Being a superstar has an awful lot to do with timing. . . . Around here, we don't think of ourselves as individuals doing too much on our own. We think of ourselves as people working together to get things accomplished.[3]

Stewards, in Kelly's idiom, rarely stand out as superstars. They do not necessarily hold positions of authority, yet they are typically critical players in their social networks, often found helping their colleagues by offering ideas, bringing knowledge resources to their attention, or connecting them with others who are doing similar work. They are the people who are most noticed or missed when they are absent, often because they represent the glue that holds the group or network together.

In stewardship and in collective leadership, people think of themselves in the context of the community. Stewards are not typically interested in "beating out" another person in an effort to get to the top. They always consider the good of the whole. Accountability for action falls to each and every member. At one point during a hearing on the Iran-Contra affair, then-Secretary of State George Shultz was asked what he learned from the incident. He answered: "Never give responsibility to someone who can't live without it." Communities governed by stewardship flourish when *everyone* feels they can't live without the responsibility for the entire community.

Peter Block sees stewardship as arising from a partnership among members of a community.[4] Building such a partnership takes work that requires four ingredients: (1) the purpose for the community must be mutual; it cannot be imposed; (2) everyone assumes responsibility for his or her own work and has the right to say no to any assignment; (3) everyone also assumes accountability for the work of the entire community; and (4) people act with integrity toward every other member.

In this era, we are often exhorted to take control of our own career; no one else will. Although we can applaud the need to lift ourselves from a dependency on others, a stewardship approach would not endorse fulfilling one's ambitions at the expense of others. Yet, this is precisely what a so-called individual careerist orientation seems to advocate. Consider the following advice, offered under the most innocent guise of self-development, and presumably attributed to a well-known management guru: "Read just one book on a subject you're interested in and you're ahead of more than 80% of other people; read two books and you're ahead of more than 95% of everyone."

A stewardship perspective would find great fault with this approach, in particular, the use of the metaphor "to be ahead of," as if our mission in life is to compete in the organizational game. The implicit careerist orientation in this message is that one reads for the purpose of getting ahead. Should we not rather say how much more *all* of us could know together if we share the books we have read or the knowledge gained from them?

Stewards put others' interests before their own. They are sincerely concerned about the welfare of their associates. Their motivation comes not from a subtle need to "win them over," but from genuine concern and integrity. Robert Greenleaf believed that wanting to serve was a natural feeling in human beings. Converting this instinct into leadership produces what he called "servant-leadership," which asks: "Do those served grow as persons; do they, while being served, become healthier, wiser, freer, more autonomous, more likely themselves to become servants?"[5]

Servant-leadership teaches you how to communicate with subordinates to gain their commitment. It subscribes to the democratic premise that people should have a say over the projects they commit to. Given that the servant-leader allows people this choice over their commitments, what is the leader's role in "supervising" a subordinate? Can and should a leader "help" another person? The answer is, yes, but not necessarily in the form that supervision normally takes, namely through direction and advice. The servant-leader is more interested in listening first in order to open up avenues that might help the subordinate solve his or her own problems. No one is a better expert on a problem than the person with the problem, so advice from a supervisor may not only be naive but it may even be counterproductive.[6] The supervisor typically does not know the countless factors that impinge on the problem. Further, it is the subordinate's prerogative to choose what to share. The servant-leader's task is to determine how to make it possible for subordinate sharing to occur.

Since many of us tend to work in large organizations, the sheer act of soliciting counsel and commentary from subordinates can seem a daunting task. Servant-leaders tend to derive personal methods to elicit feedback. General William C. (Gus) Pagonis (retired) wrote about a technique that he used in his military career and still uses to this day.[7] He would make available 3 x 5 inch index cards to everyone in his command. He guaranteed that he would consider all questions or comments written on the cards and would move them through the chain of command until they reached someone with the knowledge and authority to respond to them. Responses and commentary would then be guaranteed to be returned to their authors within twenty-four hours.

Although the servant-leadership philosophy is to be admired for its altruistic disposition of serving others before oneself, it veers from stewardship—and by association from leaderful practice—in its focus on the inviolate traits of the individual leader. Indeed, Robert Greenleaf suggested that servant-leaders seem equipped with special powers that are not necessarily available to followers. Among these, he included the servant-leaders' foresight, or the ability to foresee the unforeseeable, their intuition or feel for patterns, and their creativity and confidence in facing the unknown. To Greenleaf, these special powers made them superior. Unfortunately, though entirely benevolent, with this single belief he undermined the opportunity for collective leadership, espoused an elitist stratification among people, and advocated for followership dependency. Here is Greenleaf in his own words:

> Servant-leaders are functionally superior because they are closer to the ground—they hear things, see things, know things, and their intuitive insight is exceptional. Because of this they are dependable and trusted, they know the meaning of that line from Shakespeare's sonnet: "They that have power to hurt and will do none."[8]

Stewards appear far less divine than servant-leaders, less conspicuous, and, consequently, less interested in permanent leadership positions. Consider the ranking of leadership behaviors put forward by the ancient Chinese philosopher Lao-Tsu, who as far back as the sixth century B.C. seemed to have understood the art of stewardship. The lowest order of leadership fell to those who were despised, followed by those who were feared. A higher third level was reserved to those who were loved and revered. The fourth, highest level of leadership was associated with very few wise people who even in the less pluralist world of ancient China were acknowledged as the ones "who were barely known."

The Leader as Learner

Since we have described the leader as potentially any intimate member within the community, we would not expect such a leading member to take the community off track. But how would we handle someone emerging to save a community from his vision of "impending doom"? We can best address this challenge by inserting a value fundamental to leaderful behavior—the value of learning, or what Heifetz referred to as learning without "easy answers."[9] Heifetz asserts that a leader cannot emerge by providing a neat, quick solution that only provides an illusion of accomplishment. Tough problems require rigorous examination that can only come about through learning. By this, I refer to a level of collective consciousness that goes beyond attending to symptoms of a problem. Rather the community becomes willing to examine the fundamental assumptions behind its reasoning, carrying it to a scrutiny of successive layers of the problem, leading to as close an examination as possible of its core. This may mean reconsidering even the premise of a given belief.

The process of learning at this level is often painful in not affording a pat answer. It also takes longer because it subjects alternatives to collective examination, which often involves conflicts among competing ideas. Learning leaders, however, are unusual in their willingness to subject their assumptions to public scrutiny. They are willing to face their own vulnerability, knowing that they may lose control, that their initial suppositions may turn out wrong, or that they may not find a solution, at least in the short term. But, as W. Brian Arthur of Xerox PARC once said: "It is not what people know that counts; it's what they take for granted."

Even more, learning leaders are willing to face the reality that they not only do not know the answer but that such a revelation to others, especially to their colleagues, might suggest incompetence, not to mention their own fear of not knowing. Here's how famous theatre director Lev Dodin puts it:

> [It] is an ongoing process lasting the whole of our lives. Just before yesterday's show, we had another rehearsal of the same play and still we criticized each other and discovered new things. This means that the process is not over and can never finish, that the truth has not been discovered and that there is always a great space to go on and to discover.[10]

The key to learning is to transform the attribution of incompetence in not knowing the answer to that of competence in the capacity to learn. Learning does not have to always reside in the expert or in the "leader." Learning is a mobile, continuous, and collective process. Relying on any one person to produce it can make it stale. We need to exalt the value of inquiry in our lives and admire the person with the question as much as the person with the answer. No one needs to feel incompetent for not knowing an answer. Incompetence, to the leaderful manager, is when one does not have the courage to find the answer.

Ralph Larsen, chair and CEO of mammoth Johnson & Johnson—comprised of nearly two hundred distinct operating companies—exhibited a learning orientation when the company introduced its *FrameworkS* strategic process.[11] The capital S signifies the multiple frames through which the strategic team using the process would view its project mission. Accordingly, the company invites ten to twelve people from its various operating divisions to join the executive committee in a significant strategic undertaking. The new team members—chosen for the geographic, technical, or organizational perspective they bring to bear on the issue at hand—may not necessarily be high-ranking executives as much as people with talents to add value to the project deliberations. The team typically goes off to a remote location for a week to work on the project. Meetings are run democratically with no one imposing rank or exerting status privilege. After the initial gathering, additional subcommittees and task forces are organized to continue to research the issues and take the necessary actions. FrameworkS teams have thus steered the company into new markets, new technologies, new businesses, and even new values (such as their "what's new" program focusing J&J on innovative practices). Larsen has referred to FrameworkS as "a proven means of releasing energy throughout the corporation," and writer and coach Donald Laurie has ventured that the program "brings employees onto the balcony with [Larsen], thus widening the Johnson & Johnson panorama in previously unimagined ways."

The Leader with All the Answers   The heroic tradition in leadership makes most of us feel that when named as a leader, we receive that position because of our independence and decisiveness. The last thing we want is to be dependent on others. If we show doubt, we believe that others will begin to question our authority and respect. Before we know it, there will be an insurrection to replace us because we have come across as weak and uncertain. Indeed, the heroic expectations of our CEOs have probably contributed to their increasingly short tenures, which now average between two and four years. If they can't deliver continuously progressive results, especially reflected in a growing stock price, they can be sacked for poor performance, regardless whether they—as a single individual—had any impact on that very performance.

Along with certainty comes the need for speed. Leaders have to act fast to show their decisiveness. Inquiring with others, even slowing down to collect their own thoughts, can be seen as another sign of weakness. Yet, leaderful managers realize that they often have to slow down in order to go fast. Consider this biographical account from Ann Bancroft, one of the first women, along with teammate, Liv Arnesen, to cross Antarctica's landmass by foot. I hope you will see how Bancroft's experience in Antarctica can apply to everyday business predicaments.

Slowing down comes naturally when you're hauling a 250-pound sled across Antarctica. From the beginning of our trek, Liv and I were behind schedule by about 12 days. We needed to cross the continent within 100 days, before the winter set in. Pacing was critical; we were always tempted to go faster. And when the wind was right and the conditions safe, we prepared the sails and glided across the ice to make up for lost mileage. Sailing, we could achieve up to 70 miles in a day. Pulling, we could cover 12 miles, at best. We constantly had to rethink our strategy, depending on what card Mother Nature dealt us that day. And the slow days were the most critical days; they were our recouping days.

Liv and I constantly changed roles, depending on the day and our strength. Every hour we took a 10-minute break from pulling, replenished our supplies, and changed positions so that one person wasn't always leading. On trips like this, you strive to be equal all the time. But the reality is, you're going to have down days, even in the most severe climate. Several times, I had to swallow my pride and admit that I couldn't keep up with Liv. Sometimes I needed to slow down or stop, even though she could go another five miles.[12]

From the world of finance, Beth Sawi, executive vice president of Charles Schwab relishes the opportunity to slow down and re-connect the company to its bearings. "Most creative break-throughs happen when you break for reflection," says Sawi. She also finds that pauses in the world of action can allow managers to ask some critical questions, such as: "What's working and what's not? Where are we offering value? Where do we need to improve? What services are no longer relevant to our clients? What challenges demand our attention three months, six months, two years down the road?"[13]

Learning is preferably a collective process because it needs to extend beyond the individual. If only one person in the commu-nity learns, the remaining members are deprived of a creative op-portunity and instead subjected to dependence on the individual learner. Here's how an IT management consultant described his role as a developer of learners among his client group as they worked with him to implement a new accounting system:

> In trying to play the role of learner, I attempted to create an environment where the accountants wanted to learn the details I felt they needed to know in order to use the system effectively. Through a series of training sessions to transfer my knowledge about the system and its maintenance, I tried to instill a curiosity about how the system functions, and an ethic of experimentation in order to improve understanding. Moreover, in any project, it is important to maintain a list of project issues that serves to codify knowledge—i.e., a detailed record of issues, actions taken, and their resolution so that, when others in the organization experience similar issues, the learning is not lost. The mark of a very successful implementation is a self-sufficient client user community. My goal in acting as learner was to create learners out of the client staff—something that I believe they need to be truly successful.

In the knowledge society, the person with all the answers looks more the fool than the one who defers to the community. To illustrate, Scott Adams of Dilbert fame recounts an allegedly true story.[14] The senior management at a high-tech company presumably became angered when they discovered that two important R&D projects were entitled Ren and Stimpy, after the cartoon characters. Henceforth, they declared that names of projects would have to be submitted to a master namer who would approve only names taken from famous rivers. This would ensure the use of only appropriate and dignified names. The process worked well until some engineers presented a briefing on their most recent projects. Their names: Ubangi and Volga.

Lao-Tsu, referred to earlier, believed that people like to work in their crafts without much interference because leaders who interfere disturb the natural order of things. Oftentimes, such presumed leaders don't even know the inner workings of the task or job, thus, their interference will be viewed as unnatural and will lead to resistance from the workers. If carried on, it can even tear apart the fabric of the community. In the *Tao Te Ching*, he wrote:

> People are difficult to lead
> Because they are too clever.
> Hence, to lead the organization with cleverness
> Will harm the organization.
> To lead the organization without cleverness
> Will benefit the organization.
> . . . .
> Whoever substitutes for the Master Carpenter in carving,
> Rarely escapes injury to his hands.[15]

Double-Loop Learning   Although impressions of weakness are real within communities that have existed for years as controlling systems, we can reverse the trend of what Chris Argyris has called a Model I world.[16] In Model I, leaders resist learning by needing to be in control, by maximizing their own winning behavior (at the expense of others), by suppressing emotion, and by demonstrating that they have their act together—in other words, by remaining rational. Such a model has enormous costs because it comes at the expense of mutual learning. If you don't trust other members of your community to come up with the answers, then you'll treat them as dependent on you. This gives them the license to coast along without the need to offer suggestions or take part in the serious decisions that impact the community. Likewise, Model I leadership behavior relieves members of responsibility for any action beyond their most immediate operating domains.

A power plant employee expressed his feelings of becoming dependent quite eloquently.

> In controlling systems, you learn to stop thinking for yourself. You are never allowed to feel any feelings, except fear. You are never allowed to have inner judgment. What you learn is apathy.
>
> You are not allowed to imagine. Without the power to imagine, you are a rigid conformist. Human imagination is the power that

has forged new frontiers. . . . Without this power, you gradually become hopeless, since hope involves seeing new possibilities.[17]

Workers who are treated as dependent, when they otherwise have the talent to act with both autonomy and integrity, can occasionally use their talent to thwart the efforts of an all-knowing management. Alan Randolph refers to this phenomenon as "malicious compliance."[18] In this case, individuals may choose to do what they are told—to a fault. That is, even when they know that a job is not being done correctly (or may even be the wrong task to begin with), they will do it anyway. In a way, their work-to-rule is a form of defiance based on a conditioning that expects people to not think for themselves.

A variant of the behavior of malicious compliance is the "yes-man" mentality. Yes-men or women, knowing that their boss only wants to hear good news, willingly participate in a conspiracy of compliance. The effects of this non-learning orientation, of course, can be disastrous since the conspiracy can lead to a poor performance that most everyone could have predicted. Supervisors and executives need to eradicate the "yes-man" mentality by endorsing truthfulness at every corner. William Rockwell, former president of Rockwell International, expressed it bluntly: "If you want the truth, you have to convince people of your willingness to accept it."[19] Contrast this with a humorous quote that has been attributed to Samuel Goldwyn of Hollywood fame: "I want you to tell me the truth, even though it may cost you your job!"

Tom Peters pitched perhaps the most eloquent defense of the "good news" mentality in his classic article "Leadership: Sad Facts and Silver Linings" in the *Harvard Business Review*.[20] According to Peters, hiding bad news from chief executives is a prime example of sad facts that nevertheless typify managerial behavior. However, there is a silver lining in having subordinates deliver good news, namely, that it can, according to Peters, "deliberately reinforce desired patterns of action or response." In other words, through the process of good news reviews, senior managers can get those down the line to share their priorities. Although this is likely a true statement, it represents the nonlearning orientation that I believe leaderful managers would prefer to limit in their communities. It suggests that policy making and real strategic thinking need to occur at the top. In this event, the job of senior management is as much to "sell" subordinates on this policy as to engage them in determining what it should be. Are not subordinates capable of making and voicing their own judgments on policy? What kind of real contribution can they make when they begin to see their role as figuring out what the chief executive wants?

Are not subordinates capable of making and voicing their own judgments on policy? What kind of real contribution can they make when they begin to see their role as figuring out what the chief executive wants?

Bradford and Cohen question the toughness of leaders who make all the decisions.[21] It is not necessarily tough to make a decision all by oneself believing that "the buck stops here." What is tough is having the courage to put issues out on the table for all to argue about, not knowing the outcome. What is tough is being willing to submit the community to a conflict of views rather than suppressing the inevitable disagreements that will occur. Perhaps the most tough-minded leader is the one who can let the community make the ultimate decision, knowing that the decision might be wiser than the one the position leader could have come up with alone.

Jack Welch, the former indefatigable and sometimes controversial CEO of General Electric, was paradoxical in exhibiting both conventional and leaderful brands of toughness. He seemed nonleaderful in his apparent lack of compassion for the "also-rans" of GE, those who couldn't keep pace with the pack. He also, perhaps tacitly, liked to spice up his language with macho military metaphors. He constantly spoke about "winning" in the marketplace, about "nailing" subordinates when they didn't make their numbers, about getting rid of people who didn't adopt a quality mind-set, or about counteracting rivals' e-strategies using "destroyyourbusiness.com." Yet, behind this tough exterior perhaps lay a leaderful predisposition. In particular, Welch acted as a passionate learner and a true team facilitator.

During his tenure at GE, Welch openly encouraged grabbing ideas from anywhere and running with them—a practice that he proudly called "legitimate plagiarism." He also invented the now-popular notion of the "boundaryless" learning culture, based on an assumption that someone, somewhere, always had a better idea. As a manager, he would help people find the idea, learn it, and put it into action. He did this by pushing to delayer the bureaucracy at GE and by trying to refashion the culture into one with an insatiable desire for knowledge that might be available not just among GE businesses but also among other stakeholders external to the company. As for whether the available knowledge would come from the top, he cautioned that

> the quality of an idea does not depend on its altitude in the organization. An idea can be from any source. [If GE had to rely on me for all its ideas], this place would sink in about an hour. The only way to be more competitive is to engage every mind in the organization. You can't have anybody on the sidelines.[22]

GE's remote CT scanner, created by its Medical Systems division, which allowed GE to detect and repair an impending malfunction on-line, serves as a good example of the boundaryless learning culture fostered at the company. The technology underlying the scanner was shared with other GE businesses. In short order, Jet Engines, Locomotives, Motors and Industrial Systems, and Power Systems used it to monitor the performance of their product lines.

In contrast to Model I learning, we might ask whether our

leaders can become practitioners of what Argyris calls Model II. In a Model II world, there is a belief that the entire community can search and learn together and that all members become mutually responsible for the decisions and actions of the community. People at all levels of the community no longer feel the need to protect themselves since the leader opens him- or herself up to the challenge of others. Not that the leader is a "pushover" in a Model II world. On the contrary, a learning leader will advocate strongly for a position but *at the same time* will combine that advocacy with inquiry and self reflection. The leader does this by constantly behaving in ways that demonstrate caring, support, respect for others, and honesty. Though fallible and, thus at times, unwittingly subject to Model I behavior, the leader attempts to encourage both self and others to say what they know or what they fear to say. Furthermore, by persisting in self-reflection and inquiry, the leader imposes a check to stay the course and subsist in creating a learning environment for all.

What we have, then, is a risk-reward paradox in adopting a learning orientation within your community. If you take the risk of subjecting your assumptions to scrutiny, you risk embarrassment or an impression of incompetence. On the other hand, this very risk can reap rewards if the resulting scrutiny can lead to greater understanding and learning. A project manager in a pharmaceutical firm addressed this very paradox.

> In a meeting consisting of executives from Quality, Regulatory Compliance, and R&D, we were discussing the follow-up activities required by the FDA. A task list was formed for my group and we were about to adjourn. I thereupon asked if I could summarize my own duties. However, after each task, I asked the officers involved if they could explain to me the significance of the task and how it would benefit our responses to the FDA. I approached the questioning by stating that I was new to this entire framework, and I was just asking to clarify my own personal understanding of our group's activities as a kind of learning incen-

tive. Of course, I knew that I was vulnerable to embarrassment and the thought of these VPs thinking I was incompetent, but I did it anyway. The risk was also elevated in that I was supposedly the technical expert on the product and should already have known about the specific requirements.

To make a long story short, as the officers began to respond to my questions, there were some tasks that did not need attention because they were already being performed! Miscommunications were also uncovered, which in the end reduced our group's task list to a few simple experiments that needed to be performed. After reflecting on the situation, I believe I was able to project a learning-based approach to this group in such a way that the thought of my incompetence was never raised. I believe I demonstrated that my learning interest was stronger than the risk of embarrassment. In the end, my own boss and director both showed their appreciation of my questioning of upper management since it reduced the overall task list of the department. I was more pleased with myself for taking the risk and getting the desired result, learning more and not seeming incompetent.

In a study of cardiac surgical teams, Edmondson and her associates found that some teams adopted a new technology (in this case, minimally invasive heart surgery) far more effectively than others. Again, learning was core, but it was real-time learning that was critical. Neither the educational background and surgical experience of the team members nor the debriefs or after-action reviews following the performance made much of a difference. Rather, it was the commitment of all team members to experiment with new ways of doing things during the actual procedure itself—without endangering the patients—that led to success. Further, the technical acumen of the lead surgeon and other team members had minimal impact compared to their ability and willingness to learn together, even if it meant confronting one another, regardless of status.[23]

Motorola institutionalizes dissent by allowing employees to

file minority reports whenever they object to any business decision, even if it means going over the head of their immediate supervisors. As it turns out, a number of their technology successes can be attributed to these minority reports. In a similar vein, 3M encourages its employees to actually defy their supervisors. New employees hear stories about victories won in spite of the boss's opposition. Even former CEO Desi DeSimone was reputed to have tried to kill a project on five separate occasions only to see it unrelentingly re-emerge and ultimately become an extremely successful product.

It is nevertheless a high task to create an environment that offers psychological safety when covering up has been the dominant reaction to contrary or contradictory information. A controller describes as follows the predicament he confronted when he was put in charge of a Production Control (PC) team that needed to review its own scheduling and planning processes.

> At one of the first group meetings, the members were naturally curious as to why I was involved in this project. I told them that management didn't understand why so many scheduling problems had occurred over the past several months and that we thought it may have been caused by inexperience with the com puter system. Basically, I was blaming the cause of the problem on the computer system, not the group. In trying to gain acceptance from them, I was trying to cause the least discomfort attributable to the intervention, allowing members to basically save face. In actuality, the members were in the best position to change any inefficiency in the system. I probably would not have had to intervene if the group members had taken it upon themselves to change the system for which they were responsible. I wanted to tell it like it is because no true learning will occur if you try to sugarcoat issues. I must admit, however, that it is very difficult to tell it like it is unless your organization is truly learning-oriented and conditioned to accept this forthrightness. Given that I don't believe my organization is ready for this type of can-

dor, I'd have to admit that given the chance, I'd probably say the same thing again in my initial meeting if I had to do it over, although this time I'd at least understand what I'm doing.

In the case of this controller, we would wish to know whether he, too, would be willing to examine his assumptions about his own need to cover up his true assessment. By doing so, was he not guilty of perpetuating the same unlearning culture that he had accused his organization of perpetuating? What were his expectations of what would have happened had he brought up the problems with the PC group? Perhaps the key question for the leaderful manager is when and where does one take the first step?

Learning is intimately tied to a collective consciousness that encourages a constant re-examination of meaning. The learning leader is not content merely to solve an immediate problem. With the involvement of fellow compatriots, learning leaders uncover the implicit procedures and assumptions in use—referred to as "double-loop learning"—and then proceed, on a periodic basis, to explore the premises behind the assumptions, what we might call—"triple-loop learning."

So, let's say you need to trim staff in your organization, and are governed by familiar contractual obligations to lay off on the basis of seniority and performance. As a learning leader, acting within contractual constraints, might you be willing to question whether these criteria are useful or even whether they should be used at all? Might you find creative ways to trim staff without resorting to a traditional downsizing mentality? Perhaps you could encourage some entrepreneurial employees, for example, to go off on their own and start independent businesses, which could initially rely on some contracts with your company.

In order to invoke triple-loop learning, you might probe even deeper into the premises of the proposed strategy. In this case, you could ask: Why do we need to downsize in the first place? What are the long-term implications, especially in terms of our knowledge base, of laying off some of our staff? Have we run our company with too much fat to begin with? If we're lean enough, what nonpersonnel factors might have led to our market or financial instability? Are we guilty of resorting to a layoff mentality as an easy solution to instability? Have we looked at our own plans and actions; that is, have we looked into ourselves?

Triple-loop learning is admittedly quite difficult to institutionalize within an organization. It requires individuals to risk their reputations on exhibiting a learning orientation. At first others in the organization may say, "This just proves that so-and-so doesn't know what he's doing." Yet, if we really believe that collective change has to begin with our ability to upset standard ways of thinking and tried-and-true operating assumptions, we may have to take this risk. There's no better place to start than with the position leader.

Daniel Kim fears that not addressing the underlying causes of problems and instead relying on stopgap measures often ends up exacerbating the problem.[24] For example, let's say a manager initiates a marketing promotion campaign in order to soften a slump in sales. Although the new campaign may provide an interim spike in sales, it may do little to address the real problem, perhaps an aging product line. In time the original symptom might reappear, but by then, the manager who "saved the day" may have been offered a promotion. Meanwhile, his or her replacement may have to take the blame for the subsequent drop in sales.

Learning leaders have the courage to probe beyond the symptoms of problems at the expense of short-term improvements. Consider a scenario featuring a human resource manager involved in introducing an HR intranet in her company. She and her team had to consider whether the intranet would really be an effective resource for answers to general human resource questions within the employee population. Many employees did not own PCs. Further, the team could see that many employees preferred to speak face-to-face with a human being. During a planning session, this same HR manager, though acknowledged as the champion of the intranet project, asked: "Is the HR intranet a feasible resource for this population?" By this very question, she was willing to subject the fundamental assumptions behind the very goals of the project, which had already amassed hundreds of hours of time and commitment from her staff, to team scrutiny. There was no more demonstrative way she could have proved to her community that she valued learning above all other ends, even if it meant dislodging the very foundation of the project.

Co-Learning   Noel Tichy proclaims in *The Leadership Engine* that the one characteristic that differentiates the successful from the unsuccessful company is whether its leaders nurture the development of other leaders at all levels of the organization.[25] Rather than just worry about today's organization, they build one that can remain successful even when the top manager is no longer around. Larry Bossidy, former chair and CEO of Honeywell, once put it this way: "You won't remember when you retire what you did the first quarter or the third. What you'll remember is . . . how many people you helped have a better career because of your interest and your dedication to their development."

In order to create and sustain a learning orientation, everyone in the organization has to be seen as a co-learner. Bradford refers to a "two-hat theory," in which each employee wears two hats.[26] One represents the job they are responsible for and the other is their responsibility to have a perspective as the owner of the firm. The co-learning idea has been also institutionalized in a process known as "open-book management," which expects employees to view themselves as partners in business. At Springfield ReManufacturing, CEO Jack Stack, co-author of *The Great Game of Business*, believed in this idea deeply enough to turn over the company's financial information system to all employees so they could understand their role in the overall performance of the company.[27] Similarly, at Frito-Lay, any employee can gain access to the sales volume of each of its product lines by logging onto a computerized product development system. The Honda plant in

Marysville, Ohio, prints up a large scoreboard that regularly gives updates about the plant's performance.[28]

Jan Carlzon, famed CEO of Scandinavian Airlines, used the phrase "moments of truth" to describe how critical it was that each of his company's employees interacted successfully with SAS's ten million customers. On the basis of contact with SAS employees, customers would form an impression of the airline. Realizing the impact of each encounter, Carlzon wanted his employees to have the necessary resources and confidence to make decisions that would please the customers and develop their loyalty to SAS.

Perhaps the most widely publicized method of involving employees in the learning of their own organization is through employee stock ownership. The idea is that with ownership comes natural or intrinsic responsibility. On the other hand, ownership does not always translate into collective leadership. One has to commit to real involvement, as seems to have occurred at Herman Miller, the innovative furniture manufacturer that is 100 percent employee owned. In his well-known *Leadership Is an Art*, its former CEO Max De Pree maintains:

> Stock ownership is a marvelous vehicle for involving an entire family in the career of those of us who work for corporations. There is a certain morality in connecting shared accountability as employees with shared ownership. This lends a rightness and a permanence to the relationship of each of us to our work and to each other. There are also clear implications. There is a risk. . . . [W]hile it's great to work for gains, one also has to be ready for the losses. We must be more accountable. Owners cannot walk away from concerns. Ownership demands a commitment to be as informed about the whole as one can be.[29]

One way to inquire about the level of co-learning in your community is to ask executives what would happen to the organizational unit or the organization as a whole if they went down in a plane crash. Would everything be in place for the community to continue on its own? If not, the executives may not have built learning and development into its natural operating practices. Developing others, however, is not just a defense against the turnover of key leaders, whatever their position in the hierarchy. Development should become a natural process, embedded within the organizational system as a function of ongoing organizational learning.

Work-Based Learning   The question turns to *how* to create a learning environment where collective leadership may flourish. So many individuals equate learning with classroom education, whether in a school or a university or at a training site. Although we can pick up some useful concepts and practices in a classroom, often it represents a sterile environment far removed from the wild and woolly world of the workplace. Without a real-time demonstration of an illustrated tool or concept, the effectiveness of any classroom lesson could be at best temporary. Only through work-based learning can we integrate theory with practice and knowledge with experience. Otherwise, we can conveniently "unlearn" classroom lessons once the training is over. Why? We unlearn them because typically the back-home work environment is not prepared for any new approach; indeed, it is often unreceptive. The individual trainee may have learned, but not the surrounding department or organization. Not that any change is easy to introduce. However, when we build change into the process of work itself, it can be introduced not as an antiseptic lesson but as part of a system-wide endeavor involving the stakeholders necessary to the change.

In my book on the same subject, I introduce work-based learning as learning:

- acquired in the midst of action and dedicated to the task at hand.
- that views knowledge creation and utilization as collective activities wherein learning becomes everyone's job.

- that demonstrates a learning-to-learn aptitude that frees users to question underlying assumptions of practice.[30]

Learning can be accomplished, then, just-in-time and in the right dose to facilitate practice. Furthermore, it does not have to become disassociated from the notion of place. It can be designed to assist leaders in navigating through the cultural and political land mines of their own communities. It can be dedicated to solving actual problems faced by the business in question.

Leaderful managers make it their business to learn continuously and collectively as part of their everyday experience. They work incessantly to create an environment where people freely exchange knowledge. Their communities are characterized as learning cultures in which there is less reliance on expertise lodged in single individuals. Rather, everyone becomes a partner in creating and expanding the sources of knowledge. No view, no matter the source, is sacrosanct. As knowledge is adapted and enriched in this way, it transforms into learning.

Consider a statement by a team member, whom I'll call Dave, that I recorded during a learning team meeting of a project team working on an advertising campaign:

> It looks like we have pretty much endorsed the direct marketing approach for this advertising campaign. As you know, I have pretty much pushed for it as well, but we all remember what happened on the Rane project. I would have to admit that it still feels right to me, but to be honest with you, I still have some reservations. Do you think we might take one more look at this? I'm afraid I might have overlooked something.

Notice how Dave has not only invited open commentary with his inquiry but has also openly second-guessed himself—an exposure that in some organizational cultures would be considered overly vulnerable. Leaderful managers, interested in building a culture of learning, are nevertheless willing to take this risk.

The Leader as Meaning-Maker

What do we ask of our position leaders? If we don't need them to control work processes in a community that already knows how to do it, if we don't need them to heroically lead us out of trouble in a community that assumes this job as part of its leadership, then what behaviors can leaders exhibit that are of assistance? Besides the historical task and maintenance practices detailed in the last chapter, there may be no more critical function than to perform meaning-making for the community. Supportive of collective leaderful practice, anyone in the community can perform this role. To make meaning one has to merely help the group make sense of what people do when they work together.[31]

Visioning   Some management consultants might have you believe that meaning-making and visioning are one and the same. In most circles, however, creating a vision is a job reserved to the designated leader. One gets the impression that this leader holes up in an enchanted office and receives or constructs some anointed vision of the future, bringing it back to the community like Moses offering the Israelites the tablets of the Ten Commandments.

According to Bert Frydman, Iva Wilson, and JoAnne Wyer, the visionary gets crossed-up when he or she becomes a "true believer," someone so convinced of his or her vision that it becomes solidified into an unquestioned ideology. They go on to say that the "visionary, convinced of his or her vision, can become a *knower* who then ceases to see clearly and who does not inquire into nor seek to understand or learn from the sources of resistance."[32]

The conventional view of visioning as a cognitive process occurring within the mind of the "leader" is so implicit in our culture that we don't see that it can become an antidemocratic process. Even Secretary of State, General Colin Powell, seems unaware that by compressing vision into the mind of the "leader," he might thwart another noble leadership characteristic that he embraces, namely, having the courage to question authority. Here's how Powell describes the visioning process:

> [Effective leaders] articulate vivid, over-arching goals and values, which they use to drive daily behaviors and choices among competing alternatives. Their decisions are crisp and clear, not tentative and ambiguous. They convey an unwavering firmness and consistency in their actions, aligned with the picture of the future they paint.[33]

Does this sound like a man you would want to cross? Notice also his choice of words, especially the familiar *drive*, suggesting that people need to be driven to the vision—a vision pre-formulated and now firm, not tentative, not ambiguous.

We tend to expect our leaders to perform the mission-setting process for us. Such phrases as *aligning the organization with the strategy*, or *cascading the vision down the ranks*, have been coined to depict this process of sending the vision down to the staff where it will get implemented. The tacit operating assumption is that the staff does the doing and the leaders do the thinking.

In a consultant report that I recently read about an organizational change initiative, the leaders of the firm were advised to build consensus and commitment to some new strategies, to create energy, and to make the firm's vision real. The report continues: "[I]n essence, they would have to build ownership of the vision throughout the firm—a process that would entail communicating values associated with the vision, translating overarching strategic objectives into local initiatives, and aligning support systems to reinforce [those] objectives." The consultants, as can be seen, remain unaware that the so-called visioning process that they recommend is still a top-down endeavor. Later in the report, they take certain middle managers to task for not "buying in" to the new vision. They continue to be unaware that the "alignment process" is not mutual and that lack of buy-in may signal stifled dissent.

It could be John Kotter who initially called for aligning people with the leader's vision. In his view, top managers first need to "get people to comprehend a vision of an alternative future." However, their job does not end there. Their next challenge is what Kotter refers to as sustaining credibility, namely, "getting people to believe the message." Finally, people need to be empowered to carry out the vision. Kotter's view of empowerment, however, is constrained. He sees workers as empowered when they acquiesce to the vision.

> When a clear sense of direction has been communicated throughout an organization, lower-level employees can initiate actions without the same degree of vulnerability. As long as their behavior is consistent with the vision, superiors will have more difficulty reprimanding them.[34]

This quote is striking in that it suggests that employees operate in a punitive system to begin with. It is their assent to a vision, through so-called empowerment, that protects them from further punishment. Another example of the unintended disrespect accorded lower-level employees through the strategic alignment process was manifested by Robert Branford, president and CEO of the Center for Simplified Strategic Planning. In *Executive Excellence*, Branford recommended that the way to get people aligned with strategy is to make it their strategy. However, he cautions that you have to make the strategic planning process practical. You can't have too many people present. His solution: "What you want are ways to make people feel that they are contributing to the strategic decision-making process, even when they are not directly involved in the decision making."[35]

Meaning-Making　Visions are preferably co-created. Minimally, they arise out of the community in its very work. The leader doesn't walk away to create the vision; it is often already present. It just needs articulation. This is where the meaning-maker surfaces. A former student of mine, a CFO, distinguished the

difference between visioning and meaning when, after an acquisition, he endeavored to bring his bank's new subsidiaries into all
aspects of the business operation. This required an in-house
financial management training program, frequent visits to the
subsidiaries, and a business leadership forum. As he worked
through his project, he noted the following in his journal:

> I had originally thought that meaning-making was all about pro-
> viding vision. I came to find out that it was more directed at
> drawing out thoughts and ideas that already existed from indi-
> viduals and groups. My project proposals are not new ideas. I am
> simply trying to change the current business focus in order to
> draw upon and leverage the knowledge and information that cur-
> rently resides at the subsidiaries but have never been fully utilized
> to make informed business decisions. As a meaning-maker, I am
> focused on what Margaret Wheatley refers to as "creating mean-
> ing from work, meaning that transcends present organizational
> circumstances. As long as we keep purpose in focus, we are able
> to wander through the realms of chaos."[36]

The meaning-maker has no special powers other than his or
her own awareness. Chinese philosopher Lao-Tsu (referred to in
the last section) also depicted insight of this nature when he
warned against leadership that moved against the grain of nature
and against the direction of social evolution. Leaders who stand
above the crowd, Lao-Tsu argued, would only bring chaos to the
world. Instead we need meaning-makers because:

> [They] make the mind of the People their mind.
> [They] attract the world and merge with its mind.
> The People all focus their eyes and ears.

In retrospect we have a tendency to anoint the meaning-maker
with special powers for having distinguished a unique vision, but
the meaning is often there for the taking but for the courage necessary to detect and then act upon it. In the field of strategic man-

agement, a so-called deterministic approach suggests that the role of the leader is not so much to establish a vision as it is to reflect the organization's cultural predispositions. Strategic choice is not a matter of single-handedly predetermining a vision as much as providing a post hoc meaning and understanding to organizational actions.[37] Even in presidential politics, it is far more important to detect meaning than to create it. David Gergen, the "adviser to the presidents" (having served on the White House staffs of four presidents) has explained:

> A president's central purpose must be rooted in the nation's core values. They can be found in the Declaration of Independence. All of our greatest presidents have gone there for inspirational strength. Lincoln said he never had a political sentiment that did not spring from it. It was not intended to be a statement of who we are but of what we dream of becoming, realizing that the journey never ends. It is our communal vision. That's why a president . . . need not reinvent the national vision upon taking office. He should instead give fresh life to the one we have, applying it to the context of the times.[38]

Acknowledging this process of capturing an already existent meaning offers a unique retrospective of many historical accounts that seek to display the heroic qualities of our leaders. Often these accounts leave out the interconnectedness of the leader and his or her community in order to chronicle the leader's distinct and superior skills.

Consider another story, this time from the Bible. Most of us are aware of King David's elevation to royalty as a result of his battle with Goliath, but many of us do not know about another key event in David's ascent to the throne. Although he warmed the hearts of the Israelites with his deeds in battle, David was not King Saul's choice as successor since the old king resented this young lad's popularity. Indeed, Saul tried to discredit David even to the point of convincing the people of Israel that he was disloyal and should be hunted down and even killed. As luck would have it, one day David came across Saul alone in a cave at Adullam. At that moment, David could easily have overtaken and slayed the defenseless Saul. Instead, David merely cut off a corner of the king's robe. Later, he confronted Saul and, showing the king the slit in his robe, professed his loyalty, saying that had he been vindictive, he could have easily taken Saul's life.

Commentary on this biblical story of Saul and David use the episode to point out David's godlike powers—in particular, his virtue and extraordinary vision—attributes necessary to become a king of all Israel. Richard Phillips, for example, makes the following observation: "David [became] the heroic champion. He was the one the Israelites could trust, who could be counted on to lead the people to victory. To follow David was to observe his brilliance shine forth, to watch in wonder as his magic unfolded."[39]

But was David so extraordinary? Had he thought up this scheme of saving Saul on his own? True, some of David's soldiers would have been content to see Saul meet his Maker. It is further likely that had the roles been reversed, Saul would not have been so lenient. But there are always cooler heads that prevail at times like this. It may also have occurred to David and his community that killing Saul might have precipitated a civil war, pitting countryman against countryman. The real meaning may *not* have been to seek revenge leading to a vicious struggle but to seek unity so as to defend the nation against its real enemies. David knew this from his intimate involvement in his own community. Furthermore, his "vision" may not have been unique to him. Indeed, no one else sought to dispatch Saul after David's humanitarian act. All David did was articulate its ultimate meaning. It was a leadful act that made sense to the community.

Managers as meaning-makers are as much responsible for encouraging others to articulate the meaning of the community as for doing it themselves. They become welcomers or carriers of meaning. Authors Alain Godard and Vincent Lenhardt acknowledge the complexity of this role.[40] At times managers may need to articulate the meaning they see, especially if their colleagues are in a state of healthy dependence. At others times, they may need to endorse and even personify the meaning when less boisterous community members have only faintly articulated it. Finally, at times they enable others to detect the meaning in their work together or position themselves to reflect with others on the emerging meaning of the community.

The meaning-maker's role is complex because members may be at a different level of agreement at any point regarding the community's mental models. Shared meaning in the community may in turn depend on such variables as how long the members have been together or what prior experiences they have had in this and in other teams.[41] In their role as meaning-maker, leaders can ask a number of questions to stimulate the search for common meaning.

When it comes to content, they may ask:

What are our aims?
What are the stakes?
What are we to do?
What are we deciding?
Why have we reached this point?
Why is it important?

When it comes to process, they may ask:

How should we go about it?
What methods should we adopt?
What are the roles?
Who decides?
How do we link together?

The meaning that emerges from these questions is typically not a collection of fact-filled rules and procedures. It tends to represent a higher order of thinking and feeling that "re-presents" the facts in a more encompassing view. In this way, meaning can cohere a comprehensive set of activities and judgments. Antoine de Saint-Exupéry once wrote: "If you want to build a ship, don't drum up the [crew] to gather wood, divide the work, and give orders. Instead, teach them to yearn for the vast and endless sea."

In this sense, the meaning-maker functions not so much as a "practical scientist" who crafts rules and procedures to facilitate group integration but rather as a "practical author" who crafts words and metaphors that lend meaning to the community's collective purpose. This leader possesses the ability and, most particularly, the courage to attempt a framing or a reframing of the situation at hand. The leader's first attempt may not work. People in the group may be contending with vague and conflicting feelings. However, in speaking from the heart, the meaning-maker may provide a path that can lead the group through its contested terrain. What seemed indefinite can become clear. What seemed conflictual can become harmonious. The leaderful meaning-maker, by the sheer act of framing reality, consolidates the prevailing wisdom of the entire community.

In speaking from the heart, the meaning-maker may provide a path that can lead the group through its contested terrain. What seemed indefinite can become clear. What seemed conflictual can become harmonious.

In *A Company of Leaders*, Gretchen Spreitzer and Robert Quinn advise managers that empowering their workers does *not* mean turning them loose.[42] To do so would not only produce disabling uncertainty and ambiguity but also, in their words, "could degenerate into a system plagued with chaotic self-expression that has little alignment with the collective vision." They therefore recommend that workers be given clear goals, clear lines of authority, and clear task responsibilities. As an example, they point to Marriott's use of "safe zones," which set boundaries for empowered behavior. A hotel manager may without approval call maintenance to fix a light, but purchasing a new light may be beyond the safe zone. Although I subscribe to the need to develop leaderful communities (as described in chapter 4), I don't think one can ever be truly leaderful when having to operate under others' rules and regulations. It is far preferable to participate in a community in which all members create meaning and in which this meaning lends its own vision for coherent work.

In light of the tragedy that occurred in New York, Washington, and Pennsylvania on September 11, 2001, meaning-making might be accorded an even greater significance as people search for ways to redefine what they find of value in the workplace. Instrumental values, those that only serve as a means to an end—such as working hard to make money or to earn a fast promotion—may no longer be sufficient to lend meaning to the workplace. People may expect meaning to originate from the community's ability and commitment to provide a haven for security and belongingness. The sense of real community or family, however, though desired, may not become apparent until articulated.

Robert Greenleaf used to tell the story about John Woolman, an American Quaker reputed to have single-handedly rid the Society of Friends (Quakers) of the institution of slavery.[43] What Woolman did was to find the inner meaning of the Quaker family and communicate that sense of justice and equality throughout the community. He did this over thirty years by visiting slaveholders, traveling hundreds of miles at a time by foot and on horseback. His leadership did not consist of censuring members of his community. Rather he engaged them in dialogue, asking such questions as: What does slave ownership do to you as a moral individual? What kind of institution are we that holds slaves? What are we saying to our children about our heritage? In time, the Society of Friends became the first religious group in American to formally condemn and forbid slavery among its congregations.

Since the notion of meaning tends to run deeper than instrumental attributes, it is an intrinsic property. It's what helps give members a sense of identity and responsibility. Randy Komisar in *The Monk and the Riddle* advises people to "[w]ork hard, work passionately, but apply your most precious asset—time—to what is most meaningful."[44]

Meaning-makers may seem to emerge "out of nowhere," but in fact, they are intimately involved in their communities. They also tend to be particularly observant people. They question such things as how the community arrived at its current moment in time and what the commitment of each individual to the community might be. They also tend to see things through the eyes of others as well as through their own eyes. In this way they affirm that meaning is a co-created process rather than an individualistic thought.

Daniel Goleman recounts the case of a floundering national pizza restaurant whose senior managers were at a loss.[45] The managers would get together to strategize only to come up with the same limited options. Then at one meeting, the vice president of marketing, Tom, made a bold move. He made an impassioned plea that they alter their perspective and think of themselves not as a restaurant but as a distribution business. At that moment, Tom filled the vacuum for meaning with a conceptual breakthrough so powerful that it became the core of the restaurant's future strategy. Within weeks, local managers responded to the new strategic initiative by finding ingenious locations to open new branches: street corner kiosks, bus and train stations, hotel lobbies, and the like. Although Goleman refers to Tom in this story as a visionary; in my view, he is more likely a meaning-maker. His vision did not "come in from the cold," but came out of a community in a struggle to find the core of its identity. In this instance, Tom acted as the carrier of this vision.

Meaning-makers are rarely individuals who burst in from the outside and disrupt things. That process might sound appealing, but such individuals likely do not possess the credibility to sustain commitment from the community. They can at best direct action. Meaning-makers, on the other hand, function best when they articulate ideas within the flow of the community as it performs its work. Consider the transformation that occurred at Wyandotte High School in Kansas City over a five-year period.[46] The school had the usual M.O. of inner-city schools: low attendance, high dropout rate, low test scores. What seemed to have turned the school around was the arrival of a forward-thinking principal and a supportive superintendent, both of whom had genuine respect for frontline educators. What got things started was the blunt charge of the principal, who simply exhorted the staff to "design a school you would want to send your children to." And that's exactly what they did. They divided Wyandotte into eight mini-schools, called "small learning communities." The mini-schools and the staff became a family. Teaching and professional staff formed into teaching teams that had full autonomy to decide how to address the problems of their school—a school they would now send their children to.

Meaning-makers also appreciate that the value of leadership itself is subject to an interpretive process. They appreciate that any expectations about what a leader does or what leadership represents are open to a process of what is often called "social constructionism."[47] All this signifies is that the reality that people in an organization experience is as much due to their experience of that reality as to some objective preconception of it. Some leaders may tell their members exactly what they expect to do as leaders. Others may recognize that leadership is tied up in how they and others collectively behave in their daily interactions. Leaderful meaning-makers tend to fall into the second group. They tend not to take their leadership for granted. They know that leadership is bound up within the culture of their community and can change from day to day as new experiences arise and as challenges are confronted.

Communities-of-Practice Leaderful practice also flourishes in communities known as "communities-of-practice" (CoPs). These evolve as people united in a common enterprise develop a shared history as well as particular values, beliefs, technologies, ways of talking, and ways of doing things.[48] They come together not so much on the basis of formal memberships or job descriptions as by being involved with one another in the process of doing a job. A key to the informal membership of any CoP is the need to know what other members know. Thus, such communities are defined by knowledge rather than by task. They form around professional identities and can therefore be just as easily found across companies as within. They don't necessarily follow any pre scribed regimen, yet, in time, their efforts as a community become natural. As an example, consider how Tracey Kidder, in *The Soul of a New Machine* (about the design of a minicomputer at Data General), described the Eclipse project team:

> The entire Eclipse Group, especially its managers, seemed to be operating on instinct. Only the simplest visible arrangements existed among them. They kept no charts and graphs or organizational tables that meant anything. But those webs of voluntary, mutual responsibility, the product of many signings-up, held them together. Of course, to a recruit it might look chaotic. Of course, someone who believed that a computer ought to be designed with long thought and a great deal of preliminary testing, and who favored rigid control, might have felt ill at the spectacle.[49]

Since members of a community-of-practice have learned how to work with one another as part of their mutual tacit understanding of what needs to be done, they have no need for formalized leadership. Members commit to one another in order to do what's needed; and that may include leadership. The leader in a community-of-practice becomes the person who articulates what needs to be done, especially during times of change.

Consider the performance of a jazz band. To the observer, it oftentimes has no apparent leader in the conventional sense. There is often no conductor, for example, nor is there even a musical score; yet, the best jazz bands play with seemingly perfect timing and orchestration. Their transitions into new themes and solos appear seamless and effortless. If you ask the musicians how they accomplish this unity of performance, they will point out that, having played with one another for so long, they can detect implicitly where each of them wishes to go. Through a casual glance or a transitional series of notes they tacitly allow each other to lead the group in new directions as they see fit.

Although it is yet unclear whether an organization's executives can actually create communities-of-practice, it appears possible to minimally encourage their emergence. For one thing, executives can encourage and reward CoPs, even though they may have a membership of people external to the company. They might also extend the necessary infrastructure to sustain the ongoing collaboration of CoPs through, for example, intra- and internet resources, collaborative on-line technologies, and shared databases.[50] Perhaps the best method to encourage CoPs is merely to give them your blessing. Kermit Campbell, former CEO of Herman Miller, used this tack. He endorsed the ad hoc creation of numerous committees all over the company in order to promote initiative and responsibility. In his words:

> They are all doing their own thing, and most of the time, I don't even know what they are doing. . . . But in a team of thirty people, a few will realize they have common interests around an issue. They'll come together the day that they realize they have a need, settle the matter, make the decision, implement it immediately, and get on with life. And I don't even need to know about it. When someone gets into trouble or needs my help, then they call me.[51]

Transcendent Meaning An important meaning-making leadership role is to "see" emerging realities before they occur. Claus Otto Scharmer refers to this ability to see what does not yet exist as "self-transcending knowledge."[52] This futuristic meaning-making is often associated with artists rather than with managers. For example, we might recall the famous quip uttered by Michelangelo in describing how he carved his famous *David*: "David was already in the stone. I just took away everything that wasn't David." Applying this idea to leadership, we can imagine how leaders within their communities articulate where the group may be going even prior to getting there. And yet, the key question may be not so much Where are we going? as What do we plan to care about? Meaning-making managers have an uncanny knack for bringing out this collective consciousness in the community mainly because of their ability to act and observe at the same time.

Michael Tilson Thomas, the famous and still relatively young American conductor, used this sense of meaning-making when he served as guest conductor with the Chicago Symphony. Although the role of symphonic conductor is often interpreted as a directive practice in which members of the orchestra are asked to carefully follow the direction of the conductor, Tilson Thomas used a more collective approach in his rehearsal with the orchestra of Tchaikovsky's Sixth. "Of course, they had played the *Pathétique* hundreds of times," recounted Tilson Thomas.

> [But] when we got to the second theme, instead of beating it note by note in the typically international schoolmaster way, I raised my hands into the air and gently indicated a breathing space that would precede this phrase. At first they were baffled. "Let's breathe together, hold the first note slightly longer, and then let the melody gracefully fall away from it." I couldn't make the music happen alone. We needed to share the feeling, we had to find that shape together, and we did. It was miraculous.[53]

I have often been asked if the meaning-maker is the person who can awaken the spirituality in oneself and in each of us. For example, Neal has defined spirituality in the workplace as being "about integrity, being true to oneself, and telling the truth to others." She goes on to suggest that spirituality also helps an individual "live his or her values more fully in the workplace."[54] Although leadership can start with the pursuit of a meaning that helps you define your own values, the meaning-maker is ultimately concerned about the meaning of the community as it works together. Lee Bolman and Terrence Deal refer to any spiritual journey as one that begins with ourselves but not necessarily *by* ourselves.[55] So, in addition to an internal exploration of soul, our spiritual quest should also entail an external search for communion.

Furthermore, meaning-making in the leaderful tradition does not have to exhibit a transcendental quality. Although each individual may find deeper insights that connect with the universe in some way, the meaning drawn by the meaning-maker is a here-and-now phenomenon that captures the essence of what the community finds purposeful in its current work together. At times, the articulation of this purpose provides members with an ethereal sense of well-being, but members are as likely to feel a connection toward each other and their mission, accomplishment, and collective effort as toward the universal. The sense of well-being may also derive from the value of the work, which may have extended beyond the immediate problem to the organization and to society. Perhaps a group, for example, in remediating an environmental hazard has saved its company a fortune. However, the members feel proud that their breakthrough may be responsible for ultimately contributing to a cleaner planet and a more sustainable environment. In this sense, the meaning created for the group might have a spiritual quality in its interconnection with a greater societal good.

8 Collaborative Leadership

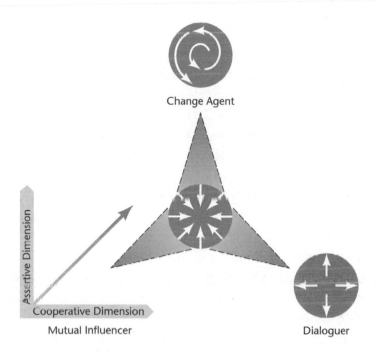

Change Agent

Assertive Dimension

Cooperative Dimension

Mutual Influencer

Dialoguer

COLLABORATION AS A LEADERSHIP CONDITION MAKES INHERENT sense. As we shall discuss throughout this chapter, when people who implement changes are involved in the design of these changes, they tend to do all they can to see their plans fulfilled. In addition, when fully involved in the implementation of change, they tend to commit themselves to seeing the change through to the end. What a great way to work in a dynamic environment.

There may be a concern that leaderful managers cannot flourish or even survive in a nonleaderful culture because competitive associates will "eat them up." Although working within a competitive culture can pose challenges, leaderful managers can advocate their viewpoints with the best of them. What distinguishes them from pure competitors is their keen ability and wholehearted commitment to listen to others and, subsequently, change their minds or build on a new contribution.

In this way collaborators can model an alternative to influence strategies built on competition, bargaining, or exchange. Their influence skills can be instructive when groups wish to invent new ways of operating that can lead to innovative outcomes.

There are three predispositions associated with collaborative leadership that are worth modeling for others. First, collaborators begin any dialogue with a stance of nonjudgmental inquiry. In other words, they express genuine curiosity about events and have no hidden interests. Any interest that they might have in intervening in an engagement derives not from an obsession with an intervention method nor from a need to be seen as "the helper." Rather, they are guided by their interest in a salutary outcome, in particular, in increased individual, group, or organizational effectiveness.[1]

Along with nonjudgmental inquiry, which relaxes any initial preconceptions about an idea, comes the predisposition to submit one's own ideas and views to the critical inquiry of others. In this way, collaborators become receptive to challenges to their own ways of thinking, even to discovering the limitations of how they think and act. Last, collaborators entertain the view that something new or unique might arise from a mutual inquiry that could reconstruct everyone's view of reality in an entirely new way. They are willing to disturb their own preconceived worldview on behalf of a common good.

One of the most illuminating examples of collaborative leadership comes to us via the world of classical music under the auspices of New York's Orpheus Chamber Orchestra. Critically acclaimed as one of the world's foremost performing ensembles, it has adopted a unique approach in its rehearsals, recordings, and performances: it has no conductor! Built on the principles of individual participation and self-governance, it has set out to achieve high standards through the democratic process of artistic collaboration among its members. Executive Director Harvey Seifter explains the orchestra's collaborative approach.

> Central to our distinctive personality is the process of sharing and rotating leadership roles. For every work, the members of the orchestra determine the concertmaster and the principal players for each section. These players constitute the core group, whose role is to form the initial concept of the piece and to shape the rehearsal process. In the final rehearsals, all members of the orchestra participate in refining the interpretation and execution, with members taking turns listening from the auditorium for balance, blend, articulation, dynamic range and clarity of expression. In recording sessions, the entire orchestra crowds into the production booth to listen to the initial playbacks.[2]

Collaborative practice, then, is inviting to all members of a community. As an influence process, it asks all stakeholders to come into the circle and fully advocate their views, but to be prepared to listen to and deeply consider those of others. As such, it recognizes that the contribution of each member of the community, no matter what his or her social standing, can only arise from civil dialogue that permits open disclosure of each person's beliefs, feelings, and assumptions.

Collaboration represents a fundamental condition underlying leaderful practice. The following three sections indicate how to develop collaborative leadership within your community.

The Leader as Change Agent

It may seem contradictory to espouse a leaderful view of leadership and at the same time propose that leaders be agents of change. The concept of agency, however, does not presuppose a method of change-making. An agent can be as much a servant as a director. An organization or a community is always in motion.

So, a leaderful leader does not force the organization where he or she wants to go; rather, the leader may shape the direction of where it wishes to go. In addition, the leaderful leader can serve as a model of changeability, someone willing to face personal vulnerability on behalf of constructive change. Such a leader tends to be predisposed to creating a psychologically safe environment for other community members.[3] Such a leader also recognizes that as members of an organization, it is our choice to remake it to cherish our human inclination to work in harmony while achieving our personal potential.[4]

We need to start, though, with the acknowledgment that community members perceive the utter reality of motion—there is no such thing as standing in place. Change is a fact of organizational life. Former CEO of W. R. Grace, J. P. Bolduc, was known to have said that the only security blanket a company has in our era is "to live outside the sandbox." Nevertheless, changing old habits or policies is difficult, at times even gut-wrenching. Fortunately, leaderful practice can make any transition easier to tolerate owing to at least two processes associated with its commitment to collaborative action. First, when people participate in designing a change that they see as desirable, their self-identity often becomes tied to the successful implementation of the change. Hence, they become intrinsically motivated to see the change not only implemented but implemented successfully. Second, when individuals participate in a change effort, they typically structure the change to be ultimately desirable to them. Essentially, by involving people in change, leaderful managers by their very behavior and instincts overcome a good part of the natural resistance that most people have toward change itself.[5]

Unfortunately, many change efforts, though well intentioned, don't follow the leaderful prescription about involvement suggested above. Often, managers form design teams and commission consultants to spearhead the change effort, but in this process, they forget to include all the internal and external stakeholders affected.

They may begin to direct rather than facilitate the process. They use team members as sources of information rather than work with them to design and implement the desired changes.[6] Leaving out key stakeholders—especially those most directly affected by the change—leads to resistance later. Yet the directive change agents are often the first to question why key stakeholders resist.

John Nirenberg and Patrick Romine reported on a case of this nature.[7] A senior marketing team from a mobile phone company pushed forward on a plan to expand sales. It was simply a matter of pre-installing batteries in their phone that would allow customers to use the phone right away. The team prepared sales figures showing a steep rise in revenue from this simple step. A "no-brainer" as far as the team was concerned, they couldn't figure out why they were getting resistance from both manufacturing and customer service departments. What they neglected to incorporate into their planning, by failing to involve these other operating staffs, was the effect this change would have on assembly and shipment processes. In particular, the size and weight of the battery would ultimately alter shipping costs, packaging, and warranty fulfillment. Further, service issues would arise if charged batteries were installed in unused phones.

In extreme conditions, whether a sudden crisis or adverse competitive pressures, top managers may claim that they simply do not have sufficient time to involve employees in the organization. Although drastic action may be called for in some circumstances, centralized change without employee involvement probably indicates prior uninvolvement. After all, if employees are involved to begin with, they shouldn't be that much more surprised by events than the top executives. Given an understanding of an impending crisis, they would likely have gone along with centralized action rather than have resisted it.

Resistance Whether a program of change is revolutionary or evolutionary, it typically poses a legitimate challenge to what already exists. Kurt Lewin referred to this as the "unfreezing" stage of change.[8] A leader's role during this stage may merely be to present data that disconfirm the apparent value of keeping the present course. Lewin called this confronting the resisting forces of change. It is often during times when change is plainly required that leaders can be most bold in initiating a fruitful examination of new strategic possibilities.[9]

Many scenarios for change can be introduced, and they should involve all affected parties. Overcoming resistance is a joint undertaking that occurs as part of an open dialogue. For example, a leader may suggest to his or her colleagues that when puzzled about what to do, they may have learning anxiety. This state occurs when you find that you currently possess insufficient knowledge to solve your problems. Another approach is to point out that success inevitably breeds its own resistance. Rather than fight it, you may prefer to incorporate it into the change.[10] What would happen to a corporation, for example, if it needed to reassess its efficient production processes because of objections from its neighbors?

One of my former students had served as a Peace Corps volunteer in Guatemala, where one of his principal assignments was to work with local farmers to implement soil conservation and organic farming techniques. Initially he reported that he faced quite a bit of resistance to some of the conservation and agroforestry systems that he espoused. However, once he earned the farmers' trust sufficiently to conduct a demonstration, he first worked on only a fraction of their land. He did this because he "wanted them to be able to make a comparison between the new way and the old."

Similarly, a line supervisor, assigned to help a team make its production goals, started by examining its processes. He discovered that team members unnecessarily turned the power off every time they changed positions. When they balked at his suggestion to keep the power going, he offered the following rationale:

Team, we're here to make money, we're here to make [the product]. We're not making schedule; we're the lowest line on schedule realization. . . . We're the most over budget of any line. This [stopping the line to rotate] is a contributing factor, a factor that we can control directly, and this is why we need to stop it.[11]

Leaders, such as the above former Peace Corps volunteer and plant supervisor, can help community members understand that forces for stability and forces for change exist in every organization. Some of these forces will have lots of influence whereas others will have little impact. Assessing the strength of each force as well as determining whether the force facilitates or resists the change in question are critical diagnostic points for the change agent. For example, a project might be undertaken in the area of mergers and acquisitions. Particular departments might very much favor the acquisition because of the synergies it might bring. Perhaps the new partner might offer a product that will significantly complement the company's product line. On the other hand, other departments might resist the change for fear of losing staff, resources, or prestige. Perhaps the new company has a comparable staff that will cause redundancies once the acquisition is completed.

Lewin originally characterized the balance of forces depicted above as a force field and their diagnosis as a force-field analysis. In order to move toward a changed or new state, one has a choice of increasing the strength of the facilitating forces or reducing the strength of the resisting forces. Lewin was clear that it is preferable to try the latter since increasing the strength of the facilitating forces can produce in-kind, often unintended, counter reactions. Continuing the example from above, perhaps the manager of the department fearing layoffs from redundancies as a result of the acquisition could have his or her fears allayed by a promise that natural attrition would be used to reduce head count, followed by a commitment to reassign all other redundant staff.

Faced with disconfirming data and an understanding of the resisting forces, community members may still not accept the change emotionally, even if they have begun to understand it rationally. Often, they need time to mourn before embracing a new state of affairs. Change inevitably translates into letting go of old and safe ways of doing things. People and groups respond differently to this transition process, often depending upon their psychological security. Helping people overcome the losses typically associated with change can serve as an important contribution on the part of change agents. People need to express their feelings and share their experience. It is important to air concerns about any prospective change in order to address them in a forthright manner. Some of the questions that community members might want addressed include:

> Why do we have to change?
>
> What will happen if we don't change?
>
> What do we get to keep?
>
> What will we lose?
>
> Who is inducing this change, and what are their agendas?
>
> What will we become after the change?
>
> What assistance and resources are being provided to help us?

An operations manager charged with heading up a process improvement project in his company, a global consumer products corporation, admitted that he effectively canceled the opportunity for his team members to vent their emotions on the mistaken belief that such an airing would frustrate them. He explained:

> As local implementation leader my initial approach during early meetings with my team members was to tell them what we needed to do and what was expected from them. Because there was no debate whether or not this project was going to take place (it was handed down from corporate), I did not find it necessary

to ask the members what they thought about the situation. I did this because I did not want to give them the impression that they had a choice, because they did not.

I now know that this was not the approach to take. I received negative responses back from my group members, and I began to feel they blamed me for recommending the need for a new system. I had unknowingly positioned myself in an adversarial role and felt my group meetings were transforming into win/lose battles in which I was the advocate of the new system while the rest of the group was the defender of the current one.

It is preferable when embarking on an unpopular change project to allow a sharing process that might solicit community members' feelings about the change. Scott and Jaffe indicate five types of losses that employees might experience when facing change.

1. **Security.** They may not feel in control or may no longer feel that they know where they stand.
2. **Competence.** They may not know what to do or how to do it, which, in turn, may cause them considerable embarrassment.
3. **Relationships.** They may fear the loss of old customers, co-workers, or managers, which might then affect their sense of belonging to a group or organization.
4. **Sense of direction.** They may lose a sense of where they are going and why.
5. **Territory.** They may fear they will lose the area that used to belong to them, such as a work space or job assignments.[12]

It is important to openly confront these losses since people may experience self-doubt, anger, depression, or any number of manifestations of anxiety. Kerry Bunker and David Noer with the Center for Creative Leadership have encountered three prototypes who react with unproductive anxiety when faced with change.

1. The *overwhelmed*, unable to let go of old ways, withdraw and seek shelter by blocking out what is happening around them. They typically go into deep denial.

2. The *entrenched* might go along with the change but do so in a narrow and limited manner. Overidentifying with the past, they can be found lecturing their co-workers on how things used to be.

3. The *BSers* appear comfortable with the change but are really just fooling people with their seeming smooth demeanor. They appear confident that they can handle any crisis by shooting from the hip.[13]

To replace such unfortunate reactions, Bunker and Noer recommend that people help each other, in the collaborative tradition, to develop a learning response. Learners respond proactively to change. They accept the need to let go of the old and take action in the face of uncertainty. They use their inner resources and skills to take a positive outlook and act with both prudence and enthusiasm.

It is possible that the resistances that individuals and members of groups erect may be unconscious to themselves. If these resistances prevent them from achieving what they hope to accomplish, leaderful change agents may need to help them confront the psychological assumptions behind their resistances. Robert Kegan and Lisa Laskow Lahey present such an instance in a case about a highly collaborative video production team that had decided to undertake a target-market strategy that would require individual members of the team to take responsibility for overseeing distinct market segments.[14] Even though all members had agreed to the strategy, it never seemed to take hold, even after a year of concerted effort.

In a reflective session with all team members present, a most curious contradiction came out. By pursuing the new strategy, even though they expected it to help them develop needed new markets, the principals worried that it would drive them apart functionally and emotionally. In other words, they seemed to have unconsciously agreed to undermine the very strategy to which they had consciously committed! Yet, they did not share their apprehensions with one another since they were, for the most part, unaware of them. Only when they openly confronted their assumptions did they realize that they had implicitly worried that the new marketing strategy would have "created the silos we have long happily avoided and would have left us more isolated from one another. We also assumed the strategy would have made us more competitively disposed toward one another." Once recognized and brought out into the open, the contradiction became manageable; namely, the team constructed ways to pursue the new strategy while preserving the collegial atmosphere the firm had created.

Stages of Change Lewin conceives of change as a stage between unfreezing—addressed in the last section—and refreezing. In the change stage, a new method or policy may be tested, perhaps on a subpopulation. For example, in order to prove a new development technology, an e-business program manager contracted with a new vendor to test out a core legacy system. Although the new system worked, the test site provided the contractor with some useful feedback to even more finely customize the product for a subsequent organizationwide adoption. In some cases, the change agent might seek out a role model who is already practicing a version of the anticipated new process or behavior. For example, as I pointed out in chapter 6, most teams in organizations are not inherently self-directed. However, one team may have made the transition from a standard team to an empowered one. If this team has achieved some success in its self-direction, it can serve as a "teacher" to other prospective teams that wish to consider a comparable transition.

In Lewin's "refreezing" stage, a new policy or program becomes institutionalized. Gaining this level of acceptance can occur only when the new practices become endorsed as natural features of the emerging culture. People refocus on a new mission and build action plans to make it work. They renegotiate their roles and expectations and reshape their values and actions to the new era. The organization may even applaud or make an example of behaviors that emulate the refocusing occurring during this stage. Managers need to keep in mind, however, that refreezing can be momentary; indeed, perhaps the most one can hope for in this last stage is a jelling of new processes or practices. Jelling offers only a temporary state of stability because reverberations from the original change sometimes emerge very late in the process or because future demands may require significant adaptation.

We can expand Lewin's three-stage change process into a five-stage model that picks up on the denial and confusion surrounding the unfreezing phenomenon. If people within the community feel content, it seems natural that many would hardly choose to experience change. This very state occurred at Digital Equipment Corporation (DEC) in the mid-1990s, shaking this high-flying manufacturer of minicomputers to its knees. Founded on supporting the technology and technical expertise of the minicomputer, the company missed out on the emergence of the PC and an industry moving toward more standardized systems favoring low-cost producers. Robert Palmer, the CEO brought in to try to turn DEC's fortunes around, found it enormously difficult to get his business units to focus on a customer orientation rather than on an engineering supply orientation. He remarked:

> One of the more difficult things we had to do, but it was one of the most important, was to get the organization through the denial phase about the marketplace and everything we had done here, and get it to accept the world as it is, not as we would prefer it to be.[15]

One way to help people confront their own denial of an impending change is merely to give them time to mourn, which often entails allowing their emotions to catch up to their rational understanding. Denial can also be confronted by having people impacted by the change examine their mindsets and behavior. Accordingly, they might evaluate the underlying assumptions behind the behavioral styles that characterized their past practices. Anderson and Anderson reported how difficult it was for the managers of a utility to shift from a regulated to a fiercely competitive deregulated business.[16] The change in mindset began with their learning to give up a prior culture of entitlement in favor of a style characterized by entrepreneurship and service.

In the five-stage model, depicted in Figure 8-1, the denial phase falls between contentment and resistance. Resistance is captured in its two components: counterproductive and nonproductive. In counterproductive resistance, the resisters exhibit energy but focus on measures counter to the direction of the proposed change. Change agents often find it easier to work with counterproductive resisters since they bring energy to the table that might be reframed. Under circumstances that tolerate resistance for a reasonable period of time, counterproductive resisters can also be thought of as "productive" resisters. The reason for this alternative interpretation is that in a leaderful environment, resisters can be viewed as people who are comfortable opening up and maintaining debate on controversial issues and processes. They are "productive" in the sense that their questioning of recommended changes may end up altering the changes in useful ways. For example, a manager might object that a diversity program to actively recruit minority candidates might be insufficient because the firm had not made plans to aggressively post job openings in minority communities.[17]

In nonproductive resistance, the resisters may have lost energy or hope or have become alienated, and thus resist more by inaction than by counteraction. Such resisters are frequently too disaffected to become open to alternatives to their past experience. Nonproductives often end up in an alienated state because they have not had sufficient time to mourn.

STAGES OF CHANGE

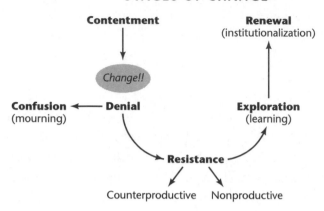

FIGURE 8-1. Stages of Change

Once people reach some level of comfort about the inevitability of change, they can begin to articulate the steps toward ultimate renewal or institutionalization. Individuals can consult new information, take cues from the environment, and even try out some new behavior. This represents a learning process that can generate its own feedback. As people try out new ideas and practices and get feedback, they make adjustments as necessary. Part of the learning process is often a question of knowing what to keep as well as what to change. By reflecting with others, leaders in the community might discover or rediscover those inalienable values that have distinguished the organization and made it unique.

Leaders may also, during the learning phase, suggest the creation of data-gathering groups, such as task forces, to inquire about both the technical and administrative aspects of the change. Since some people may nevertheless experience this learning stage as confusing and unsettling, change leaders can assist organizational members by organizing brainstorming and support sessions.

Communication of Change The leaderful manager becomes embedded within the community as its members experience the change effort. Working out of this vein, a change leader might observe and manage the process of inclusion through what change circles refer to as the CUSP model.[18] Accordingly, you might ask whether people feel that they have *control* over their situation. Do they *understand* what is happening to them and why? Are they receiving sufficient emotional and practical *support*? Finally, do they have a sense of *purpose* to give meaning to their experience and actions?

A financial system manager in a large health care organization used this model to assess his leaderful contribution to a change project that he and a cross-functional team had initiated. The project was designed to transfer voluminous yet critical storage files onto CDs using laser and optical technology. In his journal, he wrote:

> In the pilot phase of the project, the end-users of this technology were fully involved in all the team meetings and felt like they had control (C) over which reports were going out to CD and when. Through education and demonstration by my team, the users understood (U) the advantages of this technology and that they had the complete support (S) of the team, as we assisted them in writing test scripts and documenting results of those tests for them. Also, as we helped to make the users' lives more enjoyable and as we automated the many hours of their manual data entry, they began to understand the purpose (P) of the project team's efforts and the advantages that could be achieved by utilizing this technology.

During times of transition, it becomes all the more important to address people's needs and communicate with them as openly as possible. Unfortunately, because of the chaos that typifies organizations in transition, managers often conceal information from employees to protect the enterprise from security issues. For example, alerting workers to a plant shutdown might disrupt current production. Although security issues of this nature are real, managers are often guilty of not giving employees enough credit in collaborating with them through the process of change. One manager referred to such a condition in his journal.

> At my company right now, things get changed and never communicated. For example, my expense reports were being rejected months after submission because they changed the whole process to a SAP model. But no one, even the administrative assistants, were told. The decisions are being made by corporate in Dallas but no one has bothered to involve the Massachusetts people. If you need help from Human Resources, they have been instructed to only provide the employee with an 800 number which is an automated system that mails you brochures—no human being.

The Land Mines of Change   Consider an all-too-familiar vignette that probably occurs daily within the world of change. This vignette has been referred to as the "Catch-22" of change. A formerly autocratic manager turns over a new leaf and professes to become more democratic. Hence, he or she decides to delegate more responsibility to a worker. Naturally, the worker, having lived under the autocratic thumb of this boss for many years, mistrusts the boss's motives. In the past, whenever subordinates took some initiative that appeared to fail, the boss punished them in some way, such as by taking away all opportunities for enterprise. So, the worker takes a wait-and-see attitude, knowing that in due course, the boss will tell him or her what to do. Meanwhile, the boss perceives this worker's hesitation as a sign of dependency. The boss further decides that this worker is lazy and can't be trusted to assume responsibility. Taking back the project, the boss vows never to assume a risk like this again. The worker, meanwhile, feels vindicated that the boss has behaved exactly as expected and vows, in turn, never to take responsibility if it is offered again.

This vignette points out a number of land mines in the business of change that leaderful managers need to be aware of. The first land mine occurs when one goes directly into a change action without allowing unfreezing and mourning and without acknowledging and working through workers' natural resistance. Many of us enjoy the security of familiarity. So it is difficult to part with what has become customary. As we learned in the Catch-22 vignette above, you need to know what you are giving up and what you are moving toward. How will the change possibility benefit you? Clearly the manager in the vignette would need to have a series of informed dialogues with the workers if he or she were to suddenly embark on a "participation program." This manager needs to realize that it is often perceived to be far easier to take a dependent position within the hierarchy than to "stick your neck out" and face the consequences of taking initiative. Responsibility often is accompanied by risk and accountability. Why take a risk if all the critical decisions are being handled by those above you?

The change toward a leaderful model of leadership can be viewed as especially suspicious if a manager has previously operated as an autocrat. Such a manager cannot expect that a collaborative offer will "take" without a substantial delay to allow the employee to assess his or her truthfulness. The latter will certainly "wait out" the boss, knowing full well that during any moment of stress, the manager will most likely resort to the expected old ways. What can make the wait so frustrating from the manager's point of view is that while leaderful behavior may be taking hold, as people learn that they can assume leadership, there are bound to be mistakes and performance lapses. Enduring these errors is often the most difficult task of all during a transition period. Bill O'Brien, former CEO of the Hanover Insurance Company, once described his experience this way:

> [W]hat kept me up at night? It was when I had to deal with poor performance. I said to myself, "If I'm going to do this, I'd rather take a little more time and do it too late than do it too early be-

cause I have a human being's life here." Finally, you get signals that tell you you've waited too long. Some of your direct reports are coming to you, trying to drop hints that . . . there are missed deadlines—a whole host of things. I erred by being too late. I was late partially by design because I wanted to minimize the fear. For the most part the fear in corporations today is very debilitating so I wanted to keep us at a very low level of fear. I would rather have a lot of other people say, "It's about time O'Brien woke up!" than having people say, "Where is O'Brien going to strike next?"[19]

A related land mine is that change efforts are often dependent on the readiness of the system to change. In our vignette we have a system that has rarely, if ever, experienced participative management. The worker in question is not even curious about taking responsibility for actions, never having been given the opportunity. Hence, this worker and the system as a whole are in a low readiness state. In what we might call a medium readiness state, the members of the community at least express curiosity about a possible change, enough to remain open-minded about the change, though they may continue to feel uncertain about how to do it and what outcome it might bring. In a high or primed state of readiness, the members may have already begun the process of change but may just need a final word of encouragement as well as support and resources.

It might be noted that the manager and the worker in the vignette are hardly primed to engage in the change effort. Perhaps the manager has been "told" to be participative or delegatory with his or her workers. Exacerbating the change dilemma, this manager may have gotten no more opportunity to prepare for the change than the workers have.

Consider the case of an account director of cosmetic department counter managers within a large department store chain. She was interested in a change effort to transition the managerial staff from independent entrepreneurs into a self-directed work team that could support one another. She first describes a

Managing for Results (MFR) program that was designed to share leadership within the team.

> The program was designed to empower consultants and managers by letting them find solutions to the problems innate to the industry rather than having me hand them answers. This was a significant departure in leadership styles for me. When MFR was first introduced, I often felt as though I didn't have time to let managers and consultants devise their own solutions to problems at the counter. My immediate response was to give them an answer rather than challenging them to be creative. While this response was the easiest and fastest, it did not foster independence and learning on the part of the employees. I expressed this to the team and asked them not only to be aware of the change I hoped to make, but to tell me when I reverted back to my old habits, as it would be a disservice to both parties. They were encouraged to include their observations of my leadership style in our conversations during our weekly meetings.
>
> Well, the technique was only somewhat successful. I feel as though the women were not as honest or as specific as I needed them to be. In fact, during the subsequent series of meetings, there was only one manager who questioned me. She stated, "You seemed to be trying not to tell me how I should be tracking my data, but you ended up leading me toward your ideas." While this comment aided my personal growth, my leadership development could have been more significant if the women participated more in this process.

In addition to perhaps needing to exercise more patience, this cosmetics manager seems to not have recognized that expecting people to give their boss honest, descriptive, and critical feedback was quite counter-cultural in an environment that had formerly rewarded compliance.

The potential to create a leaderful culture is expedited, as was pointed out above, when a community has already reached a primed state of readiness. High-readiness conditions, however, tend to be more likely in creating new organizations than in resurrecting old ones. Why? Ted Lawler, in his study of high-involvement organizations, points out that in new organizations, the whole system may at least start out as a congruent system.[20] Change agents don't have to work in subunits of the whole; rather the whole itself can commit to leaderful practice. New employees, furthermore, can be hired with an expectation that their values be compatible with the new system. Finally, as the culture is new, there is no inherent resistance to change because of a need to uphold the status quo. On the other hand, there is no guarantee that leaderful practice will be embraced without the necessary learning conditions and commitments from those who have founded the new community.

Another land mine in change is the view that people and organizations can be changed through fix-it techniques that have been successful when working with capital. However, human beings don't react the same way as physical and financial capital. What makes us different, and of course more complicated, is that we have feelings! So, we can't expect that applying one action, say x, will automatically produce a change, say y. Not only do people sometimes not do what they're told, especially if they determine that it is not in their best interest, but they may also be affected by others who have their own agendas. Change-making, then, has to consider the feelings, values, and behaviors of people in addition to the physical processes that operate on the system in question.

Change rarely occurs when it is merely commanded. People will undertake change when they feel committed to both the process and the goal. Leaderful managers understand this basic human phenomenon and hence are not interested in commanding change. As Peter Senge likes to illustrate, leaders work like gardeners, even seed carriers, who plant the seeds for releasing the energy of others.[21] They are not so ego-involved as to have to be at the center of all change efforts. They allow change to evolve, often initially in small doses, until it becomes contagious and spreads to other locations. Robert Galvin, famed CEO of Motorola, vowed during his tenure to resource any leader (who could be anyone in the company, not just an executive) who could create a "legacy of something that would never have been accomplished if he or she had not done it (assisted by a team, of course)."[22]

Galvin put the need for a team in parentheses, but in reality, it is often the main ingredient to success. In a project to upgrade a university's web page, a manager reflected on her need to involve some key stakeholders in the process.

> I had an idea that I wanted to advocate, but I also wanted feedback from the others about their thoughts. I wanted to create excitement about the initiative but at the same time create an environment where they gravitated to where they wanted to go. I repeated to myself, "pull, don't push." I had to work very hard at ensuring my advice didn't ring too loudly. As I have described in my journals, I have a tendency to see myself as a lone champion of a cause in a win-lose manner. I realize that this attitude and methodology can be destructive to a project. Fishman bluntly writes, "And what happens to pioneers alone on the frontier? They get shot."[23]

Senge's view of the change agent suggests that leaderful consultants of change can occupy a number of diverse roles in their change-making. They do not have to be at the epicenter; they may not even be the principal champion. In some cases, for example, the leaderful change agent can serve as a sponsor to others, providing them with either pecuniary or nonpecuniary support to facilitate their change actions. Gordon and Ron Lippitt characterize eight possible roles for the change consultant, ordered from a directive to a nondirective style of intervention.

1. advocate
2. information specialist
3. trainer/educator

4. joint problem-solver

5. identifier of alternatives and linker

6. fact finder

7. process counselor

8. objective observer[24]

The choice of role may very well depend on a number of contingencies, such as what kind of contract has been arranged, the goals of the intervention, the norms and standards of both the client system and the consultant, past practices, and whether the consultant is internal or external to the system. The key is that the consultant display flexibility based upon the readiness level of both the system and the individuals committed to the change process.

Viewed as a collaborative process, change-making does not have to be a daunting task. It can become a natural ecological process embedded within our human condition. Land mines are in some ways barriers that we impose on ourselves only because we create an "us against them" dynamic in our belief that no one will go along with us. What if you created a leaderful environment in which your fears and aspirations, as well as your collaborators', could be brought to the table?

The Leader as Mutual Influencer

In classic leadership, influence is viewed as a means of control that, though not dictatorial, expects compliance from a cast of subordinates. For example, Joseph Olmstead explains in *Executive Leadership* that the executive influence system rests on four processes: (1) establishing goals, (2) exerting authority, (3) maintaining control, and (4) engaging in communication.[25] Established from the top, these processes work their way down to the bottom of the organizational hierarchy. So, for instance, the chief executive sets goals and then communicates them to the rest of the organization. The influence system, according to Olmstead, is based on an additional principle, that of coordination of actions. Coordination relies on several compatible elements, including:

- willingness on the part of subordinates to have their behavior guided by some overall concept
- willingness of these individuals to have their behavior guided by their superiors, with this willingness resting upon the acceptance of authority
- control of personnel behavior to ensure compliance with the concept
- communication of relevant requirements to each individual

Influence as a process within leaderful practice does not need to rest on the exertion of control through authority. It can be collaborative when all parties have an equal weight to affect the flow of communication and decision making. The full community, not just the leader, can set the fundamental mission of the community. Thus, compliance becomes unnecessary since everyone shares control. People contribute on the basis of their commitments to one another and to the community as a whole.

Joseph Rost believes that coercion is antithetical to an influence relationship since it deprives some people—typically followers—of their freedom to direct the flow of the relationship, which *should* be mutual.[26] For Rost, leadership is very much tied to mutual influence processes that, though unequal, can be multidirectional. Thus, although leaders are distinguished from followers—since the former initially set the pace of the relationship—followers can become leaders and vice versa. The key is that both parties influence each other to effect changes that reflect their mutual purposes.

Influence as an Exchange Process But we are getting ahead of ourselves. Some might suggest a middle ground exists between seeing influence as a bureaucratic control process and as a mutual collaborative endeavor. Influence can also be interpreted as an exchange process between individuals of relatively equal status and power. Leaders in this exchange are thought to be those who sway the group with their superior logic or reasoning or who demonstrate an ability to integrate the various perspectives presented. In this conception, leaders may or may not hold positional authority. If they are in authority, they may realize that their influence derives from critical mediating skills that serve to bring people and their ideas together. If they're not in authority, leaders may recognize the opportunity to influence people because of other skills they possess, such as knowing how to establish a compromise among parties.

Allan Cohen and David Bradford establish a rationale for the influence process described above, especially when it arises among employees without authority.[27] They argue that when faced with a condition of limited authority, the law of reciprocity should take over. By reciprocity, they suggest that people tend to be bound by the universal belief that they should be paid back for what they do. Other familiar maxims that illustrate this view are: "one good turn deserves another," or "you scratch my back, and I'll scratch yours."

Cohen and Bradford go on to suggest that reciprocity accounts for much of what goes on in organizations; in other words, people expect compensation, sooner or later, in some form of currency for their contributions. In fairness to the authors, they define currencies broadly, not just in monetary terms. For example, they discuss inspiration-related currencies and personal currencies, as well as currencies defined by task, position, and relationships.

Stephen Covey illustrates the law of reciprocity by suggesting that relationships in organizations can even be likened to bookkeeping accounts.[28] When we do something for others that they value, we make a deposit into their account that stays there until they make a withdrawal by doing something for us. We have to be careful, however, according to Covey, not to overdraw our account, for sooner or later our credit will come due.

Unfortunately, a leaderful perspective finds that this exchange process presents a rather crude view of human nature. Although I admit that some transactions can be defined by reciprocity, I certainly hope that it does not represent the engine of conscience in our communities. Are there no occasions when people do things just out of the goodness of their heart, or when they make commitments on behalf of a community without expectations of any return? To think such creatures naive is to view humanity as being in a pretty dismal state of affairs. I would hope that we can rely on leaderful members in our communities who can make commitments on the basis of personal integrity, interpersonal sensitivity, societal judgment, and community consciousness.

The leaderful perspective is concerned as much with the means of discourse as the outcomes. It is insufficient to find less than ethical behavior acceptable provided it is done in the interest of ethical outcomes. Yet, this seems to be precisely the approach that Jean Lipman-Blumen and Joe Badaracco advocate in their leadership approaches, referred to respectively as "connective" and "quiet" leadership.[29] Accordingly, leaders use pragmatic instrumental action as a means to bring diverse groups together or to overcome ethical challenges in the workplace.

Although I endorse the outcomes that these authors desire, I am less sanguine about their endorsement of "denatured" Machiavellian strategies, such as "focusing on self or relationships to get what one wants," "calculating the political capital being risked before tackling tough problems," or "exploiting people and processes to solve group problems." Machiavellianism deceives constituents regardless of how it is presented.[30] It is a philosophy that has become synonymous with manipulation, where leaders are encouraged to act without scruples to accomplish their ends. In a Machiavellian world, virtuous qualities are used but only to achieve the leader's goals. So such qualities as faithfulness, humanity, or sincerity are seen as necessary for the prince, according to Machiavelli—not to actually have them but "to seem to have them. I would even be bold to say that to possess them and always observe them is dangerous, but to appear to have them is useful." Machiavelli goes on to advise the prince that he should also be "so disposed that when it is needful to be otherwise, you may be able to change to the opposite qualities."

The notion of reciprocity is no less clear in modern discourse. It has a common meaning of a psychological obligation that each of us, upon receiving a gift, must repay in kind.[31] So the instrumental orientation is concerned with repayment. The basis of human identity derives not from mere giving, but from giving in conjunction with receiving. There is suspicion of people, call them altruists, who give just for the sake of giving, whose fulfillment rests on an intrinsic need to make the world and those in it a better place.

I hope that we have not reached such a point of cynicism in our culture that we view with suspicion anyone who gives just for the sake of giving. The leaderful manager does not expect a return for making a contribution toward the betterment of the community beyond witnessing others achieve their own fulfillment. Former United National Secretary General Dag Hammarskjöld had this in mind when he shed light on giving as a form of spiritual uplifting.

> When you have reached the point where you no longer expect a response, you will at least be able to give in such a way that the other is able to receive. When love has matured and, through a dissolution of the self into light becomes a radiance, then shall the lover be liberated from dependence upon the Beloved. [32]

Bruce Lansdale, former president of the American Farm School, echoes Hammarskjöld's sentiments by enjoining leaders to share what they have.[33] As we share what we have, we learn the distinction between "having" and "being." In the end, for a leaderful manager, what we are is far more important than what we have.

Robert Cialdini finds that the making of a commitment can be a very powerful influence strategy because most people try to behave in congruence with their commitments.[34] Although they may be made as part of an exchange relationship, it is just as commonplace to make them out of a sense of personal honor or integrity. Moreover, we tend to be viewed as trustworthy when we honor a commitment and as untrustworthy when our behavior contradicts what we said we would do.

I hope that we have not reached such a point of cynicism in our culture that we view with suspicion anyone who gives just for the sake of giving. The leaderful manager does not expect a return for making a contribution toward the betterment of the community beyond witnessing others achieve their own fulfillment.

Cialdini describes a simple experiment to prove his point. An investigator goes to a beach, lies down on his beach towel, and begins to listen to his portable radio. After a few minutes, he walks away and out of sight. A bit later, a colleague appears, takes the radio, and runs away. The intent of the study was first to determine how many "bystanders" would attempt to catch the "thief." In twenty trials of this experiment, only four bystanders attempted to apprehend the thief. In the second phase of the study, the investigators acted out the same scenario with one change. The initial investigator asked someone nearby to keep an eye on his radio until he returned. Cialdini conceptualized this interaction as the solicitation of a commitment. Well, it turned out that in the second instance, a full nineteen of the informed bystanders attempted to question or restrain the thief.

Consider another scenario in which reciprocity may govern the relationship: you are a line manager in a large company with four levels of management above you, including the CEO, Bob

Brooks. You are a nationally ranked amateur squash player but have not made it known throughout the company except to your close friends. It has come to your attention, however, that the CEO, Bob, is an avid squash player, though a mediocre player at best. Should you try to arrange a game with the CEO?

This is clearly a situation that is convertible into exchange currencies: you exchange the position currency of advancement or recognition for the personal currency of increasing (athletic) competence on the part of the CEO. But does this exchange process square with your view of how you wish life to be in your organization? Do you want people to get ahead on the basis of who they know rather than on the basis of what they do? Would you be content in an organization where people conspire to advance on the basis of what Kelley Reardon calls "the secret handshake," meaning "the subtle admission signal given to those who manage to pass muster and finagle their way to the top"?[35] Will our organizations survive if they operate on the basis of nepotism rather than merit? What implications does this hold for those in our community who have been marginalized or denied access to the same clubs as those in the majority?

Are there not wider consequences for transactions between two people who occupy different hierarchical roles, especially when one holds substantial power? For example, what reactions might peers have toward an individual who wishes to be noticed or get ahead on the basis of his or her athletic prowess? You might say that they could give credit to the person who, after all, bothered to take this kind of initiative. But is this an initiative that all could take advantage of?

Beyond the question of consequences are ethical principles that this form of behavior clearly violates. In particular, most of us subscribe to the view that the ends should not justify the means. We also like to believe that we can form our communities on the basis of the Golden Rule, which asks whether you would like similar behavior done to you. You might further ask what would become of your community if everyone acted this way. You might ask whether you would be proud to report this so-called use of initiative to your family.

Rather than build relationships based on exchange, why not build them on the basis of trust and integrity? In such a relationship, collaboration between the parties becomes prime. No party places his or her interests above those of another. Each party can be counted on to fulfill responsibilities to others without reservation. If a qualification arises, the parties come forward to communicate it to one another. Thus, they seek to build the relationship by sustaining the confidence that each has in the other's integrity.

The road to building such a trusting relationship is hardly easy. Conflicts will likely occur along the way. One rule of thumb to use when things bother you is to always let others know what the behaviors are that are of concern. It is also useful to let them know your intentions, goals, and feelings. If you're open in this way, others will likely openly share compatible ideas and feelings with you. If things continue to break down, you might try asking the other parties whether they are meeting their goals. If not, you can offer to help them figure out why not. You can also ask if you're part of the problem. These queries can make it easier for others to be forthright. They are based on the human instinct to take some responsibility for a problem when others are willing to do the same.[36] Christopher Avery adds one additional checkpoint to reinforce the value of trust in a relationship. He advises establishing the rule: Never be the first to defect.[37] If each member holds to this rule, trust can never be undermined.

Influence, then, constitutes a number of diverse strategies and leadership behaviors beyond exchange behavior. Leaderful practice may not be consistent with classic influence if the traditional definition of influence holds. Classic influence is often seen as getting person B to do what the influencer, person A, wants B to do. This perspective suggests that power is a finite quantity. Although

B may not have minded doing what A wishes, ultimately A gets B to do what A wants. In this sense, A obtains power over B.

Power is not finite but infinite.

In leaderful practice, there need not be an exchange of power in this classic sense. Consistent with a more collaborative process, A and B continuously attempt to meet each other's as well as their own needs, all toward the aim of serving the mission of the community. Power is not finite but infinite. The more they do for each other, the greater the opportunity for benefit for all. The ultimate aim of influence of this expansive type is to see everyone in the community striving for the same purpose. As I have shown throughout this book, however, the process of achieving mutual influence does not come automatically and takes considerable development.

Influence Strategies   When dealing with actors outside your immediate community—people, groups, and other organizations—classic influence often comes into play. Why? Those outside your community may have different goals than you have. They may see the world differently. For example, some parties may use a top-down approach in presenting their position; whereas you may prefer a bottom-up approach. They may be capable of reaching an immediate agreement with you; whereas you may need to check back with your membership. People representing other organizations may further need to honor the role of agent and thus cannot act as genuinely as someone *within* a given community. In other words, they may need to play a role as a delegate, being careful not to disclose too much information.

In such a setting, in which you must learn to work with the numerous stakeholders affecting or being affected by your own organization, it may take longer to develop the trust that leaderful practice requires. In this instance, external influence of the classic variety—one in which traditional power dynamics are present—may be the primary means of communication. The setting may call for the use of bargaining tactics in which offers are made in order to meet the other party at least halfway to achieve a suitable compromise. It also may require networking skills. Both bargainers and networkers know that they need to understand the requirements of their own community well enough to seek opportunities for an exchange.

While bargainers generally don't tend to stray too far from their own community's immediate preferences, networkers might be more interested in creating new forms or relationships that could alter how interacting organizations relate to one another. Hence, networkers are as much architects or designers as negotiators. They need to design what an emerging network might look like and how the parties will relate to one another. For example, in the 1960s and 1970s, most textbook publishers got out of the printing and binding businesses, and in fact many also drastically cut back their in-house art and graphics capabilities. In place of these businesses, they spun off production and design facilities that eventually contracted their services back to the publishers. Not only does a networker have to design an operation, but once it's in place, he or she has to ensure its successful operation both in the present and for the future.[38]

To better understand where collaboration fits among a range of influence strategies, let's consider the conflict handling modes proposed by Ken Thomas.[39] Thomas depicted five modes based on the degree to which each possessed assertive and cooperative behavior.

1. **Avoiding** represents a withdrawal from conflict such that neither party's concerns are satisfied.

2. **Accommodating** happens when individuals or groups demonstrate a will to cooperate in satisfying others' concerns while at the same time act unassertively in addressing their own needs.

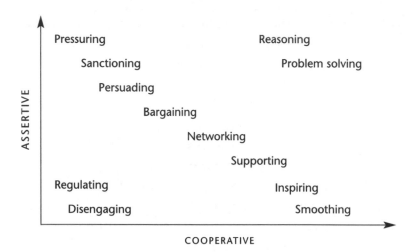

FIGURE 8-2. A Theoretical Mapping of Influence Strategies

3. **Compromising** represents an intermediate behavior on both the assertiveness and cooperative dimensions. It calls for the sharing of positions but not to the extremes of assertiveness or cooperation.

4. **Competing** occurs when individuals or groups try to satisfy their own concerns while demonstrating little willingness to satisfy the concerns of others.

5. **Collaborating** emphasizes maximum satisfaction for both parties such that each exerts both assertive and cooperative behavior. Both parties encourage the mutual expression of their needs and concerns.

Using a two-dimensional space, we can expand on the five conflict-handling modes by displaying some influence strategies associated with these conflict-handling modes.[40] Figure 8-2 illustrates twelve influence strategies according to their approximate position on a graph with cooperative behavior on one axis and assertiveness on the other. Table 8-1 categorizes the strategies according to Thomas's five conflict-handling modes and defines them.

TABLE 8-1.   Definitions of Influence Strategies

Conflict-handling mode	Influence strategy	Definition
Avoiding	Regulating	Using or becoming a third party, delegating the issue to someone else, applying standard operating procedures
	Disengaging	Reducing tension by changing the conditions of an interaction or even by backing away
Accommodating	Smoothing	Highlighting areas, values, interests in common, taking the initiative in giving in
	Inspiring	Contributing to a vision by highlighting the group's common interests, articulating exciting possibilities or ideal outcomes
Compromising	Supporting	Soliciting different views, listening, and disclosing your own needs while not giving up your interests
	Networking	Mobilizing allies and coalitions to support/gain a request or information
	Bargaining	Displaying willingness to go halfway, fighting for your side but hearing others out, giving way on things you don't need
Competing	Pressuring	Specifying the consequences you control in order to gain compliance or agreement, stating why your position is essential
	Sanctioning	Using rewards, sanctions, or appeals to higher authorities to get your way
	Persuading	Using soft competition, such as facts, suggestions, or ideas to support your own position and counter the other's
Collaborating	Problem solving	Stimulating and engaging one another to provide information, being willing to explore alternatives mutually
	Reasoning	Establishing a rational process, providing factual data, and using objective criteria to arrive at a mutually satisfying solution

As we can see, the bargaining and networking influence strategies are associated with the compromising posture, which is consistent with an exchange orientation. In the interdependent world in which we live, compromise may nevertheless be insufficient as a basis for effective influence. Parties may need to share full information with one another rather than use a gamesmanlike approach, providing only selected information.

Collaboration is thus called for under a number of conditions:

When a solution needs to be maximized since the concerns of the parties are too important to resort to a compromise

When the objective is to learn

When insights from many sources and perspectives need to be merged

When commitment is required of all the involved parties

When the parties need to work through any feelings that have interfered with their ongoing relationship

Although collaboration typically takes more time than bargaining strategies, since each party seeks to maximize its needs, it can lead to innovative solutions that may produce positive value to the parties. Indeed, it may generate a "richer, more comprehensive appreciation of the problem among the stakeholders than any one of them could construct alone."[41] Further, collaboration tends to humanize the parties rather than depict them as opponents with the attending stereotypes. It leads to empathy and goodwill that can lay the groundwork for an ongoing productive relationship.

In one company, the presidents of two product divisions decided, after numerous conversations in which they laid out the pros and cons, to share customer lists rather than keep them to themselves. Although there was a fear of diluting some formerly exclusive contacts, the presidents reasoned that the whole company would benefit from customers having a wider array of products and services to choose from.

Collaboration might even occur among stakeholders who do

not necessarily belong to the same enterprise. Briggs & Stratton, a small engine producer, now uses a collaborative extranet to share information with its customers, dealers, and distributors. The offerings include a searchable library that contains its product brochures and marketing kits; an interactive engine-replacement application that can help dealers select correct replacement engines for their customers; a module containing two- and three-dimensional engine drawings; and an on-line calendar of training classes for dealers and distributors.

Another situation that might call for a collaborative approach is when merged entities need to reach an agreement on their services or functions in spite of differing worldviews. According to Drath, if each worldview is understood as autonomous and self-justifying, it might be suboptimal to negotiate a compromise among them.[42] For example, what would happen if two training groups with dramatically different worldviews merged? One group believes in the integrity of the classroom to provide in-depth, concentrated training, while the second prefers an action learning approach that encourages people to learn and reflect while working together. A compromise solution would be for each of the training groups to use their respective methods with particular employee populations. A more collaborative solution might entail finding opportunities within a project-based curriculum to provide "just-in-time" training for project groups to help them work through and learn from their project interventions.

In figure 8-2, the practice of persuading is displayed among the competing influence strategies. Persuading or convincing often tends to be associated with "strong leadership." Accordingly, this kind of behavior suggests that a single actor has some knowledge that the rest of the community is deprived of. It assumes that the knowledge is sufficiently foreign to others who, without convincing, are unlikely to be amenable to the information. In some cases, however, it may be either premature or too late to use this type of persuading strategy. It is premature if the knowledge hasn't been sufficiently shared within the community so members can appreciate its merits. It may be too late if a presumed leader has made a decision without first involving the community members. Michael Hammer and James Champy of reengineering fame lament the mixed success of reengineering when they write:

> Most reengineering failures stem from breakdowns in leadership. Without strong, aggressive, committed, and knowledgeable leadership, there will be no one to . . . convince the people affected by reengineering that no alternative exists and that the results will be worth the agony of the process.[43]

Notice in this account how, for these authors, the leader needs to convince his or her followers and be strong since the latter presumably haven't bought into the process to begin with.

Other accounts suggest that persuasion is merely a set of tools to make one's case within a community of believers.[44] One can deploy reputation, prestige, personality, bargaining skills, decision-making style, and other such power resources to make a case. Yet, we need not presume that the parties to the debate must accept the alternatives that the persuader has in mind. As long as there is freedom to walk away from any prospective agreement, the strategy of persuasion can radiate away from competition toward the domain of compromise. Furthermore, if the persuader is just as committed to listening to others' preferences as convincing them of his or her own, then the persuasion might also begin to assume collaborative properties.

More closely aligned with collaborating are problem solving and reasoning. The definitions for both of these strategies, found in table 8-1, indicate that the parties are interested in mutual exploration and development. In problem solving, each party willingly provides information to help reach a mutually satisfying solution. In reasoning, the parties try to work out an objective process that can help lead them to a successful resolution. Except in instances when a given party's power must be preserved and time is not of the essence, a collaborative approach tends not only to lead to maximum satisfaction and outcomes but also to emulate leaderful practice.

As a culminating example of the collaborative influence process, consider the efforts of a director of marketing at a small communications company on the West Coast. The company's valuable vice-president of operations, James, planned to resign his position because of a move on behalf of his family to a city some 500 miles away. The company scheduled a meeting to talk about James' replacement. Realizing how difficult it would be to replace James, Kay, the marketing director, quietly began a campaign to "keep James." In spite of efforts by the president to move ahead with a new hire, Kay spoke to all the staff members regarding their feelings toward keeping James. Although she felt strongly about her views, she encouraged everyone to voice his or her opinion to get all the pros and cons on the table. She wasn't looking for a vote of confidence; she wanted to determine if the company could arrive at a mutual consensus. She not only documented staff concerns about replacing James but also began to record a number of suggestions regarding how he might continue to be effective in his position from a distant location. Not only were there ample alternatives using audio and video technology, but she also found out that James would not object to traveling for critical face-to-face engagements. By the time the meeting came around to replace James, lo and behold, everyone, including the president, unanimously believed that the subject of the meeting had changed. Instead, the focus would now be on planning how to work with him from his new remote location.

The Leader as Dialoguer

Being a collaborative leader requires you to let down your guard. It means seeking wisdom through others' eyes as much as through your own. It means being willing to engage in dialogue. Accordingly, rather than mount your arguments to win a debate, you learn to share your reflections and solicit those of others. You become sensitive to why things are done in a certain way. You inquire about the values that are being manifested behind any behavior. You wish to uncover discrepancies between what people say and what they do. You show an interest in probing into the forces below the surface that may shape actions and outcomes.

Ultimately, as a leaderful leader, you engage the entire community in a dialogue about the community's goals and aspirations as well as its current behavior and practices. In doing so, you don't need to hold back your own assumptions and views. You are willing to expose these, but at the same time, you also commit to finding out how others in the community see them.

One of my students, whom we'll call Matt, a middle manager in a high-tech firm, was invited to attend a public forum with his CEO. At the forum, in which everyone present was invited to pose whatever question they would like to the CEO, Matt volunteered the following: "Sir, given Moore's Law that short of splitting the technology atom, we will reach the apex of speed in our devices in under twenty years, where does that leave us in terms of maintaining our market share growth in the future?" The CEO's curt response to this query was: "I am not trying to be a wiseguy. But, Matt, that is your problem!" Many in the room, according to Matt, believed this showed that the CEO was unwilling to offer a prediction or steer a process of which he would have no part. Although one might consider the CEO's reaction noble, at the same time, it suggests a vainglorious orientation that whenever an opinion is offered by the top, it will inevitably be followed. For sure, it will not be viewed as a single opinion among many.

Although we may acknowledge how difficult it is for senior executives to create an egalitarian culture that reduces their viewpoint to one among many, dialogic leadership requires a commitment to sustain a reflective culture that considers all views, wherever they may arise, as hypotheses to be examined. No leaderful senior executive should allow his or her view to reign as gospel. King David of biblical fame found this out according to an account in the Book of Samuel. David had just become king but was embroiled in a battle against the Philistines when, longing for water, he uttered: "Oh, that someone would get me a drink of water from the well near the gate of Bethlehem." He had drunk from that same well as a boy, and part of his thirst was an expression of loneliness for that innocent and lost time. So three of his mighty men broke through the Philistine lines, drew water from the well near the gate of Bethlehem, and carried it back to David. When he saw what his soldiers had done, risking not only their lives, but also the element of secrecy about his troops' whereabouts, he remarked: "Far be it from me, O Lord, to do this! Is it not the blood of men who went at the risk of their lives?" And David would not drink the water.[45]

Van Vlissingen based his entire philosophy of management on "management by letting go."

Returning to the present era, we see the yearning to create a collaborative culture in the leadership of Paul van Vlissingen, CEO of SHV Holdings, a massive Dutch energy and consumer goods enterprise. Van Vlissingen resigned as CEO because, as he said, "I was getting too much power. . . . In power too long, and you lose your sense of reality."[46] Van Vlissingen based his entire philosophy of management on "management by letting go." His goal was always to hand over responsibility to the people in the field. Above all, he was a advocate for dialogue. Slide presentations were rarely used inside SHV since the goal was to promote face-to-face discussion of issues, not numbers. At board meetings, not only did he insist that all points of view be aired, no matter how controversial, but he was also willing to wait on decisions, even until after members had "slept on" the various points of view.

For CEOs like van Vlissingen, a viewpoint is just that—a perspective, an opinion. It may have a special or unusual vantage. Nevertheless, it should be one subject to inquiry. Hence, it needs to be offered and illustrated. Advice to CEOs to hold back on their opinions for fear of unwittingly swaying public consciousness can backfire, as it may create a perception that the CEO has hidden intents. You need not fear offering your own point of view as long as it is unabashedly held up to public scrutiny. The process of dialogue cannot even get started if the viewpoint is not offered.

If you wish to engage in dialogue, you need to both present your own viewpoint and, as suggested above, inquire about the views of others. In this way, you attempt to balance advocacy with inquiry. Inquiry, though, does not have to take the form of an interrogation, which frequently appears as a blistering set of questions posed to someone with a view. Although questions might be very effective, they should be supplemented by patient active listening that encourages the speaker to say as much as he or she wishes to on the subject.

I was struck by a story that Max De Pree once told when he was CEO of Herman Miller. De Pree writes about leadership as a spiritual and fragile practice in the stewardship mode; so, in *Leadership Jazz* he talked about Carla, a lift truck driver who had mounted the courage to come to De Pree and express her concern about incidents in her plant that were undermining the Herman Miller minority program.[47] De Pree asked Carla what she wanted him to do. She said, "You're the CEO. It's your job to tell us what you believe." De Pree said he would do just that, but he seemed to have finished the conversation then and there. Would this not have been a great time to probe more and learn from this courageous individual? Would this not have been a wonderful time to inquire about not only what was going wrong with the minority program but also, even more essentially, why it would take a proclamation from a CEO to fix?

Questioning can also be supplemented by asking others to

comment on our own attributions or inferences. An attribution is merely a perception that assigns a cause to a particular event. An inference is an assumption we draw about another person's or group's motives. As human beings, we cannot help forming attributions and inferences about others. Yet, these perceptions are unfortunately inaccurate at times. If you act on inaccurate assumptions, you can get yourself into loads of trouble in discourse. What can you do?

As a dialoguer, you can attempt to surface these assumptions. By bringing them into view, you can ask others to verify their accuracy. Once we agree on our common and different meanings, we can begin to reconstruct our projects together on a more solid footing. Consider this example of relying on a misplaced inference that took place within a project group working on a process improvement system for a large manufacturer. The project manager became upset when the purchasing representative apparently did not perform some required tests. Here's the manager's summary of what happened:

> I asked Fred (the purchasing rep) if he could give us a summary of the results of his testing. He said he played around with the new system, but he had no specific details to the testing except that it did not provide purchasing with the appropriate tools necessary to do their jobs and he wanted the new system to function identically to the old system. In my frustration, I let my emotions take over and I concluded from these comments that Fred had not done any testing, and I viewed him saying he needed the functionality of the old system as a "cop-out" for not doing the work. I managed to calm myself before commenting to him that this was unacceptable because we needed the testing results from his area to properly evaluate the new system.
>
> Later, after some personal retrospective reflection, I realized I could have handled the situation differently. I had viewed the observed data through my eyes, making a conclusion based upon my interpretation of the facts. I subsequently scheduled a meeting with Fred in order to try to gain some information into why he

was not prepared. During the meeting I realized that he was attempting to do his part but technical issues within the system and a lack of documentation were causing his frustration and were limiting his ability to test properly. This is not an excuse for coming unprepared and I wish he would have told me so at the meeting, but maybe my stern comments hindered Fred's ability to speak openly. I now had a better understanding of what he was thinking and I could see why he was still resisting the testing of the new system. He and I worked together to come up with an action plan that would address the system issues, which would give Fred the ability to continue his testing.

The Skills of Dialogue   The manager in this scenario ultimately displayed an ability to question publicly his assumptions. Although it took courage, it represents a skill that is fundamental to dialogue. The skill can be referred to as *being* and is among a cluster of five skills that my colleague, Robert Leaver, and I believe dialoguers can benefit from practicing.[48] The other skills are speaking, disclosing, testing, and probing. As we can see in figure 8-3, the skill of *being* is central and pervasive, cutting across the other skills, for it represents presence and vulnerability in creating a reflective climate in a community. In accomplishing *being*, you try to experience and describe situations, even your own involvement in them, without imputing meaning to them or evaluating them. You remain mindful of the moment. You attempt to ignore your habitual patterns. With such unbiased awareness, you also tend to be better positioned to learn from that moment and respond in kind. If leaders are successful in modeling or helping team members learn to "be," they can begin to explore differences and diverse experiences together and learn from one another without initial polarization. In this way they learn to explain together.

The skill of *being* can place you in a vulnerable state in the sense that you no longer rely on defending yourself against experience. You focus rather on opening up to experience and to the interpersonal environment around you. Bill Isaacs refers to this process as "suspending," in which you make the contents of your consciousness available to others.[49] You engage in such practices as withholding certainty, externalizing your thoughts, and exploring the tension of the opposites. This produces a reflective response that can be characterized by a number of attributes that are in direct contrast to the defensive posture:

- Instead of maintaining unrealistic standards, you set realistic expectations.
- Instead of expressing trepidation, you display tolerance.
- Instead of concentrating on self-expression, you use listening.
- Instead of being self-absorbed, you convey humility.
- Instead of feeling out of depth, you feel open to learn.
- Instead of feeling out of context, you become open to experience.[50]

The reflective response suggests that at times you engage your empathy with others by viewing them and listening to them as you wish them to treat you. At others times, you may wish to view others as "strange," beings so unlike yourself that they require even deeper respect and attention so that you may learn to know them. In fact, we can view *being* as a vital leadership quality that defines a deep form of listening, one that allows leaders to wait, to be patient, and to view the bigger picture. Guy Claxton talks about the need to "soak up experience," so as to extract the subtle patterns that are latent within it.[51] In *being*, then, one resists the temptation to foreclose on experience. Referring to a phrase from the poet John Keats, Claxon might consider *being* to constitute "negative capability," the capacity to wait and remain attentive in the face of incomprehension.

In the model shown in figure 8-3, *being* occupies the dimension I call the "frame" mode. Framing refers to how you think about a situation, more specifically, how you select, name, and organize facts to make a story to yourself about what is going on and what to do in a particular situation. In the collective mode, you extend your contributions and inquiry to all the members of the community, whereas in the individual mode, you hear your own voice or address one individual at a time. The cross dimensions are "staying with self" and "inquiring with others." At times, you make personal contributions to the group or focus attention on yourself. At other times, you extend and dedicate attention to others.

Being as a central skill may entail staying with yourself or inquiring with others. It is most concerned with exploring differences and diverse experiences apart from members' preconceived notions. The *being* skill models an inquisitive, nonjudgmental attitude toward group phenomena. Some of its components include inviting questions and comments, considering your own positions as hypotheses to be tested, acknowledging others' expressions of vulnerability. An example of *being* occurred in a program management team when an account manager assembled his colleagues and asked them about a new campaign that he hoped to launch to fund a major initiative with one of his "driver accounts." Rather than merely asking the team to comment on his campaign, he placed himself in a more vulnerable state by asking, Why do I need more funding for this project? This led to a conversation that he described as follows in his journal.

> My question initiated a discussion and some very productive learning. We began to question the very presuppositions of the problem; I needed more funding to get this project started. I am generally given about three percent of my total yearly account volume to fund promotions and other business-building programs at my accounts. The simple question, "Why do I need more funding?" spurred a discussion of my current situation. Maybe the access of this market data will prove to be more worthwhile than the other programs I have participated in at this account for the last two years? Maybe I need to reevaluate the programs I am currently

engaged in? Some ROI analysis might prove this project more worthwhile. I eventually decided to drop some of my other promotional activities at this account in order to fund this project.

The second reflective skill of *speaking* is in the upper-left section of figure 8-3, signifying that it seeks to articulate a collective voice from within yourself. In *speaking*, you attempt to characterize the state of the community or its meaning at a given time. It may entail summoning an image to articulate meaning, suggesting group norms, or bringing out uncertainties or unfounded assumptions. In *speaking* it is not necessary to prepare your words in advance. You craft your message in the moment as the meaning unfolds. One team never lost the image presented at an earlier meeting by their facilitator, who said the team was operating like "a cargo plane having to make its destination to Istanbul but with one engine knocked out."

In the third skill, *disclosing*, you stay within yourself and, at the same time, share your doubts or voice your passion. By using *disclosing*, you may unveil your feelings at a given moment based on what has transpired, or you may present a story to reveal the depth of your experience. The idea is to help the community learn more about its membership. Another cue to promote *disclosing* is to ask yourself what you might say to help the community know you better. A story about George Washington reveals the power of *disclosing*. Unknown to all but the most astute historians, a movement arose during the waning years of the American Revolutionary War for the military to take over the civilian government and install Washington as king. At one historic point, Washington appeared before some of these military officers to condemn this affront to democracy, the cornerstone of the entire revolutionary movement. However, his speech fell on deaf ears. Then, as he helplessly attempted to read a missive from a member of Congress, he paused to reach for a pair of glasses, something only his closest aides had known he needed. Then he quietly confessed to his officers: "Gentlemen, you will permit me to put on my spectacles, for I have not only grown gray but almost blind in the service of my country." The men wept. It was alone this statement of vulnerability that was thought to have nipped the movement in the bud; how could the men ignore this selfless commander who reminded them that he was one of them?[52]

Testing, the fourth reflective skill, is an open-ended query directed toward the community as a whole that attempts to uncover new ways of thinking and behaving. In using *testing,* you may ask a team to consider its own process or attempt to explore underlying assumptions previously taken for granted. You are trying to promote a process of collective inquiry. As a tester, you may occasionally ask for a process check or ask if someone might act out a scenario to explore an option. Perhaps my readers might be familiar with the "Abilene Paradox," an interpersonal dynamic surfaced by Jerry Harvey.[53] Harvey coined the terms when pondering why he and some family members took an exhausting trip in a dust storm to Abilene, 53 miles away, when not one person in the party actually wanted to go there. Since we have the unfortunate tendency in everyday life to often communicate the very opposite of our wishes based on our assumptions of another's desires, the testing skill can become indispensable. We need to develop the courage to inquire about our mutual desires and actions in order to successfully manage agreement.

Finally, in *probing,* you make a direct inquiry, typically to one member at a time, to find out the facts, reasons, assumptions, inferences, and possible consequences of a given suggestion or action. For example, *probing* might attempt to point out inconsistencies in members' reasoning patterns, perhaps helping them to uncover the assumptions and beliefs behind particular actions. In using *probing,* however, you need to be careful not to interrogate or make any member feel on the spot or defensive. On the other hand, *probing* may initially make some members uncomfortable if you ask them to consider assumptions that they had hidden even

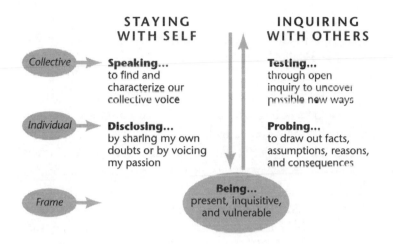

FIGURE 8-3.   Five Advanced Skills of Dialogue

from their own consciousness. As an example, consider a frank inquiry posed to Mark: "Mark, every time that we've thought about broaching our plans with Lisa, you've chimed in that no one can work with her and we should avoid her at all costs. I wonder if you've had some experiences with her that you can share that would help us, and perhaps you, too, understand what seems to be making Lisa such an obstacle. Maybe there *is* a way that would make it possible for perhaps one of us to approach her."

In the example that follows, a consultant illustrates how he *should* have used some of these skills to achieve a more favorable business outcome than he achieved using what he considers an "avoidance" stance.

> Recently I took on the role, new to me, of courting a new client based on a lead from one of our long-established vendors. After my initial contact, the client called back and left a message requesting a cost proposal. His message said he needed it in three days (though it usually takes a week to prepare). This set up several conflicts, the prospect's short schedule being the first. Obtaining approval from the senior partner to accept a figure that

would cover our scope of work but not be out of the prospect's ballpark was the second. What I chose to do was to take on the stress of scrambling to accommodate the prospect's short deadline rather than calling him to discuss how firm it was. Within my office, to avoid the likely conflict with my partners over what the client would be willing to spend, I submitted a proposal with a fee structure that acquiesced to their number even though I knew the client was likely to reject it. The client received his proposal when he wanted it but it was too expensive for him. The Senior Partner got his number submitted but lost the job.

Looking back, I can see how dialogue could have been used as a tool to reach a better outcome in this situation. Beginning with *probing*, I could have drawn out more facts. Was the prospect's deadline fixed by some other event or was it just his preference? Were there any other alternative staffing plans that could be used to build the proposal? I could have used *disclosing* on both sides. With the prospect I could have let him know the pressure his three days was creating. With the partners, I could have let on more about my feelings that price was the biggest issue for this prospect. I could have tried more *testing*. With the prospect I could have tested his position by saying, "We are looking at this fee range now; however, we might be able to sharpen the number with a few more days to refine it if you can find more time." With the partners I could have developed an alternative number and staffing plan and approached them with a more *being* as well as *testing* orientation, such as by saying: "This is what the prospect is likely to accept. Our number is predicated on. . . . How can we find an alternative to this to get in line with his expectations?" Through such a dialogic process, I could have led both sides to a better outcome.

The Conditions for Dialogue Dialoguers in their search to uncover the mental models that exist within the strategy of an organization, knowingly, and at times unwittingly, disturb the identity of the organization. They upend the image that members of the organization have about themselves as well as about their role in the community. Dialoguers may even bring the image that the community has of itself into question. Challenging anyone's identity, let alone an organization's identity, is serious business. This is why it is so commonly rejected.

Donald Laurie tells the story about an event at an annual shareholders' meeting that may have transformed the culture of the Xerox Corporation.[54] The company had halted production of its 3300 copier, which at the time was supposed to have been an answer to the more successful Japanese models. When then-CEO David Kearns opened the meeting for questions, an assembly-line worker named Frank Enos stepped up to the microphone and blasted the 3300 as "a piece of junk." He went on to say: "We could have told you. Why didn't you ask us?" At that moment, rather than punish Enos, Kearns resolved to go beyond the technical problem underlying the production process at Xerox to uncover why lower-ranking employees at Xerox had been hesitant to offer an honest appraisal of the Xerox product line to their own executives. This very insight of Kearns about the artificial yet powerful blocks to dialogue at Xerox deeply influenced the corporate culture. As the story goes, Xerox went on to overcome its problems, regain its market share, and even earn the Baldridge National Quality Award. Kearns invited Frank Enos to the Baldridge ceremony in Washington.

John Chambers, head of the networking behemoth, Cisco Systems, is another executive who seems to possess the courage to challenge the fundamental governing values of his own organization through an unusual vehicle. We hear that chief executives oftentimes feel sheltered from their organizations. Chambers, intent on avoiding this isolation, invites his employees to birthday breakfasts. At these breakfasts, he implores the employees to ask anything they want to know, to point out management mishaps, to share how executive decisions and practices affect individuals down in the trenches. Chambers considers the hour with each birthday boy or girl indispensable and once remarked, "I'm not there for the cake!"

Yet, under leaderful conditions, holding frank discussions should not be a special event nor should they be reserved for the person at the top. All managers need to at least try to create a receptive environment for bringing up the "undiscussables." Failing such dialogue, people will carry their objections either inside themselves or share them only with trusted others, typically with peers or subordinates. In these instances, commitment to action becomes unlikely since people will be operating with reservations.

The Benefits of Dialogic Inquiry   Let's complete this section by considering why open and public dialogue can establish the appropriate foundation for collaborative leadership and, in turn, for leaderful practice. Here are four benefits to reflect on:

1. People not only need to be aware of their own actions but at times need to move from a position of unawareness to awareness. Oftentimes, we are simply unaware of the consequences of our behavior. To complicate matters, our unawareness occasionally does not allow us to be open to new data or information to help us learn from our actions. We may even be unaware that our questions might produce defensiveness in others, closing off the possibility of generating new information or even new questions. Often, only through the support of and feedback from others can we become receptive to alternative ways of reasoning and behaving.

Paul Wieand, former CEO of Independence Bancorp and now principal of the Center for Advanced Emotional Intelligence in Pennsylvania, has built his entire consulting practice around this issue.[55] He is also the first to point out that he could have used a dose of this form of reflective dialogue when he was CEO. Forced to resign in 1985, he had alienated all but two members of his board. In his view, "executives, intoxicated with their own success, define themselves by their job title rather than by who they are inside. They lose touch with their emotions and become insensitive to how they affect others and become intolerant of others' weaknesses. . . . If you idealize your role," he goes on, "you fool yourself about what people really think of you. You don't know when and why you get defensive. You don't get open and honest feedback from people."

2. There is an unfortunate gap between what many of us say we will do and what we actually do. The field of action science refers to this gap as an inconsistency between our "espoused theories" and our "theories-in-use."[56] We are simply guilty of deceiving ourselves that we can practice what we preach, though what we preach may be very difficult to accomplish in particular organizational cultures. How many of us have submitted to the game called "Yes, but . . ." with a boss? "Yes, but . . ." bosses typically start out by proclaiming that they have an open-door policy. "If you ever have a problem or a question for me or about our operation, you should feel free to come to me at any time," the boss proudly avows. A series of conversations with the boss ensue over the next several months, and may go something like this.

> [one month later] "Boss, I would like to propose that we adopt the balanced scorecard approach to measuring our outcomes." "Yes, good idea, but we actually tried it fourteen months ago and it didn't work. But keep those great ideas coming!"
>
> [two months later] "Boss, rather than paying out so much overtime, what would you say to hiring Rob Evans part-time to help us out. I know he's available." "Yes, that might work, but Rob didn't get along well with Sara, so I think we best continue as we have."
>
> [three months later] "Boss, I know the group can increase its efficiency if we purchase and then receive some training in the software program, PROJ-ACT. I know a great supplier; they do a great job and can convert us in under two weeks." "Yes, but Marcy proposed that we try out the exact same program, and it was voted down just before you joined us."
>
> [four months later] "Boss, what would you say to all of us

going out to see the latest Spielberg flick?" "Yes, he's great and his current one has an important message for our group, but you can't force these social outings on people. We each have our own lives."

[five months later] No more ideas forthcoming. . . . Case closed.

3. Most of us are biased in how we obtain information, which, in turn, produces "errors" in our perceptions of reality. Errors constitute such practices as collecting data superficially, ignoring certain pieces of information and thus underestimating uncertainty, making assumptions about data rather than investigating them, believing we can control random events, or using self-confirming reasoning.[57] However, if we are interested in improving our managerial practices, we have to become aware of these judgment errors. Such an awareness is extremely difficult to awaken without involving peers who can detect the use of untested assumptions and raw biases.

You may have noted that some professional baseball managers like to use a so-called platoon system, in which they use certain left-handed batters against right-handed pitchers, but replace them for right-handed batters when the pitcher happens to be left-handed. The reason for platooning is merely that it is easier for batters to face opposite-handed pitchers. However, this general statistical rule breaks down at the level of the specific case. It is at this level where dialogic inquiry may be called for. Some batters, for example, do just as well against same-sided as against opposite-sided pitchers. Others seem to bat well against particular pitchers, regardless of their throwing arm. Some plays, such as a bunt, may call for talent that does not depend on the hand dominance of the batter.

4. Although intuition and past practices can give us very cogent clues in deciphering future situations, oftentimes the new situation presents itself in a different context. Prior solutions may not fit, even if the situations appear alike. We tend to look, however, for the similarities between the situations rather than their differences. This type of normal cognitive processing can play tricks on us. Even when we consult a repertoire of available responses, we may not find one that fits the new situation. Consider a scenario in which an executive exudes great confidence in carrying out a consolidation among two closely allied projects, having successfully linked otherwise competing projects in the past. In a relatively short time, however, the environment can change, whether as a result of economic or political conditions. Furthermore, the projects under consideration may bear little resemblance to those previously merged, perhaps due as much to elusive cultural and personal contingencies as to operating considerations. Through dialogue exercised in the presence of trusted yet discerning peers, such a manager can distinguish that part of his or her reasoning that is measured and critical from that which might be self-fulfilling and self justificatory.

These examples suggest that managers engage in public or collective dialogue with others. If managers each individually engage only in introspection, they may not be able to convert their thinking into action because of organizational rules or norms that are themselves unreflective. Reflection often leads to questioning, but not only of self. One may wish to question others in power or may wish to challenge the system as a whole. The dialogue that ensues is most genuine when it is critical and involves all stakeholders within the community.

9 Compassionate Leadership

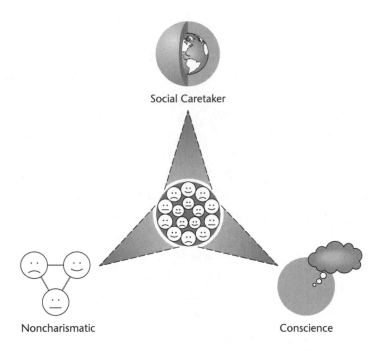

Social Caretaker

Noncharismatic

Conscience

COMPASSIONATE LEADERS DO NOT SEEK TO CONTROL OR TO AWE others because of some unmet ego needs. Transcending their own ego identity, they seek to elevate others so that the whole community can benefit. What makes them special is not necessarily their own elevation to a high state of development but an interpersonal commitment to the dignity of others. They recognize the potential contribution of each member of the community, no matter what his or her position or status.

Yet, maintaining dispassionate control over the enterprise remains a popular prescription for leadership these days since it fits with the view that we require an "orderly universe," one that eschews uncertainty and paradox. Most people do not like messes. They resist standing in the tension of opposites.[1] They want conflicts resolved and our emotions held in check. This seems to be true even when we acknowledge that standing in the tension of opposites for a while can often lead to a better solution.

If dispassionate behavior is the norm, compassionate leaders may be correspondingly viewed as indecisive and weak. Consequently, leaders with a penchant for democratic practices might choose to avoid displaying these practices for fear of not seeming "in control." Further, the Enron scandal, in which accounting irregularities led to the demise of a once-$50-billion empire, may have given top managers the impression that they operate at their own risk if they do not completely control their company. Unfortunately, direct control over behemoth enterprises that operate in countries across the globe can only be an illusion. You may reach a point where control may only apply to a few variables, leaving the less obvious but critical indicators away from the microscope. It is preferable to establish a culture of integrity that allows each operating unit the chance to manage itself while demonstrating accountability—in measures and in values—to the integrated whole.

We can view the choice of real participation as a courageous choice, especially in cultures where its component behaviors may be seen as weak. Hence, anyone making this choice tends to do so not because it is politically correct but because it has meaning to the beholder. We engage others because we truly believe in this approach to human behavior. Lawrence Bossidy, formerly of Honeywell, has been known to point out that one fundamental reason for sharing control with workers is simply because "they know their job better than you do." Another reason that compassionate leaders might offer for empowering others is because it represents a process that dignifies the human spirit to grow and achieve.

Compassionate communities are characterized as endorsing a diversity of views, even those that do not conform to existing mental models and practices. In this way, compassion extends beyond one's own culture or borders to those less privileged.

Compassionate leaders thus recognize the connection between individual problems and the social context within which they are embedded. Having made this connection, they appreciate any social transformation because they participate in it. By bridging their inner and outer worlds, they can speak with integrity in any effort taken to heal the ecological, economic, and social systems in which they live. Compassionate leaders create community out of a sense of genuine commitment to that community.

I know of no better example of the compassionate leader than Sir Ernest Shackleton, whom I discussed in chapter 6 as an explorer known not so much for his discoveries as for his leadership skills. During one two-year period he used these skills to save every one of his crew from certain death after the wreck of his ship, *Endurance.* Shakleton, or "the Boss" as he was affectionately called, took it upon himself to spend individual time with each of his crew, putting each man at ease and making him the center of attention. Always willing to place his own comforts second to those in need, he even gave up his warm bed to a seaman who was sick or infirm. He was forever optimistic, no matter how desperate the situation, and even in the gloomiest of moments, could be counted on to offer a quip or story to uplift others' spirits. Perhaps most notable was Shakleton's unparalleled ability to maintain harmony in the most wretched of conditions. By mixing duties and rotating work assignments, he fostered an air of impartiality and encouraged friendships among the entire crew. Further, he did not consider class distinctions when it came to accomplishing the critical work of the expedition; what counted was a crewman's proficiency. And Shackleton himself was not above getting down and dirty with the rest of the men, whether with the heavy lifting or the cleaning. He took his turn like every-one else with the mundane chores of the ship, including swab-bing the deck or scrubbing the floor of the main living area. In his leaderful way, he acknowledged that these activities allowed him to bond with his men and lent a sense of dignity to each job on board.[2]

In the three sections to follow, I will suggest ways of incorpo-rating compassion into your leaderful practice.

The Leader as the Noncharismatic

It has long been suggested in popular leadership discourse that personality is key to leadership and that charisma is perhaps the ultimate contributing personal characteristic. *Charisma* comes from the Greek word meaning "gift," suggesting that leaders have special gifts to distribute. So by definition, charismatics sway peo-ple and shape the future by their sheer presence and personality

Charismatic leaders are thought to differ from mere mortal leaders by their ability to formulate and articulate an inspirational vision as well as by actions that foster the impression that they are extraordinary people.[3] Some observers go as far as to assign di-vine qualities to charismatic leaders following Max Weber, who asserted that these people are "set apart from ordinary men and treated as endowed with supernatural, superhuman, or at least ex-ceptional powers and qualities . . . [that] are not accessible to the ordinary person but are regarded as divine or as exemplary."[4]

Unfortunately, even if we decided on what ingredients went into a charismatic personality, I doubt we would find that charis-matics are persuasive in all environments and for all times. The post-war demise of Winston Churchill is a sufficient case. Even more, except for quite exceptional circumstances when the com-munity is in dire straits and genuinely asks for the direction of an outspoken member, severe problems arise in allowing a given in-dividual—particularly a charismatic—to control a community.

As soon as we attempt to identify particular characteristics that constitute a charismatic personality, we begin a process of excluding a host of candidates for leadership. Here's how perennial CEO Lawrence Bossidy, formerly of Honeywell, unwittingly characterizes leaders.

> You all know the old maxim, "Leaders are born, not made." That's only half true. Some people are, indeed, born leaders, and you can spot them a mile away. The trouble is, there simply aren't enough of them to go around. So we need to find individuals with innate intelligence, an eagerness to learn, and a desire to work with others, and give them the tools and encouragement they need to become effective leaders, too. They may never run the company, but they can make enormous contributions to the success of your organization.[5]

One can see in Bossidy's comments that he has already identified in advance the "also-rans" because of his notion of what it takes to be a leader.

Drawing on the term *narcissist*, popularized by Freud, Michael Maccoby and Roy Lubit assert that though charismatics can charm the masses with their rhetoric and can draw the "big picture," they have a tendency toward grandiosity and distrust.[6] Narcissists tend to keep themselves emotionally distant from others and generally do not tolerate dissent. They are also poor listeners, show little empathy, can be brutally exploitative, seldom mentor, and are not restrained by conscience. Their excessive promotion of self and lack of concern for others can become utterly destructive to their organizations since they are prone to make reckless business decisions, divert people's energies away from their real work, and ultimately drive away the community's most talented people.

In what strikes me as a stark contrast to the democratic values and integrity underlying leaderful practice, followers working under narcissists survive by finding out what their bosses think before presenting their own views. That way, they can keep dissent to a minimum. They are advised to always let the narcissistic boss take credit for their ideas and contributions. Enough said!

Charisma is increasingly being seen as interconnected with followership. The qualities of charisma need to be appreciated by followers or by a following community. Often, the charismatic surfaces within the community as it faces some level of psychic distress. Milliken describes this in perceptual terms.[7] Distress occurs when people do not understand the direction in which the surrounding environment might be changing, what the potential impact of those changes on the organization might be, and whether or not particular responses by management might or might not be successful. Further, people might perceive that any erroneous decision on the part of management could risk the very survival of the organization. In this instance, individuals may look to a leader for psychological comfort to reduce their stress and anxiety. Such a leader might be able to turn the uncertainty of his or her followers into a vision of opportunity and success.[8]

Yet, it is precisely at this point that followers are particularly susceptible to charismatic salvation. They find themselves in a dependent state and look to their leaders to satisfy their needs. Charismatics are all too willing to comply by offering them hope and paternal direction. This is in contrast to leaderful leaders, who might choose to work with their followers to face and manage their own conflicts.

There is always a chance that followers might eventually learn to manage their affairs on their own, at which time they will no longer need the charismatic. They might even feel ashamed for having debased themselves. Under these conditions, they might develop a resentment against the charismatic, especially if they discover that he or she has an underlying weakness. This is sometimes referred to as the "feet of clay" phenomenon. It was well captured in a story recounted in one of my student's journals.

I will tell a story about meeting a celebrity. This person was a very popular singer in an 80s band. From age 12 to 18, I was obsessed with this individual. My friends weren't all that impressed with him and I got made fun of quite a bit for my big crush, but even that didn't sway my feelings. Well the 80s came and went and I moved on from my obsession because the band is out of the top 40 and really has not been heard of again. Well, just last year I found out that my co-worker's husband is my teenage heart-throb's first cousin. She offered me tickets to a concert with this band. I was thrilled, and all that excitement came back from when I was younger and more impressionable. I was after all on my way to meet the subject of my "awe." I'm sure by now you realize where this is going. Anyway, meeting this person was a big disappointment. I went back stage and actually shook his hand and talked a little bit with him. He was arrogant and conceited and his behavior made me feel stupid for even wanting to meet him in the first place. My "awe" was destroyed by this close encounter.

Capitalizing on awe, charismatic leaders offer followers a set of idealized goals. According to Conger and Kanungo, the more idealized their goals, the more likely such leaders will be credited with extraordinary vision. An idealized vision further serves to highlight the uniqueness of the charismatic leader, making him or her even more admirable and worthy of identification and imitation. Conger and Kanungo further assert that "this idealized quality of the charismatic leader's goals—supported by appealing rhetoric—distinguishes him or her from other leaders."[9]

Besides a unique vision and compelling language, the charismatic leader might also attempt to acquire the symbolic accoutrements of the role of savior. Depending on the society in question, this might manifest as a certain look or stature, particular vestments or possessions, or a relationship or lineage to prior historical figures. It was reported that during the Taliban control of Afghanistan, the spiritual leader, Mullah Mohammad Omar, rose to power by acquiring the very cloak of the Prophet Mohammed, which had been folded and padlocked in a series of chests in a crypt in the royal mausoleum at Kandahar.[10] Myth had it that the padlocks to the crypt could be opened only when touched by a true "Amir-ul-Momineen," a King of the Muslims. After the collapse of the Taliban regime, the people of Afghanistan came to know of Omar's brutality and how he duped them into obedience through the Taliban's rigid interpretations of the Koran. In the words of a young Kandahari:

> We trusted men we thought were holy and educated in the Koran, and because many of us did not know Arabic, we could not study the Koran carefully ourselves. When we saw Omar in the cloak, all of Afghanistan hoped that . . . the rains would begin. But in truth, we did not know what [he] was saying. We only followed.

We might note that charismatics need *not* be narcissistic, egocentric, or hard driving. More critical is that others see them as saviors who, through their superb vision, appeal to the masses and save the day. Indeed, Jim Collins depicts his "Level 5 Leaders" as humble and shy and as people committed to diverting credit to others. Yet they are at the same time recognized as having individually turned companies around or having led them in a strategic direction that, though unpopular, resulted in success. For example, Collins refers to Alan Wurtzel as a leader "responsible for turning Circuit City from a ramshackle company on the edge of bankruptcy into one of America's most successful electronics retailers." He cites Charles R. "Cork" Walgreen II as the iron-willed leader who transformed dowdy Walgreens by proclaiming to his executive staff: "Okay, now I am going to draw the line in the sand. We are going to be out of the restaurant business completely in five years."[11] Can you sense the silence in the room? Cork may have had a quiet demeanor, but his resolve was resolute. His followers knew that their charismatic leader had spoken. Yet, did he act alone?

Behling and McFillen, in their comprehensive review of the charismatic leadership literature, suggest that followers experience inspiration, empowerment, and even "awe" in the presence of charismatics.[12] Their model purports that these follower beliefs are created by specific acts undertaken by leaders, behaviors such as dramatizing a mission, assuring followers of their competency, projecting self-assurance, and enhancing their own image. Other accounts of charismatic leaders unabashedly assert that leaders need to engage in impression management, in image building, and in manipulation of meaning in order to bind "subordinates" most closely to them and to their vision.[13] It is no wonder, then, that followers grant charismatic leaders an enormous license to direct the community, whether in a direction of pro- or anti-social practices.

Community members do not require salvation from the top; salvation is produced by their own mutual hard work and compassion toward one another.

Leaderful behavior does not mix well with the charismatic personality. It does not see control as emanating from a single individual. Community members do not require salvation from the top; salvation is produced by their own mutual hard work and compassion toward one another. Philippe Gaulier, who uses theatrical techniques to teach leadership, would call this approach to leadership "boooorrriinng!!!"[14] The leader in his view needs to be the master of the performance, the actor who can command people's attention and steal their hearts. Note the charismatic images in this message, especially the words, *master, command,* and *steal.* The focus in leaderful practice does not need to be on the individual; it can be on the community. One folds into the community. Although the words of a community spokesperson may temporarily focus attention on the speaker, people can simultaneously see connections to themselves and to others. So, as against the charismatic who diverts attention to him- or herself by a stirring performance, I call for a boring personality who leads by succumbing to the spirit of the community.

James Meindl goes as far as to suggest that charisma is no more than a romantic notion that people conjure up to lift their spirits [15] We know from basic attribution theory that people tend to overemphasize a leader's prowess.[16] As followers interact, they begin to define a social reality of leadership that represents special mythical qualities endowed in only very special people. Although these qualities may *not* exist, they are often ascribed to the leader either by an implicit or a carefully conceived orchestration by particular members of the follower community. Called "carriers," these members essentially spread the news of the charismatic leader's mythical qualities throughout a society. In this way, charisma becomes a contagion. What they spread, though, is not necessarily real but rather reactions that represent no more than pre-existing shared profiles of what they expect leaders to be. And we know what the profile often tends to be: "the hero who can save us!" Meindl asserts that followers may be already looking for a cause and a leader of whom they can become "true believers."

Another domain of personality often linked with superior leadership performance is emotional intelligence. Whether it should be allied with leaderful practice depends on how it is used. Emotional intelligence (EI) is variously defined as the ability to perceive, access, and use emotions to facilitate one's reasoning processes.[17] Equipped with EI, people can appraise and express their emotions, understand or empathize with the feelings of others, appreciate what causes emotions and what consequences they produce, use emotions to enhance cognitive and decision-making processes, and control their own feelings and emotions. For the most part, these abilities are salutary. For example, if "George" feels irritated because of an unpleasant encounter at home, he may know enough to attempt to block out those feelings in an interaction at work. Similarly, if he's in a positive mood, he may know himself well enough to acknowledge that, under this condition, he might exaggerate his capabilities.

On the other hand, under the aura of emotional intelligence, George may be tempted to control others in the community because of a belief in his superior understanding of the surrounding culture or of others' emotions. Here's how one authority on emotional intelligence unwittingly describes this process of control.

> By accurately appraising how their followers currently feel, relying on their knowledge of emotions to understand why they feel this way, and influencing followers' emotions so that they are receptive to and supportive of the leader's goals or objectives of the organization and proposed ways to achieve them, leaders may help to ensure that their vision is shared or collective.[18]

In this passage, the exponent seems unaware that she has endorsed an instrumental view of the tool of emotional intelligence. Through a superior command of this ability, one can shape followers' views and actions. This, of course, is counterleaderful. Emotional intelligence need not be used for such control purposes. Rather, it should be used, under leaderful conditions, to encourage others to rely on their emotions as a means of participating in free and open dialogue that can become the basis of democratic action.

I see charisma and occasionally emotional intelligence not necessarily as a set of personality or emotional characteristics that define the attributes of leadership. They are as much sociological processes often implicitly set up between follower and leader to keep the leader in power. Charismatics rely on the social processes described in this section to sustain their charismatic effect. They enjoy enhancing romantic images of themselves.

Nor is charisma particularly helpful in many settings, especially if the charismatic is content to set the vision from on high rather than to pitch in and help from below. A director of marketing with a custom publishing firm wrote in her journal that the "high [charismatic] view of leadership does not remotely reflect the business world I live in." She went on:

> Success is in the execution. Perhaps in an immensely large organization, the leader can be this charismatic individual whose sole purpose is to visualize and revolutionize, but in a small, creative-driven company like mine, that revolution must come from within. We just cannot afford this "superperson" to make things happen.

One has to question whether the large organization in the dynamic markets characterizing today's business environment can likewise afford this "superperson."

It is important to deconstruct the romantic view of leadership embedded in the idea of charisma. Not only can its effect deprive a community of its own power and utility but if left unexamined, it can also lead to demagogic behavior and deleterious effects on groups not affiliated with the leader. Some believe that using the term *transformational* can alter our perceptual concerns about the charismatic because the transformational leader is more concerned with a group's accomplishment than with his or her personal advancement.[19] Nevertheless, even if the leader's purposes are entirely constructive, romanticism can lead to carrier abuse among the leader's followers, who can exalt the leader's image either without the leader's knowledge or after the leader steps aside. In extreme cases, the leader's death may even spur his or her martyrdom, a hyper-romantic construct that can be used for practically any purpose. The ultimate end of charismatic practices of this ilk is disempowerment. People no longer control their own destiny, having handed it over to their saviors.

The Leader as Conscience

Being leaderful suggests acting with conscience, that is, with a set of ethical values. Stipulating that a leader act with values can be a loaded idea since most of us could not agree on which values to sustain. Are there any values that we could consider universal?

As values underlie our motives for acting, most of us operate with values whether we wish to articulate them or not. For example, if someone pressed a group to complete a task, that person most likely would be operating under a value of efficiency or task completion. If a manager expects subordinates to follow all instructions to the letter, that person might be operating under a value of obedience to authority figures.

The values underlying leaderful practice, in that acting leaderfully signifies behavior done in conjunction with the members of a community, have to be democratic in character. Going back to a fundamental tenet of humanism, leaders do not make decisions without including people who are affected by that decision. Although this tenet is centuries old, minimally Athenian in origin, it has held an honorable space in the conscience of American business, though often forgotten. William Given, the president of the American Brake Shoe Company, noted more than fifty years ago: "save in cases of rare managerial genius, the pooled judgment, initiative, enterprise, and ideas of an organization produce better progress . . . than does the autocratic administration of an individual."[20]

There are a number of subsidiary values to democracy that we need to enumerate, but it should be clear that solving the issue of values clarification is critical to the subject of leadership. Let's consider the value of fairness. Perhaps you might stipulate that laying off a worker might not be fair because the individual has been working under hazardous conditions. Or what if this performer were affected by someone else who didn't do her or his part? During Jack Welch's tenure as CEO at General Electric, he was known to make tough calls using what became known as a "feed or weed" human resource policy. GE's 85,000 managers and professionals would be graded annually on a curve and the lowest scorers would be fired. His rationale: "You have to go along with a can of fertilizer in one hand and water in the other and constantly throw both on the flowers. If they grow, you have a beautiful garden. If they don't you cut them out. That's what management is all about."[21] The only problem with this approach, of course, is that the gardener has to be darn sure that he or she is cutting out the weeds and not the young sprouts that are doing poorly because of a neighboring weed or an overgrown plant.

The Ocean Group, a British freight transport company, devised a somewhat fairer method of working with poor performers.[22] Then-CEO Nicholas Barber had managers give out "yellow cards" to staff who did not live up to the company's or team's values. He derived this system from the penalty system used in soccer, in which referees "card" players who are guilty of an infraction. At Ocean, an infraction might include a team member forsaking the value of trust by not doing his function to the best of his ability and/or letting the team down by putting himself first. Barber encouraged the executive staff to card him as well, if he deserved it. Implicit in the card system, however, was a belief by the "carder" that the "cardee" did not intend to damage peers, subordinates, or customers and that any carding done was out of concern for a colleague or the organization as a whole.

Although the carding system had a direct impact on the practice of key values within the company, in my mind it also signified compassion, a recognition that we can occasionally fail to live up to our best intentions. On that basis, we deserve a second chance not only to demonstrate that we can improve, but also to show that we can learn from our mistakes. No one is fired peremptorily for an infraction except in the most grievous of cases. Rather, we are grateful to work in a leaderful culture that recognizes the value of fairness.

Values also affect how we approach our jobs and how we deem success or accomplishment. Hence, we may apply values to either the processes or the outcomes of our relationships. In the first instance, we may use ethical criteria to determine if we have treated one another well or with respect. In the second instance, we become concerned with the effects of our actions on the multiple stakeholders with whom we interact. We may have met our economic goals as an organization, for example, but done so without paying sufficient attention to the community in which we operate.

Leaderful Values   Are there particular values that tend to be associated with compassionate leaderful behavior? Perhaps among the most important is the value of humility articulated best by Gandhi in the form of a talisman for decision making. He implored the decision maker, regardless of the setting, to think of the poorest and weakest person and ask whether the alternative in question would help him or her. Humility holds that no person has any inherent or predestined superiority over other human beings. Practicing this value may require giving up some of the trappings of the executive suite.

Consider what Jan Carlzon did when he took over as chief executive of Linjeflyg, one of SAS's affiliates.[23] He was welcomed with a large, airy office with an adjoining personal dining room. Feeling that this privileged space conveyed a false sense of his identity, he converted it to an office and conference room, which he made available to anyone. Devoid now of a personal dining room, he and his executive staff began to eat their lunch in the company cafeteria with everyone else. This modest expression of humility sent a huge message to his company that, though a chief executive who had to interact with other officials, he would not use his status for personal advantage.

The value of humility is consistent with that of respect for the individual. Regardless of whether we hold a managerial position, we endeavor to treat everyone with respect, upholding their intrinsic dignity as human beings. Jim Clawson proposes a provocative check on whether we are capable of treating others with respect. He asks us merely: "given your behavior toward the other person, would you be willing to trade places with that person immediately?"[24] Michael Abrashoff, one of the Navy's most successful and popular commanders and captain of the USS *Benfold*, associates the behavior of listening to others with the value of respect. When he took command of the *Benfold*, he "vowed to treat every encounter with every person on the ship as the most important thing in [his] world at that moment."[25]

There is a utilitarian value implicit in the practice of humility. Those managers who practice it come to realize that they do not have a monopoly on good ideas. They rely on their community to work toward mutual solutions to problems, be they in their operations or markets. They seek to build the confidence of their members to express themselves and to exert the necessary autonomy to run their own operation without fear of being second-guessed or punished, even when they make a mistake. In this way, the community is blessed with leadership at every corner, leading to a highly efficient and effective operation.

Placing confidence in other people to produce successful results isn't necessarily a natural talent bred in most managers. For example, it took Andy Pearson, former CEO of PepsiCo, some twenty years to change from one of the toughest bosses in the United States (according to a *Fortune* survey in 1980) to a tough-"minded" and humble executive with Tricon Global Restaurants, the largest chain restaurant in the world. Instead of finding fault with employees, he became obsessed with trying to determine how to unleash the power of everybody in the organization. Pearson now believes that the human heart is responsible for a company's success—one person at a time—and that it can't be imposed from the top but must be kindled through attention, awareness, recognition, and reward. He explains that the manager's job is to "get results and to do it in a way that makes your organization a great place to work—a place where people enjoy coming to work, instead of just taking orders and hitting this month's numbers." Pearson and CEO David Novak have actualized compassionate values at Tricon through programs such as CHAMPS, which rewards employees for recognizing the best practices of *fellow* workers. Pearson also has become a mentor to countless leaders inside the company, spending a day every so often with them.[26]

Perhaps one of the greatest examples of humility was the stance former CEO of Chrysler, Bob Eaton, took with his number two, then-president and COO, Bob Lutz.[27] Lutz had coveted the top post only to be passed over in 1993 with the naming of Eaton as CEO by Lee Iacocca. Nevertheless, Lutz stayed on and worked with Eaton to transform Chrysler, until its merger with Daimler-Benz AG in 1998, into one of the most admired companies in the United States. Where other successful companies during this era were linked with their CEOs—Microsoft with Bill Gates, Intel with Andy Grove, IBM with Louis Gerstner, or GE with Jack Welch—Chrysler had co-leaders. This was in large measure due to Bob Eaton's insistence on allowing Lutz to flourish as the rather outspoken, brash, risk-taking maverick that he was. Indeed, Eaton not only approved the company's five-year plan, largely developed by Lutz and his team, but also gave Lutz free rein to execute it. For Bob Eaton, then, there was little to be gained by wielding power as "number one." Indeed, he had no problem with Lutz being quoted in *USA Today* saying that: "Sometimes I do aspects of the chairman's job, sometimes Bob does aspects of my job."

It may seem difficult to find an example of humility from the competitive entertainment industry but the classic example has to be the "straight man" who subsumes his or her own talent for the benefit of a partner and the entire performance. Among the notable straight men, Jack Benny and George Burns come to mind. Roger Rosenblatt writes:

> The essence of the straight man is that he gives. He gives the best lines; the stage; the spotlight. By giving, he creates the show—the entire show. It takes a certain kind of person to do that—one who is willing to diminish his part for the good of the whole.[28]

In conjunction with humility, the leaderful leader maintains a consistent commitment to participative values that speak to the empowerment of all involved actors. These participative values prescribe such behaviors as sharing power and responsibility, consolidating the "planning" with the "doing" of any job, opening access to the data underlying business decisions, and encouraging team and organizational members to solve problems on their own and in conjunction with one another.[29]

These values, especially the sharing of power, speak to the question of *who* is participating. When we say that participation should be "full," for example, we mean that all participate, even groups or individuals normally excluded, whether on the basis of demographics (i.e., race and gender) or on the basis of expected norms of practice. In bureaucratic practice, we tend still to organize by division of labor, which separates the doers from the thinkers, the doers being the managers, and the thinkers the workers. Such an environment fosters little opportunity to distribute leadership in a leaderful manner. The manager or supervisor will assume the leadership, and his or her success will hinge on the extent to which the workers can be cajoled to do the work assigned. In this instance, the boss may be dependent on the good graces of the workers to comply with his/her wishes. Oftentimes, coercion or pay may not be sufficient to effect compliance. This leadership problem can be exacerbated if the supervisor is recruited right out of the ranks. Consider the plight of this young supervisor, newly promoted to manage a call center:

> If I wanted to keep supervising, I had to prove I could keep order, run the equipment, and above all, keep numbers from falling so sharply that I would be blamed. How can you ask your chums to get back to work without turning them against you? I thought I knew, but I didn't. Here's one instance:
>
> "Gina, I've got to ask you to watch the downtime."
>
> "Oh, I get it," my former co-worker (and friend) scowled. "Work harder. I understand."

"It isn't like that," I answered. "Make us both look good."

I don't think she talked to me again, though she did talk about me, which is something, I suppose.[30]

The thinkers are often further sub-divided into top and middle levels of management. Have you heard the comical explanation of participation under this division of labor? "Participation is what the top get the middle to do to the bottom!" The distribution of power in an organization is, of course, more complicated and dynamic than a mere three-way split. Dominant coalitions emerge informally as well as formally whenever they obtain preferential access to both material (budgets) and symbolic (budget approvals) resources. Power is a fact of life in organizations where people assemble, and no last experiment in social engineering can do anything beyond wishing it away. Leaderful managers, however, recognize the emergence of power dynamics and try to convert it into mutual gain. This can occur through the dialogic processes that I discussed in our last chapter. In dialogue, people willingly open their beliefs and values to the scrutiny of others. In this setting, as noted late-modernist Habermas put it, all participants have a symmetrical distribution of chances to effect the flow of the conversation.[31]

I would be remiss if in any catalog of leaderful values I did not include the value of trust. As an organizational concept, trust resides on a continuum somewhere in the middle between faith and confidence.[32] To have confidence in a leader means that one's conviction is based on hard and substantial evidence. To have faith in one's leadership is to accept their decision on emotion and in the absence of evidence. To have trust is to accept the leader's actions based on incomplete evidence.

How do leaderful managers earn the trust of their community members? There are three ways: (1) to display competence, (2) to have integrity, and (3) to exhibit goodwill toward others.[33] The first tenet derives from conviction on the part of others that the leader knows what he or she is doing. This doesn't mean knowing how to do others' jobs; rather it's knowing how to do the manager's job. Integrity derives from a perception, based on past behavior, that the manager is not self-serving but rather has the best of the organization in mind. To Wayne Calloway, former CEO of PepsiCo, integrity, one of Pepsi's key values, means to be open and willing to put yourself on the line, to say what you think, and to not have any hidden agendas.[34] Focusing on its contrast, Gordon Bethune of Continental Airlines takes a tough stand on lying. He asserts: "You never lie to your doctor, you never lie to your *own* lawyer, and you never lie to your employees."[35] Leaders of integrity, then, share information, whether good news or bad news, whether things they understand or things they don't. They also are willing to disclose their feelings, whether high or low.

Finally, a trustworthy leader displays goodwill by maintaining personal relationships with the members of the community. All should feel they are valued in the community. Goodwill also implies not having favorites or playing one group off another, which creates winners and losers. Leaderful practice does not require staged controversy or adversity as a basis for its emergence.

Impressionism and Loyalty   The art of "impression management" has been making the rounds of leadership practice. According to this approach, leaders must become more conscious of the impressions they make and learn to manage them more carefully. In short, they choose the image they wish to convey and plan how to convey it.[36] The use of impression management is non-authentic and hence quite contrary to leaderful behavior. What makes it particularly troublesome is that many practice it under the guise of authenticity. I submit that most colleagues and employees are sufficiently worldly to dissect whether a manager is creating impressions or being authentic and trustworthy. Consider an example from an article by Goffee and Jones in the *Harvard Business Review*. They espouse authenticity as a fundamental precept of leadership; yet, they also advise leaders to protect themselves by selecting out only those weaknesses in their practices that they want the public to talk about. They go on to say:

> Knowing which weakness to disclose is a highly honed art. The golden rule is never to expose a weakness that will be seen as a fatal flaw—by which we mean a flaw that jeopardizes central aspects of your professional role. Consider the new finance director of a major corporation. He can't suddenly confess that he's never understood discounted cash flow. A leader should reveal only a tangential flaw . . . pick a weakness that can in some ways be considered a strength, such as being a workaholic. When leaders expose these limited flaws, people won't see much of anything and little harm will come to them.[37]

This excerpt from Goffee and Jones makes the point. The leader on the pedestal should not expose any glaring weaknesses for fear of appearing vulnerable, which presumably would lead to loss of control. You need to look good while deflecting blame, exaggerate your successes while cloaking your failures. Yet, it is precisely vulnerability that exposes one's integrity and humanity. Would a group not feel grateful that its leader admitted a shortcoming, assuming it even is a shortcoming, of having forgotten his cash flow analysis? Leadership will not be embraced by others when they see through the mask constructed by Goffee and Jones' leader. They are more likely to say, "Okay boss, I understand who's in charge." This sets in motion a dependency that reduces all the more the opportunity for leaderful practice.

It is preferable in a leaderful world to have a frank discourse about things that community members care about. From such discourse can emerge a sense of trust among members and between groups within the community. However, trust requires a fairly steady diet of truth-telling on any decision-making process or decision that is deeply held, no matter how uncomfortable that truth-telling may be. William Peace, a former executive with Westinghouse and United Technologies, maintains that exposing oneself to personal vulnerability that might arise from employee criticism, though thought by some to be "soft," can actually be very hard. For instance, at one point in his career, against the advice of his closest colleagues, he chose to meet alone with fifteen people who had just received pink slips. The encounter was an emotionally battering experience for Peace as he had to submit to former employees pouring out their grief, anger, and bewilderment. When he got a chance, he tried his best to explain that the survival of the business required their release, even though there was absolutely nothing wrong with their performance. In the end, the business was sold but the remaining entity flourished sufficiently so that Peace was able to offer the chance for half of the dismissed employees to return. Without exception, every person offered the chance to return accepted, even those who had found other jobs in the meantime. In retrospect, Peace explains his so-called "soft" management in this way: "Unlike the classic leaders of business legend with their towering self-confidence, their unflinching tenacity, their hard, lonely lives at the top, I try to be vulnerable to criticism. I do my best to be tentative, and I cherish my own fair share of human frailty."[38]

There may be occasions when the goals of the organization and of the individual conflict. In such circumstances, the organization's representatives, typically in the form of management, often give dissenting members a voice so they can freely share their objections without repercussions. The management also endeavors to consider these objections as possible suggestions for change to current policy. Minimally, such dissenters are also granted due process, privacy, freedom of conscience, and other civil liberties.

A difficult decision for a leaderful manager is what to do about community members who exemplify consistent dissent. Such members should be able to remain and contribute to the organization provided they do not attempt to sabotage the community's livelihood. Dissent intended to expand learning opportunities, as opposed to that which merely serves one's individual needs, can surely be accepted. Those of the latter persuasion who seek self-aggrandizement without regard to the integrity of the whole community may be asked to leave. Corporate organizations are purposeful entities. They act on behalf of a mission that is even chartered through the laws of the state. They can expect their members to adhere on general terms to their mission. If the values of the organization, as initially constructed, and those of the individual diverge, the parties may need to separate in order to pursue their own interests. However, this divergence should not happen that frequently and should not result from mere "difference of opinion."

Leaderful practice appeals to managers to redefine the notion of organizational loyalty. Loyalty today should be thought about as an intrinsic property, given freely by community members, not as an act of obedience. Meg Wheatley asserts that self-determination is a natural right inherent in the human condition. Obedience is not, so when we ask workers to obey, they may comply but they may also shut down and become lifeless. The leader's work is not to get people to comply but to engage them, to support them, and to keep the field clear so they can be released to do meaningful work.[39] The same can be said for managers who are often asked to carry out the plans of their senior executives. Suggesting that it is preferable for the whole person to show up to work, Douglas Emond, senior vice president at Eastern Bank quipped, "As a manager, you're not paid to agree with everything your bosses decide."[40]

There is far too much need for spontaneity, creativity, and initiative for blind obedience to have value today. Indeed, loyalty in our era should incorporate dissent. Loyalty is extended to the organization to such a degree that one is willing to suffer unpopularity because of an offer of an alternative view. This reconstruction of loyalty rids us of horrible attributions of dissenters, such as "whiners," that one hears from time to time. To label someone a "whiner" is to label *oneself* an insecure soul whose stability comes from preserving the status quo. Compassionate managers listen deeply to dissenters and whiners to understand the basis for their objections. They look to dialogue with them in order to determine how to improve the community for everyone. Leaderful managers also know when such whiners are criticizing on the basis of valid principle and when they are griping to serve their own ego needs.

Acting on Leaderful Values   Perhaps even more critical than democratic values, however, is the commitment to act on these values consistent with their purpose. Espousing empowerment in name alone will only produce cynicism about your democratic orientation. If you pursue leaderful action, you need to be prepared to face review and feedback on your values and resulting behavior. This means being willing to publicly state your positions and feelings and their underlying values, assumptions, and inferences. It means soliciting the opinions and feelings of others. Occasionally, it may require having an open dialogue about consistency between emerging values and current behavior and whether decisions are consistent with these values.

Lewis Platt, former CEO of Hewlett-Packard, was one executive who practiced what he preached.[41] He believed strongly in Hewlett-Packard's culture, embodied in a set of implicit principles known as "The H-P Way." The features of this culture included such humanistic values as loyalty, honesty, modesty, and respect. But in so many explicit and tacit ways, Platt demonstrated a real commitment to these values. For example, in his many visits to HP's plants, he held informal "coffee talks," in which he answered questions from any employee. He also toured the facilities and asked people how they were, how long they'd been with the company, and what they'd like to see changed. He spent hours each week responding to voice mail and e-mail. In addition, once a year, he would have business unit managers vote on which corporate office functions added value and which did not. Among the corporate functions over the years "voted out," in his view, "were [those having to do with] getting too involved in decisions and second-guessing."

What other behaviors do leaderful managers exhibit to help them practice compassionate values?

1. Strong listening skills. They really are interested in the agendas of others and do not formulate responses to others' ideas until they are fully heard. They train themselves to give undivided attention to others as they formulate and express their thoughts and feelings. They may use active listening skills to demonstrate that they understand others' ideas and feelings and wish them to fully express themselves.

2. Sincerity. They display an unguarded sense of identity that has no hidden motives or intents. They are not interested in creating impressions but rather in maintaining a genuine interest in others. They also display caring toward people and toward the community as a whole, often relegating their self-interest as second to the needs of the whole. They tend to dedicate themselves to their associates as part of a stewardship ethic that suggests the authority they have derives only from the consent of those they represent.

3. Inner peace. They display a sense of wonder about life and about others. They maintain a positive outlook and appreciate the gift of their being. Their peace of mind appears to lighten their step.[42]

4. A joyful spirit. They bring a sense of humor even to the most perplexing circumstances, thereby acknowledging their own humility in the face of complexity. They also recognize their ultimate inability to fully know the world and thus appreciate that only in community with others can one progress through the human condition. Humor also signals their humanity and approachability. General Claudia Kennedy displayed a joyful spirit in an interview for a magazine article. Kennedy, the U.S. Army's first female three-star general, was asked by the reporter whether she had any regrets about her career. She mentioned that, unfortunately, she never had time to have a husband and children, to which the reporter suggested, "You could still get married." Kennedy quickly responded, "Well certainly—put my phone number in this article."[43]

5. Harmony. They encourage their associates to work in an atmosphere of sharing. They believe that everyone will be better off working together than at odds with one another. They look for ways to achieve commonality among member differences.

The Lure of Control   Even with the practice of the foregoing behaviors, the value of participation or empowerment will likely remain problematic in most corporate cultures because it often represents a romantic ideal of organizational life. Why do we so often espouse it but rarely practice it? I can propose a number of reasons for this popular inconsistency. Since individuals hold many different values and also waver in the values that are important to them over their lifetime, the professed value of participation may constitute merely a weak or transient value. In this instance, if such individuals confront a surrounding culture that does not endorse real participation, they may be quite willing to relinquish their practice of democratic behavior. If the participative value is particularly weak, such individuals may dispense with its practice, regardless of the context, resorting, especially under stress, to a more dominant value such as control.

The dominance of control in many cultures may, nevertheless, be tacit. In other words, its acceptance may directly depend on its subtle practice. We may no longer accept outright authoritarian control, but are willing to submit to benign control, that is, control that has a sympathetic ring to it. In this instance, most of us may not realize that we are exercising control or are even being controlled. Nevertheless, the culture of the organization, which we might define as the implicit expectations, beliefs, and shared values underlying its mission, may reward such behavior.

In some instances, the actual culture of the organization may belie what executives espouse. For example, the "press" of the organization may stipulate openness, but the manifest culture, expressed through rituals, physical arrangements, or mere day-to-day behavior, may represent control. When workers attempt to act on the basis of the espoused rather than the actual norms of the organization, they may find their behavior constricted or even punished. Yet, much of the dynamic expressed here may be hidden from view since the culture may also not promote open discussion of such cultural inconsistencies.

One of my students captured her own inconsistency in a personal reflective practice. In particular, she not only produced insightful journal entries but also accompanied her entries with drawings that captured the themes she was working on. In the specific entry below, accompanied by one key drawing (figure 9-1), this manager displayed the challenge of discovering her democratic capacity.

> After reading your comments on my last journal, I realized that drawing images can show me my hidden desires, assumptions, and inconsistencies. For example, I realized that it is going to be very difficult for me to let go of my notion that leadership is synonymous with power, authority, and influence. I realized this because (in my drawing, see below) I was trying to conduct a business meeting in which I would use the steward leadership style. However, what I actually drew was myself in a very authoritarian position standing apart and above everyone. The conflict in my drawing is evident: on the one hand I am asking them for their opinions, yet I am in a physical position of power and domination. If I were to revise the drawing, I would seat myself among the individuals in the group. As a result of the readings and participating in our learning team, I have learned that in order to encourage all opinions and ideas to surface, the participants must not feel defensive or threatened and must feel empowered. By actually using images, I have come to realize that my espoused theory (conducting an open forum of ideas in which all are equal) is

Personal Drawing

contradictory to my theory in use (conducting an authoritarian meeting in which I have power and control).

Leaderful managers need to assemble community members who can hold them to their espousal, especially of democratic values. Otherwise, they may become a victim of "value recidivism." By this, I refer to the return to moral decay once one faces the rigors of actual practice. For example, faced with laying off a very capable but senior worker, a manager might rationalize the decision by applying the commonly used euphemism, "I had to make a business decision." In this way one can excuse oneself from behavior that otherwise might be considered morally bankrupt.

Other such excuses frequently crop up to rationalize inconsistency between espoused democratic values and behavior. We can easily resort to diffusion or displacement of responsibility. For example, we can diffuse responsibility by saying, "Everyone else is doing it." Behavior of this kind can start with the most innocuous of acts but then expand into full-scale corruption. So, we might observe that everyone in the lunchroom seems to be taking sugar or sugar-substitute packets back to their offices. Since everyone is doing it, we think, why shouldn't I? From sugar we proceed to silverware and salt shakers, and then to materiel outside the lunchroom, perhaps office equipment or furniture. As the firm faces increasing moral decay, perpetrators feel comforted in knowing that "everyone else is doing it."

Then there is the moral excuse of displacement, sometimes referred to as the "Nuremberg defense," in which at the famous post–World War II trials in Nuremberg, SS officers explained their execution of millions of victims with the familiar refrain, "We were just following orders." When might we see one courageous individual emerge who is willing to say that the behavior in question is not only not right but that it also conflicts with our espoused values? Such an individual would likely confront superiors when their behavior is morally bankrupt.

Values are, in sum, inherent in leadership, even if they remain unstated. When a fan protests that "we need a leader on that team," he is saying that without such an individual, the team has become disorganized and lackluster. Someone has to control the situation before it gets out of hand. Leaderful managers seldom resort to the seductiveness of control. They don't need to. Their authority comes not from line position but from a mutual respect shared with all community members.

The Leader as Social Caretaker

Although we tend to think of leaders as inhabiting organizations, they often extend themselves beyond their organization's boundary. It would be unnatural for leaderful managers to be only concerned about their organizations and not about the wider society in which they operate. When we talk about community in leaderful practice, we initially focus on the community within reach, call it the local community. However, each community, whether within an organization or within society at large, overlaps with other communities.[44] For example, a vocational service agency may overlap with the state employment service, with community social service agencies, or with human resource officials from surrounding companies. Hence, it is nearly impossible for any community or any organization to operate as a closed system in our culture given the increasingly complex interpenetrating relationships most have with multiple stakeholders. Yet many of the effects that we have on external actors are unaccounted for or even unknown.

The concept of "externality" comes into play when neighbors of organizations experience effects—most often reported as negative but they can also be positive—that go unaccounted for or uncompensated. An externality may be quite obvious, such as when a company pollutes a river and impedes usage by anyone downstream, or it may be more subtle, such as when its development appropriates a former open space used by children in the neighborhood. Social caretakers attempt to engage in sufficient dialogue with all possible stakeholders to the extent of raising consciousness about the technologies and resources in use or proposed by their companies. They become willing to be challenged on their actions, not to the extent of ceasing all developments and innovations, but at least to the extent of considering all viewpoints within a public forum.

Sustaining Local Cultures   Social caretakers also search for "sustainable," or ecologically viable, solutions. Sustainable solutions not only persist without outside interference but also depend upon the contribution of the local environment. They respect local customs, as well as celebrate and reward them. So corporations that add sustainability to their criteria for entering global markets honor the cultures in which they consider doing business. As social caretakers, their leaders are concerned about and take responsibility for the effects their actions will have on the multitude of stakeholders with whom they interact. Carly Fiorina, CEO of Hewlett-Packard, addressed the role of social caretaker in a speech given in the aftermath of the September 11, 2001, tragedy.

Today, in initiatives like HP's World E-Inclusion effort, [we can] spread the benefits of the digital world into areas that have been excluded until now—to nations across the globe, to towns and villages and businesses everywhere, into the lives of billions who have up to now not had the tools to share their inventions with the rest of the world, and who have every right to participate in a knowledge economy. It's not about recycling PCs or imposing Western technology on developing nations. It's inherently about creating, from the ground up, locally sustainable solutions that are culturally relevant. It's about rethinking how technology can empower and sustain and liberate, rather than exclude and erode and restrain.[45]

So, in working with the indigent communities of the world, the social caretaker understands that development must arise as an internal process within the community at the local level. Leaders cannot impose solutions from above; rather solutions to local problems need to come from community leadership. Bruce Lansdale reported on a very successful community development program working with 151 villages in Thessaloniki, Greece.[46] Some of the prefecture officials involved in the program gathered after its completion to offer some observations about its success. These observations (shown here in part) provide a testimony to leaderful action within the NGO (non-governmental organizations) development community.

1. People we seek to help can teach us how to plan our help.
2. Villagers often learn more from each other about planning than from us as outsiders.
3. New programs have to "fit in" to prevalent social and organizational structures.
4. Planning new programs must incorporate, build on, and take advantage of the strengths of existing plans and programs.
5. There is synergistic value in bringing people together to share experiences and dreams in the planning process.

6. By becoming "salesmen" of their own plans, villagers understand them better, grow more committed to them, and sustain them as their own.

7. To the extent that our plan helps them to deal with *their* felt needs, to that degree will the program acquire momentum.

8. A development worker's role is to help village leaders identify problems that are important to the local citizens who must articulate solutions as their own plans.

9. Activities vertically and horizontally integrated in the fabric of a society will be assured of lasting momentum.

10. This momentum will be maintained as exogenous leaders are replaced by indigenous leaders. The status of the local leaders is enhanced by their own successes.

11. No foreigner will be any more effective than the indigenous leadership through which he/she chooses to work.

Leaderful organizations operate according to leaderful principles of compassion, collaboration, and democratic practice, and leaderful managers try to create a space in which all voices can be heard regardless of one's background or social and physical standing. Paulo Freire, for example, in his work with Brazilian peasants, was concerned with reforming systems that even unconsciously may have used power, privilege, and voice to exert influence and suppress dissent.[47]

It is the very act of extending yourself beyond your immediate self-interest that distinguishes the compassion of the social caretaker. People who care are mindful of the benefits that they enjoy within their community and so recognize the value of giving to the community. In their consideration and giving, they seek to raise everyone, including themselves, to a higher level of being— a level characterized by compassion. Consider how you would act in this predicament, which Christopher Avery labels "The Theory of the Missing Hero."[48] In driving down a country road, you come upon a traffic jam. Cars have backed up around the next curve. As you get closer to the jam, you notice cars in both lanes pulling off the road to get by something. When you get to the source of the congestion, you spot a large mattress lying in the road, apparently having fallen off a truck. What will you do?

Will you drive around the mattress like everyone else, or will you stop and move the mattress out of the road?

Let me make it easier on you. What if I said that you were not in any particular rush to get to an important engagement nor was there any personal danger to you if you got out of your car to move the mattress? Would you still have acted on behalf of your fellow "community of motorists"?

Social caretakers typically hold a commitment to democratic values, among which might be the value of building trust with and extending compassion to stakeholders within the wider community. Trust and compassion represent values that at times may not lead to short-term results. Consider the actions of many U.S. companies in the aftermath of the September 11, 2001, terrorist attacks. Many showed enormous generosity, donating millions of dollars to relief efforts and supporting their employees through employee assistance. A most creative display of caretaking occurred in Dallas where the manager of an Enterprise Rent-a-Car agency found several hundred stranded customers, but only one hundred or so cars available in his fleet. His solution: though not official company policy, he organized car pools and waived the drop-off fee for one-way rentals so people could get home to their families. Although the agency took a hit due to cars being either lost or batched in far-off locations, the Dallas manager decided to operate according to the values of compassion and trust, in spite of the short-term loss of profit.[49]

Social Caretaking and Courage   Leaderful managers are social caretakers who encourage individuals to speak out beyond their social context. They possess the courage to advocate ideas that their community might not accept. They become willing to face the utter isolation that may arise from group ostracism. Most of us have been in situations where someone has asked for a second look at a proposal. In so doing, that person may face stern rebuke from nearly everyone in the room. Yet how often does the second review lead to new critical insights? Are we not better off encouraging voice, or at least having a public debate about it, than suppressing it?

The ability to try to deeply understand communities outside of your own distinguishes the social caretaker. Once you cross your own borders of comfort, it often takes courage to let down your guard, re-examine your assumptions, and open yourself up to other cultures. Yet doing so can lead to undiscovered and innovative approaches to managing nagging problems within communities. Consider the case of urban banks in the 1960s, many of which began to disinvest in their own cities.[50] Spurred by community reinvestment laws, the banking industry began to dialogue intensely with community-based organizations (CBOs), which led a number of bankers to question the very basis for their assumptions that poor neighborhoods represent a poor business risk. Many began to realize that their original models about product lines, product development approaches, and delivery systems were at the root of their lack of success in the neighborhoods. Working with CBOs and churches, many banks revamped their business models, leading by the end of the century to both good service and profits in these formerly disinvested communities.

Social caretaking, then, explores the historical and social processes underlying our decisions and actions. In this way we come to understand how we have constructed and managed knowledge and how we have arrived at what we deem relevant or even common sense.[51] We need to examine whose interests are served by the forms of knowing in popular use today. We need to encourage our own critical consciousness by ensuring that multiple points of view are heard, leading to new ways of thinking and ultimately of acting.

The notion of social caretaking is not entirely consistent with the extant views of diversity that permeate our culture. The practice of "managing diversity" emphasizes difference, in particular, the celebration of difference. Though there is much to be valued in acknowledging differences, it is not sufficient to merely make others in our community aware of our differences. This is only a first step. We must also learn to transcend our differences to explore the basis for our common humanity. Only by freeing ourselves from attachment to differences can we ultimately dialogue with others to face the true social ills in our culture.

Admittedly, there has been much cultural and religious imperialism in the history of civilization in which one group achieves hegemony by stifling the beliefs and practices of others. What we need to do, however, is do more than merely remedy the act of exploitation by asserting a cultural relativism that leaves every culture or subculture alone to fend for itself. Rather, we need to open up avenues of discourse across all cultures to work together as a common global community. In this way, we seek new and unexplored ways to solve the world's problems. Progress is not reified in a leaderful view of the world because no one person has a copyright on the right answer. The answers come from the community as a learning entity willing to explore new ways of being. Out of this mutual exploration may arise a new solution to our problems. If these problems are solved, then perhaps we can call any solution, temporary though it might be, "progress."

10 Getting Started on Your Leaderful Quest

YOU NOW KNOW WHAT LEADERFUL PRACTICE IS AND HOW IT compares to conventional leadership. You understand why leadership as we know it has to change if we are to prosper in our twenty-first-century organizations and communities.

You also realize that leaderful behavior in organizations will not miraculously show up; rather, it needs to be developed, first by you in your own self-development, and then by your community(ies). You also recognize that leaderful practice is made up of the four C's, tenets that build toward a new paradigm of leadership. The four C's, in turn, are constituted of a number of prior leadership traditions that need to be mastered to develop day-to-day leaderful practice.

Even though you may understand all of the aforementioned considerations, are you ready to embark on a change in your behavior as early as tomorrow? You might have resolved that whether you're a manager or an employee, leaderful practice is something you can experiment with and adopt as your leadership quest. So, in this last chapter, I will address some immediate methods to get started on this quest, whether you're a manager or an employee. There's no need to wait any longer. Give it a shot. And good luck!

Tips for Managers

The first thing to consider on a quest to adopt leaderful practice is to re-assess your current leadership behavior. If you have tried out some of the techniques and practices suggested in the prior chapters and believe you have begun to change your leadership, you may wish to retake the Leaderful Questionnaire on pp. 86–87. You might also ask colleagues to assess your leaderful behavior by having them fill out the Leaderful Questionnaire on you.

Recall the tenets of leadership, displayed in Figure 1-2 on page 14, and size up your leaderful potential on each of the four continua. Do your actions correspond to your beliefs about leaderful practice? You may believe, for example, that you manage quite collectively, but are in fact seen as an individual operator (other than occasionally consulting with chosen staff). Once you have a fair assessment of your leadership behavior, you will have a road map of where to concentrate your efforts in working on the four C's of leaderful practice.

The next step is to become more leaderful within yourself. This process requires an honesty that few of us are willing to examine in ourselves without prompting. A good place to start is to become more reflective, especially if the reflective stance does not come naturally. You might start journalizing as a first step. Write down your thoughts and feelings on a periodic basis, using whatever style most suits you. Become accustomed to pausing and taking stock of your actions and feelings, both before and after an interaction, but concurrently as well. Once you develop a discipline to reflect privately in this way, try to bring your reflections gradually into the open, initially with trusted friends.

To acquire leaderful skills, many of us need to concentrate on our ability to give up control. Ask yourself and ask others if you are more able to share power and control with others. Do you believe in the capabilities of your associates? Are you willing to exhibit any vulnerability about your own actions and assumptions? Are you willing to own up to your inadequacies and to admit that you may not always have the answer?

Your work on yourself can gradually give way to helping prepare others for self-leadership. As people in a community gain confidence in directing their own work in conjunction with their colleagues, they develop the capability of mobilizing their own teams. This occurs as their self-direction incorporates feedback from others, not only on their own effectiveness but also on their contributions to the effectiveness of the whole community. So, at this point, you need to find out if you and your team are prepared to transition into a leaderful mode of operation.

Assuming you have become self-directed and now wish to see your team become self-directed, you need to ask: (1) if the position leader or supervisor of your team (if not yourself) as well as the top management of your organization are committed to leaderful practice; (2) if the team or community has access to the necessary information and resources to become leaderful; and (3) if there are opportunities for learning about and practicing the leaderful ideas and behaviors that have been extensively described in this book.

Developing Concurrent Leadership Since concurrent leadership suggests that you are willing to share your leadership with others in the community at the same time, you need to support the development of others so that sharing becomes a viable alternative to control. Continuing your work on yourself, you need to determine if you can give up control. Can you declare, like Herb Kelleher did, that "you never had control and never wanted it!" Once other members perceive the viability of leaderful practice, you then need to acknowledge their contributions by either working with them in a participative mode or by allowing them to control their own operations using full delegation. The situational model is a useful approach to help community members make the transition into leaderful practice. The decision about whether to use a "join" or "delegate" style of management might hinge on whether you have the time to be a fully involved member of the team or whether your line responsibilities require you to manage several teams and operations.

We also recognize that teams are not automatically leaderful. They need to be developed. I have suggested a number of facilitative interventions consistent with situational team leadership that managers can use to help accelerate the developmental process. Leaderful managers also need to know how to overcome some of the barriers that community members erect to make themselves unavailable for concurrent leadership. For example, managers may need to allow members to voice their concerns about past and present maladaptive behaviors among the membership as a means to build trust within the community. Leaderful managers in supervisory positions may also need to use their formal role to coordinate with stakeholders both within and outside the present organization. In this way, they serve as boundary managers that can screen and access resources to help the team do its internal work more effectively.

Developing Collective Leadership   Collective leadership requires a mindset that shifts leadership from the individual to the community, from a singular to a plural phenomenon. As the position leader, you need to assess your task and maintenance strengths and weaknesses and have everybody in the community do the same. That way, people can assume leadership roles when necessary or when called upon.

In the true tradition of stewardship, anyone in a formal leadership position views his or her role as a privilege, and that privilege is nothing more than the opportunity to serve others. When others in the community are in a position to then serve, it is hoped that they will do so. Although some proponents of stewardship like to ascribe special powers to stewards—such as foresight, confidence, or creativity—in actuality they have no special skills other than to foresee the leadership potential in everyone and to allow it to surface. To be a steward, you need to listen first and elicit the natural talent that exists in each person.

Collective leadership benefits from having a collective voice to count on when critical decisions are made and actions taken. However, this voice does not have to always sing in unison. Indeed, leaderful practice does not subscribe to neat solutions that may only provide an illusion of accomplishment. As a collective leader, you need to become committed to a learning process at the deepest level of understanding. This means being willing to probe below the surface to uncover the hidden assumptions and core premises behind key points of view. It may also mean exposing your own ignorance of some subjects, causing you to rely on others to fill gaps in the knowledge requirements of the community. However, as a learning leader, you don't need to have all the answers. What makes you tough is having the courage to put issues on the table for all to argue about, without having any preconception about the outcome. Learning leaders, then, commit to experimenting with new ways of doing things in the midst of action.

Being collective, leaderful managers don't have to do new things on their own, nor must they distinguish themselves as the sole innovator in the group. At times, it may be just as important to help make sense of what people do when they work together. This meaning-making can help a group work through difficult moments of uncertainty or through contested terrain when competing interests seem to place the group on the verge of disunity. In performing meaning-making, you don't have to feel responsible, even as the position leader, for providing the vision for the community. In many cases, the vision is present but for its articulation. Furthermore, since the vision is collective, anyone in the community can express it, though it typically will come from someone who is intimately involved (not someone who bursts in from the cold) and who is expressive in his or her use of words and metaphors.

Developing Collaborative Leadership A collaborative leader is not only enriched by difference of opinion, but also seeks it out.

Collaborators are not afraid of conflict because they recognize that affirmative change arises from an open exchange of well-considered points of view. Since change is inevitable, it might as well proceed with the full involvement of those affected. Deftly recognizing and sensitively managing legitimate resistances to change perhaps constitutes the most valuable lesson in collaborative leadership.

Collaborators also engage in mutual influence processes, meaning that all parties have an equal weight to affect the flow of communication and decision making. In particular, they tend to rely on problem-solving and reasoning influence strategies in order to engage other parties in a process of mutual exploration and development. Even more critically, they enter a relationship with others not because they expect to get paid back for what they contribute, but because they value them and wish to encourage and sustain a commitment to them.

So as a collaborative leader, you seek to discover wisdom through others' eyes and to do so requires open, civil dialogue. Dialogue goes beyond a mere exchange of views. As a publicly reflective practice, it probes below the surface to discover the assumptions behind points of view and feelings. It does this through nonjudgmental inquiry in which we relax our preconceptions about others' views and become receptive to challenge to our own ways of thinking.

Developing Compassionate Leadership   Compassion emanates from a profound respect for the dignity of every other human being. Hence, trying to shape your personality so you can deliver inspirational messages to others to hold them in awe is antagonistic to leaderful practice. As a noncharismatic, you hold those whom you serve in awe and do not take advantage of their occasional dependence. If there is to be salvation, it will arise from the hard work of everyone in the community.

As a compassionate manager, you commit to establishing relationships that embody democratic values, in particular, humility, participation, and trust. You also seek to practice consistently with these values, displaying such qualities as strong listening skills and sincerity. Compassionate managers eschew the need to control, choosing instead to elevate the human spirit to grow and achieve. They can resist the seductiveness of control because their contribution is derived not from line position but from respect and compassion shared with all community members.

Compassion is also extended to stakeholders outside of your internal operations. You take responsibility for the effects of your actions. As a social caretaker, you search for sustainable solutions that honor local customs and create a space in which all forces can be heard regardless of background or social standing. It is the commitment to deeply understand communities outside of your own that distinguishes the compassionate social caretaker.

Tips for Employees

If you hadn't read the entire book, you might find this last section a bit curious, since most people are not used to talking about their leadership as an employee. Employees as followers are supposed to do what they're told. How can they have any leadership?

By now, I hope I have deconstructed the notion of followership sufficiently that it does not have to denote passive acceptance of a leader's vision. Follower and position leader are interchangeable roles in leaderful practice. In fact, employees do not have to be followers; you are rather a member of a leaderful community that needs your leadership.

I realize that many groups may not be entirely prepared for this view of leadership, but as long as there is a slight crack of readiness in the system, you might find a way to exhort and exhibit leaderful practice in your own community. Just as managers must, you start by working on yourself.

You need to know what strengths you bring that can contribute to a healthy growing community. Are you good at finding information to help your team? Are you creative? Do you have a nat-ural sensitivity toward others that can bring them out more? Do you like to represent the team in its dealings with stakeholders? If you're willing to assume leadership functions for your community, are you aware of those tendencies that might be holding you back?

The search for self-awareness, as we know, does not have to proceed in isolation. You can initiate the process by gathering around you a close-knit group of friends who might be willing to help you in your discovery. Among the competencies that people engaging in self-learning might consider would be those that contribute to the growth and knowledge of the team. As people develop their confidence in working together, they may then need to consider the willingness of their management to permit them to share leadership.

Management, in large organizations anyway, exists at a num-ber of levels. If the top management seems unsympathetic to lead-erful practice, that doesn't necessarily doom it to extinction. Perhaps your immediate manager may be interested, in which case you could instigate a microcosm of such a practice. If you're suc-cessful in interesting your manager and team and if you become successful, then you might find it possible to spread leaderful prac-tice throughout your organization. It is my sincere hope that the prevalence of unadulterated close-mindedness among chief exec-utives is slight. Most people at the top do recognize processes that work. Many of us have morbid expectations that any initiative we take will be not only rebuffed but also punished. It is important to recognize whether such expectations are real or imagined.

Once you have performed the necessary individual, team, and system-wide assessment of readiness for leaderful practice, the next steps call for you to change your own leaderful behavior to embrace the four C's.

Developing Concurrent Leadership   As an employee you do not typically have formal responsibility for the outcome of others, other than the extent to which those outcomes affect your own work. Once you embrace leaderful practice, the community's outcomes indeed become part of your responsibility. You would also prefer that others in the community maintain this same disposition. Thus, you become interested in your colleagues' readiness to assume greater responsibility for people other than themselves. The diagnosis of readiness among your peers is not performed so much for conventional managerial purposes as for helping you recruit support for the concurrent leadership of the unit.

In a similar vein, though you may not be the position leader of your team, you can become a facilitating member as long as your supervisor does not feel threatened by this behavior. Since your leaderful behavior is not designed to assume authority, it should actually benefit your supervisor by helping him or her get the work done. Facilitative behaviors encompass a full range of competencies designed to help the team develop itself internally or relate externally to stakeholders. For example, you might serve as a team builder that encourages quiet members to play more of a role in team activities, or you might serve as a knowledge broker that helps the team interface with other units working on similar problems.

Developing Collective Leadership   As a teacher of leadership, I have found the greatest gift I can give is to recognize among my quieter students their contribution of stewardship to their teams. These students often feel that they are not capable of leadership because they are not sufficiently assertive. Yet, they become absorbed by the work of their teams, act with integrity toward other team members, typically put others' interests before their own, and often seem to be precisely the key persons who hold the team together. Perhaps the first task of collective leadership is to likewise recognize who the stewards are in your community.

As an employee, you may be a steward yourself, or you may be someone who applauds stewardship by others. Another responsibility for employees in collective leadership is to recognize the learners in the community. The learners are those who find learning opportunities in everyday experience. For them, learning is more than just technical know-how. It can also involve learning how to function more collectively as a community, how to learn from our mistakes and conflicts, or how to learn from questioning taken-for-granted assumptions.

It is possibly in meaning-making that employees can make the most critical contributions of leadership to their community without having to obtain permission from their position leader. This is because articulating the meaning of a community as its members do their work together would be seen as a natural process that comes from the heart. As a meaning-maker, your simple responsibility is to occasionally find the path that can lead your group through contested terrain. In addition, consistent with the collective property of leaderful practice, you need not be the sole meaning-maker for your community. It is just as important to recognize others' attempts to voice the meaning for the group.

Developing Collaborative Leadership   Leaderful practice assumes that those involved in a change effort wish to be involved in the planning and implementation of that change. The tenet of collaborative leadership speaks to this inherent democratic process. Oftentimes, as an employee, you don't feel that you can initiate anything without clearance from corporate. Yet, in many circumstances corporate leaders would prefer to have their employees initiate responsible changes in their own area. No one is more informed about a problem than the possessor of that problem. It is preferable that where bureaucracy is called for, those in authority commit to releasing the energy of others rather than insist on being the epicenter of change.

Even when position leaders resist, employees can still attempt to influence their own groups to consider collaborative work processes. Although our culture seems to endorse a reciprocal tit-for-tat basis of exchange, opportunities arise every day for you to do something for the common good. There is also no need to wait for authoritative permission to engage colleagues—be they inside or outside the community—in a dialogue that inquires about the points of view of others rather than proves your own. Not that you have to remain exclusively in an inquisitive mode as a dialoguer; you also learn to feel comfortable challenging the perspectives of others. This becomes possible in a community that is receptive to new thinking and to new ways that often disturb preconceived worldviews.

Developing Compassionate Leadership   A compassionate community treats everyone with dignity regardless of his or her position or background. As an employee, you might start by asserting your own worth, one which does not require someone else's affirmation. If you discover that a position leader in your organization has traded on the insecurity of others or that other associates have spread rumors of this leader's pseudo-salvation, it is your responsibility to speak out against this potential demagoguery. Leaderful employees seek charisma in the auspices of their own community, not in the auspices of single individuals.

Leaderful practice as a compassionate endeavor supports building relationships on the basis of trust and integrity rather than strictly on the basis of collecting bargaining chips. Whether we wish to recognize them or not, we all work out of our values—the principles by which we approach our jobs or define our successes or accomplishments. You don't have to be in a position of power to treat every personal encounter, as Michael Abrashoff of the USS *Benfold* does, "as the most important thing in [your] world at that moment." You might even find that your recognition and valuing of other associates in your workplace can become contagious.

Many employees find themselves in roles that are at the

boundary of their own organization and of other stakeholders. Leaderful practice extends outside your own community as you begin to realize that individual problems occur within a social context. So you commit to opening yourself up to other cultures and ensuring that their spokespersons have an opportunity to voice their concerns and aspirations in their relationships with you.

Leaderful practice, in sum, can begin in the day-to-day behaviors that people of good will extend to one another. We are all parties to leadership. Although it helps to have a sympathetic position leader get the ball rolling, we shouldn't wait for the go-ahead. There can be acts of compassionate leadership in every step you take. You may collaborate with others as soon as you begin to value their interests. You can be a collective leader when you vow to serve others and your community, and you can concurrently assume a leadership role whenever you decide to proactively enlist your teammates to forge a leaderful identity.

We bid "adieu" to the old paradigm of leadership. Leadership has served us well. But we are grown up now. We are ready to move on. Welcome everyone to the age of leaderful practice!

Notes

CHAPTER 1. THE TENETS OF LEADERFUL PRACTICE

1. The processes in the model are based on what famed sociologist, Talcott Parsons, considered the four functional prerequisites of organizations. Although credited to Parsons, the prerequisites derived from his collaboration with Edward Shils and Robert Bales. Bales, in particular, observed how groups went through these phases as they coped with any material problem. Parsons then applied the framework to larger social institutions. See T. Parsons, R. F. Bales, and E. A. Shils, *Working Papers in the Theory of Action* (Glencoe, IL: Free Press, 1953); and L. H. Mayhew, ed., *Talcott Parsons: On Institutions and Social Evolution* (Chicago: University of Chicago Press, 1982), pp. 23–41.

2. Reported in B. L. Kirkman and B. Rosen, "Powering Up Teams," *Organizational Dynamics* 28, no. 3 (2000): 48–66.

3. For more information on our high-tech military, see G. Jaffe, "In the New Military, Technology May Alter Chain of Command," *Wall Street Journal*, March 30, 2001.

4. The Home Depot example was part of *InformationWeek* Research's Information Sharing & Collaboration study reported in P. McDougall, *InformationWeek. Com News*, May 7, 2001.

5. Some of these views have also been expressed by Joseph Rost as the post-industrial paradigm of leadership. See his *Leadership for the Twenty-First Century* (New York: Praeger, 1991). Margaret Wheatley also compares leadership to quantum physics, a new paradigm in contrast to traditional views grounded in Newtonian physics. See her *Leadership and the New Science: Learning about Organizations from an Orderly Universe* (San Francisco: Berrett-Koehler, 1992). Craig Pearce,

Jay Conger, and others have also been developing an emerging view of leadership known as "shared leadership." See C. L. Pearce and J. D. Conger, ed., *Shared Leadership: Reframing the Hows and Whys of Leadership* (Thousand Oaks, CA: Sage, 2003).

6. D. T. Phillips, *Lincoln on Leadership* (New York: Warner Books, 1992), p. 139.

7. Rich Teerlink and Lee Ozley detail some of these defects within command-and-control environments and show how they addressed them at Harley-Davidson in *More Than a Motorcycle* (Boston: Harvard Business School Press, 2000).

8. The evidence suggests that workers tend to desire more influence on activities that are closer to their immediate work roles rather than on those that shape general organizational policy. However, once given some control over local conditions, their sphere of influence might expand. Increasing control by workers, furthermore, does not necessarily detract from control by top management; in other words, control might be a non-zero-sum game. See especially the work of A. S. Tannenbaum, e.g., *Control in Organizations* (New York: McGraw-Hill, 1968). Also consult B. M. Staw, "Beyond the Control Graph: Steps toward a Model of Perceived Control in Organizations," in *The Organizational Practice of Democracy*, ed. R. N. Stern and S. McCarthy (New York: John Wiley, 1986), pp. 305–310.

9. J. Lipman-Blumen, *Connective Leadership: Managing in a Changing World* (Oxford, UK: Oxford University Press, 1996).

10. The interview with Smith was conducted by Harris Collingwood and Julia Kirby and transcribed in the article, "All in a Day's Work," *Harvard Business Review*, 79, no. 12 (2001): 55–66.

11. See M. Paulson, "Catholics Drawn to Splinter Group in Wellesley," *Boston Globe*, May 1, 2002.

12. W. Bennis and J. O'Toole, "Don't Hire the Wrong CEO," *Harvard Business Review*, 78, no. 3 (2000): 170–178. Each has written many books on leadership. See, e.g., W. Bennis and B. Nanus, *Leaders: Strategies for Taking Charge* (New York: HarperBusiness, 1997); J. O'Toole, *Leading Change: The Argument for Values-Based Leadership* (San Francisco: Jossey-Bass, 1995).

13. See D. L. Bradford and A. R. Cohen, *Power Up: Transforming Organizations through Shared Leadership* (New York: John Wiley, 1998).

CHAPTER 2. THE DISTINCTIVENESS OF LEADERFUL PRACTICE

1. See Carol Hymowitz' In The Lead column, "How Cynthia Danaher Learned to Stop Sharing and Start Leading," *Wall Street Journal,* March 16, 1999.

2. The label *professional bureaucracy* was first applied by H. Mintzberg in *The Structuring of Organizations* (Englewood Cliffs, NJ: Prentice-Hall, 1979). See also P. DiMaggio and W. W. Powell, "The Iron Cage Revisited: Institutional Isomorphism and Collective Rationality in Organizational Fields," *American Sociological Review,* 28 (1983): 147–160; and J. A. Raelin, *The Clash of Cultures: Managers Managing Professionals* (Boston: Harvard Business School Press, 1991).

3. For more detail on the concept of the leadership constellation, see J. Denis, L. Lamothe, and A. Langley, "The Dynamics of Collective Leadership and Strategic Change in Pluralistic Organizations," *Academy of Management Journal,* 44, no. 4 (2001): 809–837.

4. Some writers suggest that there are pivotal transition points between the different layers of hierarchy. It is incumbent upon managers to navigate these leadership passages successfully in order to ascend successfully to top management. See, e.g., R. Charan, S. Drotter, and J. Noel, *The Leadership Pipeline* (San Francisco: Jossey-Bass, 2001).

5. See, for example, A. I. Kraut, P. R. Pedigo, D. D. McKenna, and M. D. Dunnette, "The Role of the Manager: What's Really Important in Different Management Jobs," *Academy of Management Executive* 3 (1989): 286–293; M. E. Baehr, *Predicting Success in Higher–Level Positions: A Guide to the System for Testing and Evaluation of Potential* (Westport, CT: Quorum, 1992); and S. J. Zaccaro, *The Nature of Executive Leadership* (Washington: American Psychological Corporation, 2001).

6. See E. Jaques, *Requisite Organization* (Arlington, VA: Cason Hall, 1989).

7. D. C. Hambrick, "Top Management Groups: A Conceptual Integration and Reconsideration of the 'Team' Label," in *Research in Organizational Behavior,* ed. B. M. Staw and L. L. Cummings (Greenwich, CT: JAI Press, 1994), 16: 171–213.

8. For a review of cognitive complexity theories, see chapter 2 of Zaccaro, *Nature of Executive Leadership.*

9. R. C. McPherson, "The People Principle," *The Book of Leadership Wisdom*, ed. P. Krass (New York: John Wiley, 1998), pp. 91–92.

10. For more detail on the circle structure at Harley-Davidson, see chapter 7 in R. Teerlink and L. Ozley, *More Than a Motorcycle* (Boston: Harvard Business School Press, 2000).

11. See, for example, J. Pfeffer, "The Ambiguity of Leadership," *Academy of Management Review* 2, no. 2 (1977): 104–112; and T. H. Hout, "Are Managers Obsolete?" *Harvard Business Review* 77, no. 2 (1999): 161–168.

12. See M. Schneider, "A Stakeholder Model of Organizational Leadership," *Organization Science* 13, no. 2 (2002): 209–220.

13. R. L. Ackoff, "Corporate Perestroika: The Internal Market Economy," in *Internal Markets: Bringing the Power of Free Enterprise Inside Your Organization*, ed. W. E. Halal, A. Geranmayeh, and J. Pourdehnad (Westport, CT: Quorum Books, 1993), 15–26.

14. K. E. Weick and K. H. Roberts, "Collective Mind in Organizations: Heedful Interrelating on Flight Decks," *Administrative Science Quarterly* 38 (1993): 357–381.

15. Quoted in L. S. Csoka, *Bridging the Leadership Gap* (New York: The Conference Board, 1997), p. 7.

16. For more information on Virgin and its flamboyant chairman, Sir Richard Branson, see M. Kets de Vries, "Leaders Who Make a Difference," *European Management Journal* 14, no. 5 (1996): 486–493.

17. G. Anders, "John Chambers, After the Deluge," *Fast Company*, July 2001.

18. A. Godard and V. Lenhardt, *Transformational Leadership: Shared Dreams to Succeed* (Paris, Village Mondial, 1999; transl. New York: Macmillan, 2000), p. 69.

19. Tom Kelley's quote is from an interview by John Koch, *The Boston Globe Magazine*, March 25, 2001, p. 8.

20. R. E. Kelley, "In Praise of Followers," *Harvard Business Review* 66, no. 6 (1988): 142–148.

21. For a review of the dyadic and exchange approaches, see G. B. Graen and M. Uhl-Bien, "Relationship-Based Approach to Leadership: Development of Leader Member Exchange (LMX) Theory of Leadership over 25 Years: Applying a Multi-Level Multi-Domain Approach," *Leadership Quarterly* 6, no. 2 (1995): 219–247.

22. See S. J. Wayne and M. K. Kacmar, "Implications of Member Role Differentiation: Analysis of a Key Concept in the LMX Model of Leadership," *Group & Organization Studies* 16 (1991): 102–113.

23. See the team empowerment research of B. L. Kirkman and B. Rosen in "Powering Up Teams," *Organizational Dynamics* 28, no. 3 (2000): 48-66.

24. A. Zaleznik, "Managers and Leaders: Are They Different?" *Harvard Business Review* 70, no. 2 (1992): 126–135.

25. Kotter's work on managers and leaders first appeared in 1990 but was reprised as a Best of HBR article in a special issue of the *Harvard Business Review* on Breakthrough Leadership. See "What Leaders Really Do," *Harvard Business Review* 79, no. 12 (2001): 85–96.

26. L. S. Csoka, *Bridging the Leadership Gap* (New York: The Conference Board, 1998).

CHAPTER 3. THE CHALLENGE OF LEADERFUL PRACTICE

1. This is a synopsis of a case described by Dr. Richard Boyer to Mareen Duncan Fisher and Kimball Fisher in "Leadership on Self-Managing Teams," *At Work*, May/June, 1998.

2. R. N. Lussier and C. F. Achua, *Leadership: Theory, Application, Skill Development* (Cincinnati: South-Western College Publishing, 2001).

3. For more on the social capital model of leadership, see M. Uhl-Bien, G. Graen, and T. Scandura, "Implications of Leader-member Exchange (LMX) for Strategic Human Resource Management Systems: Relationships as Social Capital for Competitive Advantage," in *Research in Personnel and Human Resources Management*, ed. R. Ferris (Greenwich, CT: JAI Press, 2000), 19:137–185.

4. R. Teerlink, "Harley's Leadership U-Turn," *Harvard Business Review* 78, no. 4 (2000): 43–50.

5. This perspective falls under the "social exchange" theory, which argues that status differentiation naturally occurs in groups that do not have authoritative leaders. See, for example, R. F. Bale, "Task Roles and Social Roles in Problem-Solving Groups," in *Readings in Social Psychology*, ed. E. E. Maccoby, T. M. Newcomb, and E. L. Hartley (New York: Henry Holt, 1958), pp. 437–447; G. C. Homans, *Social Behavior: Its Elementary Forms* (New York: Harcourt Brace and World, 1961); P. M. Blau, *Exchange and Power in Social Life* (New York: Wiley, 1964);

and C. L. Ridgeway and H. A. Walker, "Status Structures," in *Sociological Perspectives on Social Psychology*, ed. K. S. Cook, G. A. Fine, and J. S. House, (Boston: Allyn & Bacon, 1995), pp. 281-310.

6. See, for example, M. Rafiq and P. K. Ahmed, "A Contingency Model for Empowering Customer-Contact Services Employees," *Management Decision* 36, no. 10 (1998): 686–694.

7. Geert Hofstede performed the seminal work on international global values. See his *Culture's Consequences* (Beverly Hills, CA: Sage, 1980). See also B. Kirkman, C. B. Gibson, and D. L. Shapiro, "Exporting Teams: Enhancing the Implementation and Effectiveness of Work Teams in Global Affiliates," *Organizational Dynamics* 30, no. 1 (2001): 12–29.

8. For a distinction between professionals and managers, see J. A. Raelin, *The Clash of Cultures: Managers Managing Professionals* (Boston: Harvard Business School Press, 1991).

9. This model has been adapted from D. Barry, "Managing the Bossless Team: Lessons in Distributed Leadership," *Organizational Dynamics* 20, no. 1 (1991): 31–47.

10. E. M. Belbin, *Management Teams: Why They Succeed or Fail* (London: John Wiley, 1981).

11. These dimensions were initially suggested by C. Lashley, "Empowerment through Involvement: A Case Study of TGI Fridays Restaurants," *Personnel Review* 29, no. 6 (2000): 791–811.

CHAPTER 4. THE DEVELOPMENT OF LEADERFUL PRACTICE

1. See Iva Wilson's commentary in B. Frydman, I. Wilson, and J. Wyer, *The Power of Collaborative Leadership* (Boston: Butterworth Heinemann, 2000), pp. 223, 247.

2. P. Kaipa, "Developing Tomorrow's Executives Today," SelfCorp, Inc., 2001, unpublished manuscript.

3. B. Mackoff and G. Wenet, *The Inner Work of Leaders* (New York: AMACOM, 2001).

4. R. L. Lee and S. N. King, *Discovering the Leader in You* (San Francisco: Jossey-Bass, 2001), pp. 74–100.

5. K. Cashman, *Leadership from the Inside Out* (Provo, UT: Executive Excellence Publishing, 2000), pp. 36–42.

6. Cashman, *Leadership*, pp. 112–114.

7. For more on the value of coaching or mentorships, see M. London, *Leadership Development: Paths to Self-Insight and Professional Growth* (Mahwah, NJ: Lawrence Erlbaum, 2002).

8. T. Merton, *No Man Is an Island* (New York: Walker, 1986).

9. Daniel Goleman, Richard Boyatzis, and Annie McKee believe that a neural basis exists for our ability to train ourselves toward pleasant rather than toxic behavior. See their "Primal Leadership: The Hidden Driver of Great Performance," *Harvard Business Review* 79 (Special December Issue, 2001): 43–51.

10. See C. Rogers, *On Becoming a Person* (Boston: Houghton Mifflin, 1961). See also, A. Baveja and G. Porter, "Creating an Environment for Personal Growth," in *Advances in Interdisciplinary Studies of Work Teams*, ed. M. M. Beyerlein, D. A. Johnson, and S. T. Beyerlein (Greenwich, CT: JAI Press, 1996), 3: 127–143.

11. Frydman, Wilson, and Wyer, *The Power of Collaborative Leadership*, p. 252.

12. C. C. Manz and H. P. Sims, Jr., "Superleadership: Beyond the Myth of Heroic Leadership," *Organizational Dynamics* 19, no. 4 (1991): 18–35.

13. Self-leadership does not automatically extend to team leadership unless it is clear that developing personal or professional autonomy should not arise at the expense of community goals. It is thus possible to resolve the paradox between individual and group autonomy provided the group expects its members to exhibit *both* autonomous and collaborative behavior. This contention contrasts to research citing a negative relationship between personal autonomy and group cohesiveness. See, e.g., Claus W. Langfred, "The Paradox of Self-Management: Individual and Group Autonomy in Work Groups," *Journal of Organizational Behavior* 21, no. 5 (2000): 563–585.

14. D. Anfuso, "Core Values Shape W. L. Gore's Innovative Culture," *Workforce* 78, no. 3 (1999): 48–53.

15. J. Huey, "The New Post-Heroic Leadership," *Fortune* 129, no. 4 (February 21, 1994): 42–50.

16. R. Fisher and A. Sharp with J. Richardson, *Getting It Done* (New York: HarperCollins, 1998).

17. B. L. Kirkman and B. Rosen, "Powering Up Teams," *Organizational Dynamics* 28, no. 3 (2000): 48–66.

18. This case was drawn from a study by V. Urch Druskat and J. V. Wheeler, "Managing from the Boundary: The Effective Leadership of Self-Managing Work Teams," presented at the Annual Meeting of the Academy of Management, Washington, August 7, 2001, p. 34.

19. D. W. Organ, *Organizational Citizenship Behavior: The Good Soldier Syndrome* (Lexington, MA: Lexington Books, 1988).

20. J. Fahr, P. M. Podsakoff, and D. W. Organ, "Accounting for Organizational Citizenship Behavior: Leader Fairness and Task Scope Versus Satisfaction," *Journal of Management* 16, no. 4 (1990): 705–721.

21. See also, R. Forrester, "Empowerment: Rejuvenating a Potent Idea," *Academy of Management Executive* 14, no. 3 (2000): 67–80.

CHAPTER 5. THE BENEFITS OF LEADERFUL PRACTICE

1. Reported in P. LaBarre, "Marcus Buckingham Thinks Your Boss Has an Attitude Problem," *Fast Company* 49 (August 2001): 88–98.

2. D. J. Kravetz, "Increased Finances through Progressive Management," *HRMagazine* 36, no. 2 (1991): 57–62.

3. G. Hamel, *Leading the Revolution* (Boston, Harvard Business School Press, 2000).

4. Edward Lawler addressed this caveat in his classic *High-Involvement Management* (San Francisco: Jossey-Bass, 1986), pp. 12–43.

5. Lawler's *High-Involvement Management* also addressed some of these. See also, G. M. Spreitzer, "Psychological Empowerment in the Workplace: Dimensions, Measurement, and Validation," *Academy of Management Journal* 38, no. 5 (1995): 1442–1465; and S. Kim, "Participative Management and Job Satisfaction: Lessons for Management Leadership," *Public Administration Review* 62 no. 2 (2002): 231–241.

6. For a discussion of the effect of knowledge and other contingencies on participation interventions, see K. I. Miller and P. R. Monge, "Participation, Satisfaction, and Productivity: A Meta-Analytic Review," *Academy of Management Journal* 29, no. 4 (1986): 727–753.

7. E. E. Lawler, S. A. Mohrman, and G. E. Ledford, Jr., *Employee Involvement and Total Quality Management: Practices and Results in Fortune 1000 Companies* (San Francisco: Jossey-Bass, 1992).

8. From J. Schecter, "The Private World of Richard Nixon," *Time* 99, no. 1 (1972): 18–19.

9. For a multidimensional view of the cumulative effect of participative decision making, see J. S. Black and H. B. Gregersen, "Participative Decision-Making: An Integration of Multiple Dimensions," *Human Relations* 50, no. 7 (1997): 859–878.

10. Center for Creative Leadership, "The Paradox of Leadership," *CCL's e-Newsletter*, www.ccl.org/connected/enews/articles/1001paradox.htm.

11. R. J. Lee and S. N. King, *Discovering the Leader in You* (San Francisco: Jossey-Bass, 2001), pp. 27–28.

12. J. A. Olmstead, *Executive Leadership* (Houston: Cashman Dudley, 2000), p. 154.

13. H. Kelleher, "A Culture of Commitment," *Leader to Leader* 4 (Spring 1997).

14. G. W. Fairholm, *Perspectives on Leadership* (Westport, CT: Quorum Books, 1998), p. 153. See also, G. Pinchot and E. Pinchot, *The End of Bureaucracy and the Rise of the Intelligent Organization* (San Francisco: Berrett-Koehler, 1994).

15. Reported in M. De Pree, *Leadership Is an Art* (New York: Dell, 1989), pp. 7–9.

16. T. Watson and P. Harris, *The Emergent Manager* (London: Sage, 1999).

17. Ibid., p. 164.

18. Ibid., p. 165.

19. Ibid., p. 161.

20. Ibid., p. 168.

21. The case of Tex Gunning and Van den Bergh was reported in an unpublished learning history by Philip Mirvis, Karen Ayas, and George Roth.

22. This story, including speech excerpts, is reported in K. Cashman, Leadership from the Inside Out (Provo, UT: Executive Excellence Publishing, 2000), pp. 181–182.

CHAPTER 6. CONCURRENT LEADERSHIP

1. This readiness approach is formally known as "A Model for Group Leadership and Group Effectiveness," by R. L. Hughes, R. C. Ginnett, and G. J. Curphy, *Leadership: Enhancing the Lessons of*

Experience, 2d ed. (Chicago: Irwin, 1996), pp. 354–367, and, in turn, is based on the work of J. R. Hackman, *Groups That Work (and Those That Don't)* (San Francisco: Jossey-Bass, 1990).

2. P. Hersey and K. H. Blanchard, *Management of Organizational Behavior*, 5th ed. (Englewood Cliffs, NJ: Prentice-Hall, 1988).

3. See, e.g., C. N. Greene, "The Reciprocal Nature of Influence between Leader and Subordinate," *Journal of Applied Psychology* 60 (1975): 187–193; F. H. Sanford, "The Follower's Role in Leadership Phenomena," in *Leaders & The Leadership Process*, ed. J. L. Pierce and J. W. Newstrom, 2d ed. (New York: McGraw-Hill, 2000), pp. 203-205; and E. P. Hollander, "Leadership, Followership, Self, and Others," *Leadership Quarterly* 3, no. 1 (1992): 43–54.

4. Initially reported in V. Urch Druskat and J. V. Wheeler, "Managing from the Boundary: The Effective Leadership of Self-Managing Work Teams," presented at the Annual Meeting of the Academy of Management, Washington, August 7, 2001, p. 42.

5. V. H. Vroom, "Leadership and the Decision-Making Process," *Organizational Dynamics* 28, no. 4 (2000): 82–94. See also his normative approach in his book with P. Yetton, *Leadership and Decision Making* (Pittsburgh: University of Pittsburgh Press, 1973).

6. M. De Pree, *Leadership Jazz* (New York: Dell, 1992), pp. 151–166.

7. M. Morrell and S. Capparell, *Shackleton's Way: Leadership Lessons from the Great Antarctic Explorer* (New York: Viking, 2001).

8. B. J. Avolio, *Full Leadership Development: Building the Vital Forces in Organizations* (Thousand Oaks, CA: Sage Publications, 1999), p. 120.

9. See M. Kets de Vries, "High Performance Teams: Lessons from the Pygmies," *Organizational Dynamics* 27, no. 3 (1999): 66–77.

10. H. Kelleher, "A Culture of Commitment," *Leader to Leader* 4 (Spring 1997): 20–24.

11. R. A. Eckert, "Where Leadership Starts," *Harvard Business Review* 79, no. 10 (2001): 53–61.

12. See K. Fisher, *Leading Self-Directed Work Teams* (New York: McGraw-Hill, 1993), pp. 21, 27, 113.

13. R. Slater, *Get Better or Get Beaten: Twenty-nine Leadership Secrets from GE's Jack Welch*, 2d ed. (New York: McGraw-Hill, 2001).

14. G. Anders, "How Intel Puts Innovation Inside," *Fast Company* 56 (March 2002): 122.

NOTES TO CHAPTER 6   263

15. B. W. Tuckman, "Developmental Sequences in Small Groups," *Psychological Bulletin* 63 (1965): 384–399. This information on the situational model applied to team development is drawn from J. Raelin, *Work-Based Learning: The New Frontier of Management Development* (Upper Saddle River, NJ: Prentice-Hall, 2000), pp. 152–156.

16. For more information on the "Nut Island Effect," see P. F. Levy, "The Nut Island Effect: When Good Teams Go Wrong," *Harvard Business Review* 79, no. 3 (2001): 5–12.

17. A. Godard and V. Lenhardt, *Transformational Leadership: Shared Dreams to Succeed* (Paris, Village Mondial, 1999; transl. New York: Macmillan, 2000), pp. 93–94.

18. See K. Blanchard, S. Bowles, D. Carew, and E. Parisi-Carew, *High Five!* (New York: William Morrow, 2001).

19. For a definitive account of how to apply the situational model to group development, see D. Carew, E. Parisi-Carew, and K. Blanchard, *Group Development and Situational Leadership II* (Escondido, CA: Blanchard Training and Development, 1990). Another important model developed by Kozlowski and his colleagues focuses on a sequence of roles to be deployed by the team's position leader to help integrate individual tasks and team skills throughout the group's developmental cycle. See S. W. J. Kozlowski, S. M. Gully, E. Salas, and J. A. Cannon-Bowers, "Team Leadership and Development: Theory, Principles, and Guidelines for Training Leaders and Teams," in *Advances in Interdisciplinary Studies of Work Teams*, ed. M. M. Beyerlein, D. A. Johnson, and S. T. Beyerlein, vol. 3 (Greenwich, CT: JAI Press, 1996), pp. 173–209.

20. For more detail on the effect of coaching on self-managing teams, see R. Wageman, "How Leaders Foster Self-Managing Team Effectiveness: Design Choices Versus Hands-on Coaching," *Organization Science* 12, no. 5 (2001): 559–577. Additional categories of coaching behavior can be also found in J. A. Arnold, S. Arad, J. A. Rhoades, and F. Drasgow, "The Empowering Leadership Questionnaire: The Construction and Validation of a New Scale for Measuring Leader Behaviors," *Journal of Organizational Behavior* 21, no. 3 (2000): 249–269.

21. See, e.g., C. C. Manz and H. P. Sims, Jr., *Business Without Bosses: How Self-Managing Teams Are Building High Performance Companies*

(New York: Wiley, 1993); R. G. Jones and W. D. Lindley, "Issues in the Transition to Teams," *Journal of Business and Psychology* 13, no. 1 (1998): 31–40; and B. L. Kirkman, R. G. Jones, and D. L. Shapiro, "Why Do Employees Resist Teams? Examining the 'Resistance Barrier' to Work-Team Effectiveness," *The International Journal of Conflict Management* 11, no. 1 (2000): 74–92.

22. Adapted from a case presented in J. P. Kotter and L. A. Schlesinger, "Choosing Strategies for Change," *Harvard Business Review* 57, no. 2 (1979): 106–114.

23. To find out more about the organizational effects of distrust, see D. S. Reina and M. L. Reina, *Trust and Betrayal in the Workplace: Building Effective Relationships in Your Organization* (San Francisco: Berrett-Koehler, 1999).

24. The biographical account of Ross was largely based on T. Kunkel's *Genius in Disguise* (New York: Random House, 1995).

CHAPTER 7. COLLECTIVE LEADERSHIP

1. A. Edmondson, "Psychological Safety and Learning Behavior in Work Teams," *Administrative Science Quarterly* 44 (1999): 350–383.

2. M. J. Wheatley, *Leadership and the New Science: Learning About Organization from an Orderly Universe* (San Francisco: Berrett-Koehler, 1994).

3. J. Kirby, "Reinvention with Respect: An Interview with Jim Kelly of UPS," *Harvard Business Review* 79, no. 10 (2001): 116–123.

4. P. Block, *Stewardship: Choosing Service over Self-Interest* (San Francisco: Berrett-Koehler, 1996).

5. R. K. Greenleaf, *Servant Leadership* (New York: Paulist Press, 1977), pp. 13–14.

6. I recommended this approach in working with "focal persons" in learning teams but find that it applies equally well in the supervisor-subordinate relationship considered from a stewardship perspective. See J. Raelin, *Work-Based Learning: The New Frontier of Management Development* (Upper Saddle River, NJ: Prentice-Hall, 2000), p. 117.

7. W. G. Pagonis, "Leadership in a Combat Zone," *Harvard Business Review* 79, no. 12 (2001): 107–116.

8. Greenleaf, *Servant Leadership*, p. 42.

9. R. A. Heifetz, *Leadership without Easy Answers* (Cambridge, MA: Belknap Press, 1994).

10. From L. Dunham and R. E. Freeman, "There Is Business Like Show Business: Leadership Lessons from the Theater," *Organizational Dynamics* 29, no. 2 (2000): 108–122.

11. The *FrameworkS* process is discussed in depth in D. L. Laurie, *The Real Work of Leaders* (Cambridge, MA: Perseus, 2000), pp. 64–65.

12. Reported in C. Canabou, "Six Ways to Slow Down Smart," *Fast Company*, May 2001, http://www.fastcompany.com/learning/braintrust/0105.html

13. *Ibid.*

14. Reported in D. Hemsath, "Finding the Word on Leadership," *The Journal for Quality and Participation* 21, no. 1 (1998): 50–51.

15. Lao-Tsu, *Tao Te Ching*, passages 65 and 74, in *The Tao of Power*, trans. R. L. Wing (London: Thorsons, 1988).

16. See, among his many writings, C. Argyris, *Reasoning, Learning and Action* (San Francisco: Jossey-Bass, 1982).

17. From S. E. Humphries and K. F. Otterman, "The Natural Emergence of Deep Learning," *Reflections* 3, no. 3 (2002): 19–26.

18. W. A. Randolph, "Rethinking Empowerment: Why Is It So Hard to Achieve?" *Organizational Dynamics* 29, no. 2 (2000): 94–107.

19. The quote from Rockwell is in his chapter, "Reviewing Yourself," in *The Book of Leadership Wisdom*, ed. P. Krass (New York: John Wiley & Sons, 1998), p. 324.

20. See T. J. Peters, "Leadership: Sad Facts and Silver Linings," *Harvard Business Review* 79, no. 12 (2001): 121–128. The Peters account is an apt portrayal of managerial life in the tradition of research on the real working lives of managers. See, esp., H. Mintzberg, *The Nature of Managerial Work* (New York: Harper & Row, 1973).

21. D. L. Bradford and A. R. Cohen, *Power Up: Transforming Organizations through Shared Leadership* (New York: John Wiley & Sons, 1998).

22. This quote and the examples in this section came from R. Slater, *Get Better or Get Beaten: Twenty-Nine Leadership Secrets from GE's Jack Welch*, 2d ed. (New York: McGraw-Hill, 2001).

23. A. Edmondson, R. Bohmer, and G. Pisano, "Speeding Up Team Learning," *Harvard Business Review* 79, no. 10 (2001): 125–132.

24. D. H. Kim, "Fixes that Fail: Why Faster Is Slower," *The Systems Thinker* 10, no. 3 (1999): 1–4.

25. N. Tichy with E. Cohen, *The Leadership Engine: How Winning Companies Build Leaders at Every Level* (New York: HarperCollins, 1997).

26. Interviewed by Ellen Heffes in "Power Up With Shared Leadership Strategies," *Accounting Today* 13, no. 15 (1999): 8–9.

27. J. Stack and B. Burlingham, *The Great Game of Business* (New York: Doubleday, 1994).

28. G. M. Spreitzer and R. E. Quinn, *A Company of Leaders* (San Francisco: Jossey-Bass, 2001), p. 126.

29. M. De Pree, *Leadership Is an Art* (New York: Dell, 1989), pp. 98–100.

30. J. A. Raelin, *Work-Based Learning*. See esp. chaps. 2 and 3 for additional comparisons between learning and conventional training.

31. W. H. Drath and C. J. Palus, *Making Common Sense: Leadership and Meaning-Making in a Community of Practice* (Greensboro, NC: Center for Creative Leadership, 1994).

32. B. Frydman, I. Wilson, and J. Wyer, *The Power of Collaborative Leadership* (Boston: Butterworth Heinemann, 2000), p. 279.

33. From "Lesson 14" of General Colin Powell's *A Leadership Primer*, a PowerPoint presentation produced while he was Chairman, Joint Chiefs of Staff, United States Department of the Army.

34. See John Kotter's 1990 article, reprised as a Best of *HBR* tract, in a special "Breakthrough Leadership" issue of the *Harvard Business Review*, "What Leaders Really Do," *Harvard Business Review* 79, no. 12 (2001): 85–96.

35. R. W. Branford, "Strategic Alignment," *Executive Excellence* 19, no. 1 (2002): 8–9.

36. M. J. Wheatley, *Leadership and the New Science: Learning about Organization from an Orderly Universe* (San Francisco: Berrett-Koehler, 1994), p. 136.

37. See, for example, W. H. Starbuck, "Organizations as Action Generators," *American Sociological Review* 48 (1983): 91–102; D. A. Cowan, C. M. Foil, and J. P. Walsh, "A Midrange Theory of Strategic Choice Processes," in *Strategic Leadership: A Multiorganizational-Level Perspective*, ed. R. L. Phillips and J. G. Hunt (Westport, CT: Quorum, 1992).

38. D. Gergen, *Eyewitness to Power: The Essence of Leadership—Nixon to Clinton* (New York: Simon & Schuster, 2000), p. 348.

39. R. D. Phillips, *The Heart of an Executive: Lessons on Leadership from the Life of King David* (New York: Doubleday, 1999), pp. 124–134.

40. See A. Godard and V. Lenhardt, *Transformational Leadership: Shared Dreams to Succeed* (Paris, Village Mondial, 1999; transl. New York: Macmillan, 2000), pp. 93, 110–111.

41. For more coverage on the antecedents of team mental models, see J. R. Rentsch and R. J. Klimoski, "Why Do 'Great Minds' Think Alike? Antecedents of Team Members Schema Agreement," *Journal of Organizational Behavior* 22 (2001): 107–120.

42. See, esp., chap. 2 in G. M. Spreitzer and R. E. Quinn, *A Company of Leaders* (San Francisco: Jossey-Bass, 2001).

43. R. K. Greenleaf, *The Power of Servant-Leadership* (San Francisco: Berrett-Koehler, 1998), pp. 133–135.

44. R. Komisar and K. L. Lineback (Contributor), *The Monk and the Riddle: The Education of a Silicon Valley Entrepreneur* (Boston: Harvard Business School Press, 2000)

45. D. Goleman, "Leadership That Gets Results," *Harvard Business Review* 78, no. 2 (2000): 78–90.

46. The Wyandotte school case was reported by A. Jehlen, "Recipe for a Great School," *NEA Today* 20, no. 5 (2002): 1–2.

47. See P. L. Berger and T. Luckmann, *The Social Construction of Reality* (New York: Doubleday, 1966); S. Sjostrand, J. Sandberg, and M. Tyrstrup, *Invisible Management: The Social Construction of Leadership* (London: Thomson Learning, 2001).

48. W. H. Drath and C. J. Palus, *Making Common Sense.*

49. T. Kidder, *The Soul of a New Machine* (New York: Avon Books, 1981).

50. According to Verna Allee, this is common practice at Xerox. See her "Knowledge Networks and Communities of Practice," *OD Practitioner* 32, no. 4 (2000): 1–12.

51. Reported in J. Lipman-Blumen, *Connective Leadership: Managing in a Complex World* (Oxford, UK: Oxford University Press, 1996), pp. 219–220.

52. C. O. Scharmer, "Self-Transcending Knowledge: Organizing

around Emerging Realities," presented at the Academy of Management Annual Meeting, Chicago, August 1999.

53. D. Schiff, "An Older, Wiser, Humbler Wunderkind," *New York Times Magazine*, August 20, 1995, p. 31.

54. J. Neal, "Spirituality in Management Education: A Guide to Resources," *Journal of Management Education* 21, no. 1 (1997): 121–140.

55. See L. G. Bolman and T. E. Deal, *Leading with Soul* (San Francisco: Jossey-Bass, 2001).

CHAPTER 8. COLLABORATIVE LEADERSHIP

1. For additional keys in learning how to unlock unproductive group processes, see R. J. Marshak and J. H. Katz, "Keys to Unlocking Covert Processes," *OD Practitioner* 33, no. 2 (2001): 1–9.

2. See the Orpheus website for this note and for other information: www.orpheusNYC.com

3. See D. Coutu's interview of Edgar Schein in "The Anxiety of Learning," *Harvard Business Review* 80, no. 3 (2002): 100–108.

4. For more on change and the human desire to affiliate, see the interview with Peter Senge and Margaret Wheatley by Melvin McLeod in "Changing How We Work Together," *Reflections* 3, no. 3 (2002): 63–67.

5. The connection between participation and resistance is discussed at length in chap. 3 of E. E. Lawler III, *High-Involvement Management* (San Francisco: Jossey-Bass, 1986).

6. R. H. Axelrod, "Why Change Management Needs Changing," *Reflections* 2, no. 3 (2000): 46–57.

7. J. Nirenberg and P. Romine, "The Crafting of Leadership: Values, Moral Assumptions, and Organizational Change," *OD Practitioner* 32, no. 2 (2000): 1–11.

8. K. Lewin, *Field Theory in Social Science,* ed. D. Cartwright (New York: Harper & Row, 1951).

9. M. L. Tushman and E. Romanelli, "Organizational Evolution: A Metamorphosis Model of Convergence and Reorientation," in *Research in Organizational Behavior*, ed. L. L. Cummings and B. M. Staw, vol. 7 (Greenwich, CT: JAI Press, 1985), pp. 171–222.

10. According to biologist Humberto Maturana, every growth process in nature is counterbalanced by limiting or inhibiting processes.

See P. M. Senge and K. H. Kaufer, "Communities of Leaders or No Leadership at All," in *Cutting Edge: Leadership 2000*, ed. B. Kellerman and L. R. Matusak (College Park, MD: The James MacGregor Burns Academy of Leadership Press, 2000).

11. Initially reported in V. Urch Druskat and J. V. Wheeler, "Managing from the Boundary: The Effective Leadership of Self-Managing Work Teams," presented at the Annual Meeting of the Academy of Management, Washington, August 7, 2001, p. 40.

12. C. D. Scott and D. T. Jaffe, *Managing Organizational Change* (Los Altos, CA: Crisp Publications, 1989).

13. The response types of Bunker and Noer were described in the Center for Creative Leadership's e-Newsletter, *Staying Connected*, www.ccl.org/connected/enews/articles/0102selfawareness.htm.

14. R. Kegan and L. Laskow Lahey, "The Real Reason People Won't Change," *Harvard Business Review* 79, no. 11 (2001): 85–92.

15. See C. M. Farkas and P. De Backer, *Maximum Leadership* (New York: Henry Holt, 1996), pp. 210–219.

16. L. A. Anderson and D. Anderson, *The Change Leader's Roadmap* (San Francisco: Jossey-Bass/Pfeiffer, 2001).

17. For more examples of this type of resistance, see D. E. Meyerson, *Tempered Radicals: How People Use Difference to Inspire Change at Work* (Boston: Harvard Business School Press, 2001).

18. I associate the CUSP model with the work of William Bridges & Associates.

19. These comments from Bill O'Brien are from an interview in B. Frydman, I. Wilson, and J. Wyer, *The Power of Collaborative Leadership*, p. 215.

20. E. E. Lawler III, *High-Involvement Management*, p. 221.

21. See his interview with Allan Webber in "Learning for a Change," *Fast Company* 24 (May 1999): 178–188, as well as the famed *The Fifth Discipline: The Art and Practice of the Learning Organization* (New York: Currency/Doubleday, 1994).

22. The quote from Galvin is from his chapter, "Real Leaders Create Industries," in *The Book of Leadership Wisdom*, ed. P. Krass (New York: John Wiley, 1998), p. 418.

23. The journal writer is referring to Charles Fishman's "Change," *Fast Company* 8 (April–May, 1997): 64–73.

24. G. Lippitt and R. Lippitt, *The Consulting Process in Action*, 2d ed. (San Diego, CA: University Associates, 1986).

25. J. A. Olmstead, *Executive Leadership* (Houston: Cashman Dudley, 2000), pp. 81–82.

26. J. C. Rost, *Leadership for the Twenty-First Century* (New York: Praeger, 1991), pp. 102–107.

27. A. R. Cohen and D. L. Bradford, *Influence without Authority* (New York: Wiley, 1994).

28. S. R. Covey, *Seven Habits of Highly Effective People* (New York: Simon & Schuster, 1989).

29. J. Lipman-Blumen, *Connective Leadership: Managing in a Changing World* (Oxford, U.K.: Oxford University Press, 1996); J. Badaracco, Jr., *Leading Quietly: An Unorthodox Guide to Doing the Right Thing* (Boston: Harvard Business School Press, 2002).

30. N. Machiavelli, *The Prince* (New York: Signet, 1952).

31. R. B. Cialdini, *Influence: How and Why People Agree to Do Things* (New York: Quill, 1984).

32. D. Hammarskjöld, *Markings* (New York: Alfred A. Knopf, 1964).

33. See B. Lansdale, *Cultivating Inspired Leaders* (West Hartford, CT: Kumarian Press, 2000).

34. R. Cialdini, *Influence—The Psychology of Persuasion* (New York: William Morrow, 1993).

35. K. Reardon, "Learning to Leverage Workplace Politics: Are Politics Always Dirty? Not at Work!" *Link & Learn Newsletter*, http://www.linkageinc.com/newsletter/archives/od/kathleen_k_reardon_0202.shtml, 2001.

36. Some of these strategies are developed in the approach known as "supportive confrontation." See D. L. Bradford and A. R. Cohen, *Power Up: Transforming Organizations through Shared Leadership* (New York: John Wiley, 1998), pp. 330–345.

37. C. M. Avery, *Teamwork Is an Individual Skill* (San Francisco: Barrett-Koehler, 2001), p. 169.

38. R. E. Miles and C. S. Snow, "Network Organizations: New Concepts for New Forms," *California Management Review* 28, no. 3 (1986): 62–73.

39. K. W. Thomas, "Conflict and Conflict Management," in *Hand-*

book of Industrial and Organizational Psychology, ed. M. D. Dunnette (New York: Rand McNally, 1976).

40. Some of these strategies are discussed in D. E. Berlew, A. Moore, and R. Harrison, *The Positive Negotiation Program* (Plymouth, MA: Situation Management Systems, 1977).

41. B. Gray, *Collaborating: Finding Common Ground for Multiparty Problems* (San Francisco: Jossey-Bass, 1989), p. 5.

42. W. Drath, *The Deep Blue Sea: Rethinking the Source of Leadership* (New York: John Wiley, 2001), pp. 98–100.

43. M. Hammer and J. Champy, *Reengineering the Corporation: A Manifesto for Business Revolution* (New York: HarperBusiness, 1993), Chap. 14.

44. See, for example, R. Neustadt, *Presidential Power*, 2d ed. (New York: Wiley, 1980), pp. 30–35; J. C. Rost, *Leadership for the Twenty-First Century* (New York: Praeger, 1991), pp. 159–161; and G. A. Williams and R. B. Miller, "Change the Way You Persuade," *Harvard Business Review* 80, no. 5 (2002): 65–74.

45. This account of King David was cited in R. D. Phillips, *The Heart of an Executive: Lessons on Leadership from the Life of King David* (New York: Doubleday, 1999), pp. 186–188.

46. See this account in detail in C. M. Farkas and P. De Backer, *Maximum Leadership* (New York: Henry Holt, 1996), pp. 71–75.

47. M. De Pree, *Leadership Jazz* (New York: Dell, 1992), pp. 50–52.

48. These skills are also referred to as the skills of reflective practice and are discussed as well in J. A. Raelin, "Public Reflection as the Basis of Learning," *Management Learning* 32, no. 1 (2001): 11–30.

49. W. Isaacs, *Dialogue: The Art of Thinking Together* (New York: Doubleday, 1999).

50. See S. Bell, "Self-Reflection and Vulnerability in Action Research: Bringing Forth New Worlds in Our Learning," *Systemic Practice and Action Research* 11, no. 2 (1998): 179–191.

51. G. Claxton, *Hare Brain Tortoise Mind* (London: Fourth Estate, 1997), pp. 174, 192.

52. Depicted in O. Guinness, ed., *Character Counts: Leadership Qualities in Washington, Wilberforce, Lincoln, and Solzhenitsyn* (Grand Rapids, MI: Baker Books, 1999), p. 37.

53. J. B. Harvey, *The Abilene Paradox and Other Meditations on Management* (San Francisco: Jossey-Bass, 1988).

54. D. L. Laurie, *The Real Work of Leaders* (Cambridge, MA: Perseus, 2000), pp. 65–66.

55. P. Kruger, "A Leader's Journey," *Fast Company* 25 (June 1999): 116.

56. See C. Argyris and D. A. Schön, *Theory in Practice: Increasing Professional Effectiveness* (San Francisco: Jossey-Bass, 1974); and J. A. Raelin, "The Persean Ethic: Consistency of Belief and Action in Managerial Practice," *Human Relations* 46, no. 5 (1993): 575–621.

57. B. Bright, "Reflecting on 'Reflective Practice,'" *Studies in the Education of Adults* 28, no. 2 (1996): 162–184; R. Hogarth, *Judgment and Choice*, 2d ed. (Chichester, UK: John Wiley, 1987).

CHAPTER 9. COMPASSIONATE LEADERSHIP

1. I would like to acknowledge the contribution of my colleague Robert Leaver for the development of the concept of "tension of opposites."

2. M. Morrell and S. Capparell, *Shackleton's Way: Leadership Lessons from the Great Antarctic Explorer* (New York: Viking, 2001).

3. J. A. Conger, R. N. Kanungo, and S. T. Menon, "Charismatic Leadership and Follower Effects," *Journal of Organizational Behavior* 21 (2000): 747–767.

4. M. Weber, *Economy and Society*, ed. R. Guenther and C. Wittich, 3 vols. (New York: Bedminster, 1925/1968), pp. 358–359.

5. From L. Bossidy, "Reality-Based Leadership: Changes in the Workplace," in *The Book of Leadership Wisdom*, ed. P. Krass (New York: John Wiley & Sons, 1998), p. 410.

6. M. Maccoby, "Narcissistic Leaders," *Harvard Business Review* 78, no. 1 (2000): 68–77; and R. Lubit, "The Long-Term Organizational Impact of Destructively Narcissistic Managers," *Academy of Management Executive* 16, no. 1 (2002): 127–138.

7. F. J. Milliken, "Three Types of Perceived Uncertainty about the Environment: State, Effect, and Response Uncertainty," *Academy of Management Review* 12 (1987): 133–143.

8. B. M. Bass, *Leadership and Performance Beyond Expectations* (New York: Free Press, 1985).

9. J. A. Conger and R. N. Kanungo, *Charismatic Leadership in Organizations* (Thousand Oaks, CA: Sage, 1998), p. 158.

10. Reported by Patrick Healy in "Many Afghans Now See Omar As a Betrayer," *Boston Globe*, December 18, 2001, p. A21.

11. J. Collins, "Level 5 Leadership: The Triumph of Humility and Fierce Resolve," *Harvard Business Review* 79, no. 1 (2001): 67–76.

12. O. Behling and J. M. McFillen, "A Syncretical Model of Charismatic/Transformational Leadership," *Group and Organizational Management* 21, no. 2 (1996): 163–191.

13. See, for example, R. J. House, "A 1976 Theory of Charismatic Leadership," in *Leadership: The Cutting Edge*, ed. J. G. Hunt and L. Larson (Carbondale: Southern Illinois University Press, 1977); B. M. Bass, "The Inspirational Process of Leadership," *Journal of Management Development* 75 (1988): 21–31; B. M. Bass, *Bass and Stogdill's Handbook of Leadership: Theory, Research, and Managerial Applications*, 3rd ed. (New York: Free Press, 1990).

14. See an account of Gaulier's method at L'école Philippe Gaulier in H. Rubin, "Boooorrriinngll!" *Fast Company* 35 (June 2000): 228+.

15. J. Meindl, "On Leadership: An Alternative to the Conventional Wisdom," *Research in Organizational Behavior* 12 (1990): 159–203.

16. See, for example, R. Weber, C. Camerer, Y. Rottenstreich, and M. Knez, "The Illusion of Leadership: Misattribution of Cause in Coordination Games," *Organization Science* 12, no. 5 (2001): 582–598; and J. Pastor, J. R. Meindl, and M. C. Mayo, "A Network Effects Model of Charisma Attributions," *Academy of Management Journal* 45, no. 2 (2002): 410–420.

17. J. D. Mayer and P. Salovey, "What Is Emotional Intelligence: Implications for Educators," in *Emotional Development, Emotional Literacy, and Emotional Intelligence*, ed. P. Salovey and D. Sluyter (New York: Basis Books, 1997), pp. 3–31.

18. J. M. George, "Emotions and Leadership: The Role of Emotional Intelligence," *Human Relations* 5, no. 8 (2000): 1027–1055.

19. No one is more eloquent on the principle of transformational leadership than James MacGregor Burns; see his *Leadership* (New York: HarperCollins, 1985). However, he positions leaders as special people, even self-actualizers, who can raise the consciousness of followers.

20. W. B. Given, Jr., "Freedom Within Management," *Harvard Business Review* (Summer 1946).

21. Reported in C. K. Barnett and N. M. Tichy, "How New Leaders Learn to Take Charge," *Organizational Dynamics* 29, no. 1 (2000): 16–32.

22. Reported in D. L. Laurie, *The Real Work of Leaders* (Cambridge, MA: Perseus, 2000), pp. 120–121.

23. Reported in D. L. Laurie, *The Real Work of Leaders,* p. 85.

24. J. G. Clawson, *Level Three Leadership: Getting Below the Surface* (Upper Saddle River, NJ: Prentice-Hall, 1999).

25. D. M. Abrashoff, "Retention Through Redemption," *Harvard Business Review* 79, no. 2 (2001): 3–7.

26. Adapted from an article by D. Dorsey in *Fast Company*, "Andy Pearson Finds Love," 49 (August 2001).

27. The depiction of the "two Bobs" was captured by David A. Heenan and Warren Bennis in *Co-leaders: The Power of Great Partnerships* (New York: John Wiley & Sons, 1999), chap. 2.

28. R. Rosenblatt, "The Straight Man," *Modern Maturity*, July–August 1996, p. 20.

29. P. McLagan and C. Nel, *The Age of Participation: New Governance for the Workplace and the World* (San Francisco: Berrett-Koehler, 1995); J. A. Arnold, S. Arad, J. A. Rhoades, and F. Drasgow, "The Empowering Leadership Questionnaire: The Construction and Validation of a New Scale for Measuring Leader Behaviors," *Journal of Organizational Behavior* 21 (2000): 249–269.

30. Reported by C. Lowe in "Promotion to Supervisor Is an Eye-opening Experience," *Boston Sunday Globe*, March 10, 2002, p. G17.

31. For a commentary on Habermas's views of rational consensus, see T. McCarthy, *The Critical Theory of Jürgen Habermas* (Cambridge: Polity Press, 1978), or consult Habermas directly in his *Knowledge and Human Interests* (Boston: Beacon Press, 1971).

32. From K. Hart, "Kinship, Contact, and Trust: The Economic Organization of Migrants in an African City Slum," in *Trust: Making and Breaking Cooperative Relations,* ed. D. Gambetta (New York: Basic Blackwell, 1988), pp. 176–211.

33. See, e.g., R. Mayer, J. Davis, and E. D. Schoorman, "An Integrative Model of Organizational Trust," *Academy of Management*

Review 20 (1995): 709–734; and W. Q. Judge, *The Leader's Shadow: Exploring and Developing Executive Character* (Thousand Oaks, CA: Sage, 1999).

34. See C. M. Farkas and P. De Backer, *Maximum Leadership* (New York: Henry Holt, 1996), pp. 81–86.

35. From M. Brelis, "I've Got the Trust," *Boston Sunday Globe*, June 3, 2001, p. E5.

36. See, e.g., P. Rosenfeld, R. A. Giacalone, and C. A. Riordan, *Impression Management in Organizations: Theory, Measurement, Practice* (London: Routledge, 1995).

37. R. Goffee and G. Jones, "Why Should Anyone Be Led by You?" *Harvard Business Review* 78, no. 5 (2000): 63–70.

38. See William Peace's classic article, "The Hard Work of Being a Soft Manager," in the special issue of the *Harvard Business Review* on "Breakthrough Leadership," 79, no. 12 (2001): 99–104.

39. This reference to Wheatley is from an interview conducted by Melvin McLeod featuring her and Peter Senge and published in the January 2001 issue of the *Shambhala Sun*, The Shambhala Institute

40. This quote was drawn from C. Hymowitz, "When You Disagree With the Boss's Order, Do You Tell Your Staff?" *Wall Street Journal*, April 16, 2002.

41. See C. M. Farkas and P. De Backer, *Maximum Leadership* (New York: Henry Holt, 1996), pp. 138–142.

42. B. M. Lansdale, *Cultivating Inspired Leaders* (West Hartford, CT: Kumarian Press, 2000), p. 120.

43. S. McElwaine, "A Different Kind of War: A Blunt Interview with the Army's First Woman Three-Star General," *USA Weekend*, October 3–5, 1997, p. 6.

44. For a full explanation of the idea of overlapping circles of responsibility, see J. Liedtka, "Linking Competitive Advantage with Communities of Practice," *Journal of Management Inquiry* 8, no. 1 (1999): 5–16.

45. From a speech by Carly Fiorina, "Technology, Business, and Our Way of Life," Minneapolis, Minnesota, September 26, 2001.

46. B. M. Lansdale, *Cultivating Inspired Leaders*, p. 137.

47. P. Freire, *Pedagogy of the Oppressed* (New York: Seabury Press, 1970).

48. This story, which Christopher Avery reports originates from an unnamed British professor, was recounted in his *Teamwork Is an Individual Skill* (San Francisco: Berrett-Koehler, 2001), pp. 45–47.

49. Extracted from "Putting Relationships First," *Corporate Citizenship Review* 16, no. 2 (2001): 4–5.

50. The case of urban banking was developed from the work of Steve Waddell of Organizational Futures. See his "Societal Learning: Creating Big-Systems Change," *The Systems Thinker* 12, no. 10 (2001): 1–5.

51. See H. A. Giroux, *Ideology, Culture and the Process of Schooling* (London: Falmer Press, 1981); and I. Shor, *Empowering Education: Critical Teaching for Social Change* (Chicago: University of Chicago Press, 1992).

Name Index

A

Abrashoff, Michael, 221, 251
Achua, Christopher, 47
Ackerman Anderson, Linda, 165
Ackoff, Russ, 34
Adams, Scott, 124
Anderson, Dean, 165
Argyris, Chris, 125, 129
Arnesen, Liv, 122–23
Arthur, W. Brian, 120
Avery, Christopher, 181, 237
Avolio, Bruce, 99

B

Badaracco, Joe, 177
Bancroft, Ann, 122–23
Barber, Nicholas, 219
Behling, Orlando, 213
Belbin, E. Meredith, 56, 57
Bennis, Warren, 26
Benny, Jack, 222
Bethune, Gordon, 225
Blanchard, Kenneth, 93
Block, Peter, 117
Bolduc, J. P., 156
Bolman, Lee, 152

Bossidy, Lawrence, 134, 207, 210
Bradford, David, 27–28, 126, 134, 176
Brady, Tom, 36
Branford, Robert, 140
Brooks, Bob, 180
Bunker, Kerry, 161–62
Burns, George, 222

C

Calloway, Wayne, 225
Campbell, Kermit, 150
Carlyle, Thomas, 21
Carlzon, Jan, 135, 220
Carroll, Phil, 64
Cashman, Kevin, 61, 62
Chambers, John, 35, 201–2
Champy, James, 188
Chase, Bert, 67
Churchill, Winston, 209
Cialdini, Robert, 179
Clawson, Jim, 220
Claxton, Guy, 195
Cohen, Allen, 27–28, 126, 176
Collins, Jim, 213

Subject Index

A
Abilene Paradox, 198
Absenteeism, 75
Action learning, 187
AES Corporation, 68
Alignment, 139, 140, 145
Altruism, 70
American Brake Shoe
    Company, 218
American Farm School, 178
American Revolutionary War,
    197
Apollo 13, 114–15
Attitudinal resistance, 52
Attribution, 193, 215, 228
Authenticity, 77–82
Authority, concern about,
    29–33
Autonomy, 32, 58, 126, 148, 221

B
Baldridge National Quality
    Award, 201
Bargaining, 183, 185, 186
Baseball, 20–21, 204
Behavior-focused strategies, 65
Being, skill of, 194–96, 199
Bible, 142

Boston Red Sox, 20
Boundary
    function, 9, 101
    management, 90–91, 101,
        110–12
Boundaryless learning culture,
    128
Briggs & Stratton, 187
Bureaucracy, 33, 35, 128, 250

C
Cap Gemini Ernst & Young, 72
Careerist orientation, 117–18
Carriers, 215, 217
Catholic Church, 26
Center for Advanced
    Emotional Intelligence, 202
Center for Creative Leadership,
    161
Center for Simplified Strategic
    Planning, 140
CHAMPS, 222
Change
    commanding vs. evolving,
        172–73
    communication of, 167–68
    land mines of, 168–72
    leaderful practice and, 75

About the Author

When asked what led to his development of the perspective known as leaderful practice, Joe Raelin acknowledged that he has been working on it during his entire adult life. In the 1960s and 1970s, while associated with the human potential movement, he incorporated into his personal and professional life the ultimate democratic belief that no one affected by a decision should be left out of that decision, be it in its design or implementation. From that origin, Raelin extended his thinking about leaderful behavior through a counseling master's degree followed later by a Ph.D., which rounded out his ongoing consulting practice in organizational development and change.

From 1976 until 2002, Joe was a professor at Boston College in the Carroll School of Management where he dedicated his principal teaching and research to professional education and executive development. A practical scholar, Joe not only writes about but also helps organizations establish leadership development programs using action learning methodology, a human resource development approach that encourages managers and employees to learn in the midst of their very practice.

The current book is Raelin's sixth and accompanies more than seventy-five articles appearing in the leading management journals. The book grew out of a graduate course at Boston College called "The Leadership Workshop," which he taught for many years both in the full-time and part-time MBA program. In the course, he used a "perspectives" approach, exposing students not to one best way to prepare for leadership but to a variety of approaches to both think about and practice leadership. At the conclusion of the course, he attempted to integrate these many perspectives into his own view, which he would refer to as "leaderfulness." He credits his students and his co-facilitators of the course with encouraging him over time to develop his ideas into a treatise that they believed would change the face of leadership as we know it. Offered for readers here, then, is potentially a new paradigm of leadership: leaderful practice.

Joe has been a featured speaker at numerous conventions and professional meetings, and has been widely quoted in the media. He has received many honors, but he would point out that the most important one occurred just prior to this book's release. He has just been named the Asa S. Knowles Chair at Northeastern University in Boston and will be extending his leaderful practice to the new Center for the Study of Practice-Oriented Education.

Berrett-Koehler Publishers

B errett-Koehler is an independent publisher of books, audios, and other publications at the leading edge of new thinking and innovative practice on work, business, management, leadership, stewardship, career development, human resources, entrepreneurship, and global sustainability.

Since the company's founding in 1992, we have been committed to creating a world that works for all by publishing books, periodicals, and other publications that help us to integrate our values with our work and work lives, and to create more humane and effective organizations.

To find out about our new books, special offers, free excerpts, and much more, subscribe to our **free monthly eNewsletter** at **www.bkconnection.com**.

Please see next pages for other publications from Berrett-Koehler Publishers

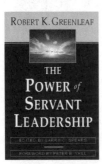

The Answer to How Is Yes
Acting on What Matters

Peter Block

Peter Block presents a guide to the difficult journey of bringing what we know is of personal value into an indifferent or even hostile corporate and cultural landscape and teaches individuals, workers, and managers ways to act on what they know and reclaim their capacity to create a world they want to live in.

Hardcover, 200 pages • ISBN 1-57675-168-6
Item #51686-415 $24.95

Stewardship
Choosing Service Over Self-Interest

Peter Block

Peter Block shows how to recreate our workplaces by replacing self-interest, dependency, and control with service, responsibility, and partnership. In this revolutionary book, he demonstrates how a far-reaching redistribution of power, privilege, and wealth will radically change all areas of organizational governance, and shows why this is our best hope to enable democracy to thrive, our spiritual and ethical values to be lived out, and economic success to be sustained.

Paperback, 288 pages • ISBN 1-881052-86-9
Item #52869-415 $16.95

Hardcover • ISBN 1-881052-28-1 • Item #52281-415 $24.95

Audiotape, 2 cassettes • ISBN 1-57453-147-6
Item #31476-415 $17.95

Empowerment Takes More Than a Minute
Second Edition

Ken Blanchard, John Carlos, and Alan Randolph

These expert authors explain how to empower the workforce by moving from a command-and-control mindset to a supportive, responsibility-centered environment in which all employees have the opportunity and responsibility to do their best. They explain how to build ownership and trust using three essential keys to making empowerment work in large and small organizations.

Paperback, 145 pages • ISBN 1-57675-153-8
Item #51538-415 $12.95

Berrett-Koehler Publishers
PO Box 565, Williston, VT 05495-9900
Call toll-free! **800-929-2929** 7 am-9 pm Eastern Standard Time

Or fax your order to 802-864-7627
For fastest service order online: **www.bkconnection.com**

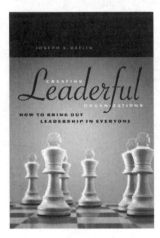